D0922304

NIGHT
MADNESS

Copyright © 2012 Richard R. Pyves
5 4 3 2 1
All rights reserved. No part of this publication may be reproduced, stored in a retrieval system or transmitted, in any form or by any means, without the prior written permission of Red Deer Press or, in the case of photocopying or other reprographic copying, a licence from Access Copyright (Canadian Copyright Licensing Agency), 1 Yonge Street, Suite 800, Toronto, ON, M5E 1E5, fax (416) 868-1621.

Published by Red Deer Press
195 Allstate Parkway, Markham, ON, L3R 4T8
www.reddeerpress.com

Published in the United States in 2013 by Red Deer Press
311 Washington Street, Brighton, Massachusetts, 02135

Cover and text design by Daniel Choi
Cover image courtesy Richard R. Pyves
Printed and bound in Canada by Goody Production

We acknowledge with thanks the Canada Council for the Arts, and the Ontario Arts Council for their support of our publishing program. We acknowledge the financial support of the Government of Canada through the Canada Book Fund (CBF) for our publishing activities.

 Canada Council for the Arts **Conseil des Arts du Canada** ONTARIO ARTS COUNCIL CONSEIL DES ARTS DE L'ONTARIO

Library and Archives Canada Cataloguing in Publication
Pyves, Richard
Night madness : a rear gunner's story of love, courage, and hope in WWII / Richard Pyves.
Includes bibliographical references and index.
ISBN 978-0-88995-464-9
1. Pyves, Ron. 2. World War, 1939-1945--Personal narratives, Canadian.
3. Dresden (Germany)--History--Bombardment, 1945. 4. Post-traumatic stress disorder--Patients--Canada--Biography. 5. Soldiers--Canada--Biography.
I. Title.
D811.P98P98 2012   940.54'8171   C2011-907148-7

Publisher Cataloging-in-Publication Data (U.S.)
Pyves, Richard.
Night madness : a rear gunner's story of love, courage, and hope in WWII / Richard Pyves.
[334] p. : photos. ; cm.
Includes bibliographical references and index.
Summary: The story of Ron Pyves, a teenage tail-gunner who fought in WWII and survived, only to battle post traumatic stress disorder caused by the memories of war. Based on interviews, archival research, and a long-distance love affair captured in daily correspondence.
ISBN: 978-0-88995-464-9 (pbk.)
1. Pyves, Ron. 2. World War II, 1939-1945 – Personal narratives, Canadian. 3. Post traumatic stress disorder – Patients – Canada -- Biography. 4. Dresden (Germany) – History – Bombardment, 1945. 5. Soldiers – Canada – Biography. I. Title.
940.54/8171 dc23   D811P98.P984 2012

NIGHT MADNESS

A REAR GUNNER'S STORY OF LOVE, COURAGE, AND HOPE IN WORLD WAR II

Richard R. Pyves

Red Deer Press

For all those who courageously served in Bomber Command in World War II, both on the ground and in the air, and especially to the crew of WL-D (for "Dog") in 434 Bluenose Squadron, who brought each other safely home through thirty-five combat missions.

Contents

Maps   vi

Acknowledgements   vii

Introduction   ix

An Auspicious Beginning   1

Chance Encounter   8

Over There   17

Heavy Conversion Unit Training   47

Combat Ready   55

Cat and Mouse   79

A Lucky Fellow   94

Lucky Number Thirteen   107

Fighter Attack   127

Birthday over Germany   135

Goodbye Halifax   146

A New Year   154

Night Madness   174

Screened   198

Reunion   224

Post Traumatic Stress Disorder   232

A New Beginning   237

A Personal War   243

Passing the Torch   250

The Crew   265

Abbreviations   284

Notes   285

Bibliography   311

Index   315

Maps

Duisburg Night Operations – October 14/15, 1944 88

Essen Night Operations – October 23/24, 1944 96

Cologne Night Operations – October 30/31, 1944 102

Oberhausen Night Operations – November 1, 1944 106

Bochum Night Operations – November 4/5, 1944 113

No. 6 Group Bases in the Vale of York 1943/1945 122

Neuss Night Operations – November 27/28, 1944 128

Duisburg Night Operations – November 30/December 1, 1944 132

Hagen Night Operations – December 2/3, 1944 136

Soest Night Operations – December 5/6, 1944 139

Cologne Night Operations – December 30/31, 1944 151

Hannover Night Operations (Second Attack) – January 5/6, 1945 158

Merseberg (Leuna) Night Operations – January 14/15, 1945 162

Zeitz Night Operations – January 16/17, 1945 164

Kornwestheim (Stuttgart) Night Operations – January 28/29, 1945 170

Dresden Night Operations – February 13/14, 1945 179

Dortmund Night Operations – February 20/21, 1945 190

Duisburg Night Operations – February 21/22, 1945 193

Dessau Night Operations – March 7/8, 1945 204

Heide Night Operations – March 20/21, 1945 210

Acknowledgements

Night Madness would not have been possible without the contributions and support of many people and institutions. First, I would like to thank all the crew members who flew with Ron Pyves in 434 Squadron, including Bill Thomson, Hal Ward, and Frank Welsh, who met and shared personal experiences and observations of their tour of combat duty. I am fortunate to have had the opportunity to personally meet with these individuals to capture events which were otherwise undocumented. Bill and Frank generously provided me with copies of their log books, which included critical information that made this story possible. Bob Henry's wife was also kind enough to loan me Bob's three log books, which covered all of his World War II flying. I must also thank Frank Welsh, who read the first draft of my story and encouraged me to carry on. I am also indebted to both Goetz Bergander and Lothar Metzger who allowed me to include their personal recollections of the bombing of Dresden, which they experienced first-hand.

Without the correspondence between Kay and Ron, and Ron's letters to his parents, some 230 letters in total, this story could never have been written. These letters provided not only an eyewitness account to history, but were invaluable in helping me understand some of Kay's and Ron's innermost thoughts and feelings as events unfolded. I must also thank my sister, Colleen Pyves, who assisted in the editing of the many versions of the first draft and provided not only constructive criticism but also encouragement and ideas to make the story better. I would also like to thank several other colleagues, including Pat Burns, John Breen, John Dogger, Terry Fallis, Tania Freedman, Gert Rosenau, Tom Edgerton, and Susan Elliott Wittrup for their advice and assistance.

Although a significant portion of the information for this account came from log books, interviews, and personal letters, this project became so much easier because of the Herculean work that Richard Koval completed over a thirty-year period. Richard distilled the information from thousands of RCAF documents available to the public through the assistance of Library and Archives Canada, and has provided in his own words a summary of the experiences of Bomber Group 6 by individual squadron, on a daily basis, for the entire period in which the Group was operational in World War II. This information is available at www.6grouprcaf.com. In addition, Richard directed me to other original sources of data, which allowed me to better understand life on an operational base as well as what had happened on each of the missions in which Ron Pyves participated. Another excellent website is www.rcaf434squadron.com, which was set up by Allan Soderstrom who helped me discover that pilot Bob Henry had an older brother, Jack, who flew with 431 Squadron and in many instances on the same missions as his brother.

A special thanks to my editor and publisher, Richard Dionne from Red Deer Press, for his sage advice and support to make this book possible.

Finally, I must thank my wife, Judy, who encouraged me to pursue this project despite the fact that I probably should have been directing my energies into finding full-time employment given the current chaotic economic times.

Introduction

Late on December 13, 2007, I received a frantic call from my sister Colleen, who lives in Magog in the Eastern Townships, informing me that our mother, Kay Pyves, had been taken to the hospital. She had suffered a heart attack. My initial reaction was one of disbelief as I had just spoken to her four days earlier by phone and she appeared to be her usual chatty self. Unfortunately, Kay had thought she only had a bout of flu so did not seek immediate medical treatment. By the time she arrived at the hospital by ambulance, some eighteen hours had passed since her initial heart attack. Kay experienced irreversible damage to her heart and passed away less than twenty-four hours later, surrounded by her loving immediate family.

What a tragic end for someone who had lived such a vibrant life and had been the cornerstone of her family, one that included four children, ten grandchildren, and six great-grandchildren. Although very outgoing, Kay had always been a very private person who took great delight and interest in what others were doing. Ironically, many facets of her own life, including her interest in writing and how she met and married her lifetime partner, Ron Pyves, were facts she kept to herself.

While settling Kay's estate, we had to clean out all the furniture and personal effects from her apartment. Through this difficult process, my sisters and I discovered an extensive collection of letters from the war years covering 1943 to 1945, which included letters that Kay had written to her future husband, Ron, letters that Ron had written to his parents while overseas, and letters that Ron had written to Kay while away on his tour of duty with the RCAF as a tail gunner in Bomber Command. As a child, I had seen these bundles of over 230 letters with the old stamps on them. They had been stuffed away in my parents' dresser drawers, but at the time I was too young to realize their significance.

In reading them now, I realized that not only had I uncovered a paper trail of correspondence that explained how my parents' long-distance relationship had developed after meeting just three times before my father was shipped overseas, but in many ways I discovered a new eyewitness account to history.

I know from personal insight that my father's wartime experience had a significant impact on him, so his letters helped me understand some of his thoughts, feelings, and experiences as he progressed through training and his tour of duty. Ron, a sensitive young man of eighteen, volunteered to join the RCAF not only to fight for his country, but also for England, the birthplace of his parents. Ron became a tail gunner. His position at the extreme end of the bomber could be terrifyingly isolated. In many instances, the first point of attack by enemy fighters was the tail gunner, which would leave the bomber vulnerable to further attack. As a tail gunner in a plastic bubble at the very extremity of the bomber, it would be difficult to comprehend the multiple effects of isolation, vulnerability, and the unceasing necessity to protect his fellow crewmates from enemy attack.

Ron's youth, sensitivity, and isolation and, in particular, his feelings of guilt for his involvement in the bombing of Dresden, would combine to seriously impact his health and quality of life after the war. Although Ron had at least survived his tour of duty while many aircrew lost their lives, in the end his personal tour of duty would turn fatal. I believe that every individual has a different tolerance for stress and life-threatening experiences; some individuals can come through highly traumatic situations almost unscathed while others, like Ron, sustain permanent damage.

Night Madness is really three separate stories inextricably woven together. The first is a wonderful love story about a growing relationship nurtured and brought to life through a series of almost daily correspondence between two teenagers. The second is the true story of one RCAF bomber crew's adventures in the last seven months of the campaign over Europe. In many ways the crew's experiences were a microcosm of the key role that Bomber Command played in helping push the enemy back into Germany. The third story covers what happened to Ron after returning home, including the ultimate loss of his ability to cope with his wartime experiences due to Post Traumatic Stress Disorder (PTSD). At first this ailment was not readily recognized by the government, medical profession, and the military as a real sickness that warranted proper medical treatment and support. Even today, with troops serving in locations around the world, it is still a challenge for soldiers, as well as non-combat personnel who support our military services, to get compensation and proper treatment when PTSD strikes. This ailment has no respect for rank, race, or gender and can manifest itself unannounced. As we'll see, Kay's and Ron's story deals with this hardship and just how difficult it can be for victims of PTSD to get proper care and compensation. The Pension Act administered by Veterans Affairs clearly states in subsection 5(3) that in weighing uncontradicted, credible evidence, any doubt shall be resolved in favour of the applicant or pensioner. In reality, the experiences of many claimants who have unselfishly served their country show the opposite. It can sometimes take *many* years to resolve a request for compensation from the combatant or spouse.

Altogether, *Night Madness* is a story about lifetime bonds of brotherhood forged through shared combat experience, a story of love built on friendship, and a story about the triumph of the individual against adversity in both wartime and in peace.

Richard (Rick) Pyves
Pickering, Ontario

1

An Auspicious Beginning

It was an auspicious beginning. Ronald Leslie Pyves arrived on December 5, 1924, twenty-one years to the month after the Wright brothers made their first successful manned flight at Kill Devil Hills in North Carolina. The newborn was welcomed by his parents, Edward Lewis and Laura, and his older brother, Edward Lewis Jr., to his new home, a modest walkup flat in a working-class neighbourhood of east-end Montreal. The young boy's parents could not have predicted at the time that in less than fifteen years the world would once again be embroiled in another all-consuming global conflict—one which would involve their youngest son in a bomber that would outweigh the Wright brothers' *Flyer* by a hundredfold.

Laura, an English war bride, had met and married Edward Lewis while he was overseas as part of the Canadian Expeditionary Force in World War I. They married in England in 1917 while he was recovering from wounds sustained at Hill 60 in Belgium—a battle that saw many of Edward's comrades killed and wounded. Edward's battalion, the Victoria Rifles of Canada, sustained in their first six months in the trenches a casualty rate in excess of 40 percent. Edward's son Ron would take up the torch again in the next Great War. And if it were not for one fatal mission to bomb Dresden on the night of February 13–14, 1945, and a chance encounter with Kay Eason just prior to embarking for England, Ron's life would most definitely have taken a very different direction.

As a boy, Ron attended Maisonneuve Public School, played with his friends in Lafontaine Park, paid frequent visits to the Montreal Botanical Garden, and spent his summers in the Laurentians north of Montreal at his parents' cottage on the shores of Lake Nantal. Ron learned how to play soccer from his dad, Edward, who was an excellent teacher of the game. Edward also worked at St. Mary's Veteran Hospital where he became one of the early X-ray technicians in Canada. As Ron and his brother got older, their mother took in foster children. She had a preference to foster young girls as she did not have a daughter of her own.

At age thirteen, Ron decided to follow in his older brother's footsteps and joined the Vickers Troop of the Boy Scouts of Canada. Although Ron's brother was five years older, as siblings they formed a close friendship that lasted throughout their lives.

By 1939, Ron had completed Grade nine at Montreal High School, which by that time was a rather tired-looking institution in the city core. That summer, he visited his Aunt Ethel in New York City. The New York World's Fair, named "Building the World of Tomorrow," opened in April of that year. Its theme focused on international cooperation. Five months later Hitler invaded Poland.

To Ron, the city, with its vibrant shows and nightlife, provided an overwhelming experience, and in Times Square he marveled at "the most wonderful display of coloured electric lights that (he) had ever seen." On July 5, Ron penned the first of many letters that he would write home to his parents over the next six years.

> *Dear Mum, After we left the house Friday morning, we didn't stop until we came to the border and we crossed that without any difficulty. I saw two minor league handball games. Monday went swimming again. Tuesday afternoon we watched a handball game and at night Uncle Bob and I went swimming. All day long from morning until night there were bangs and flashes celebrating Independence Day.*
>
> *I have slept well here but I am always thinking of you.*
>
> *I hope everybody's well at home. I think I'll close now*

because there isn't much to say. Ta-ta for the present. Your Loving Son, Ron

Two days later, the *Queen Mary*, one of the world's largest ocean liners, arrived in New York. It was a massive ship, stretching over one thousand feet and standing some eighteen storeys high. It could reach unheard-of speeds of almost thirty-three knots. Among the crew, which numbered 1,101 members, was Ron's Uncle Billy (William Garnett), a marine engineer. Ron paid a visit to the *Queen Mary,* which would soon be converted to a troopship. It would eventually carry as many as fifteen thousand soldiers on each cross-Atlantic voyage. During the war the ship would transport over seven hundred thousand passengers to Singapore, Sydney, the Middle East, the Suez, and the U.K., as well as assist in the post-war repatriation of Canadian and U.S. troops.

Upon his return, Ron decided to quit school and work full time. He obtained employment as a sheet metal worker at Canadian Vickers, a large manufacturer involved in the production of the Wellington bomber, a model that he would later fly in.

Ron was fourteen when war was declared. Hitler was intent on expanding German territory and invaded Austria in early March 1938. Hitler also wanted to regain land lost in the Paris Treaty of 1919. As early as 1938, Germany made demands for the return of the Sudetenland, an ethnic German portion of Czechoslovakia which had prior to 1919 been part of the Austro-Hungarian Empire. Through the Munich Agreement, which was signed by Britain, France, Italy, and Germany, the Czechs were coerced into surrendering the Sudetenland in September 1938 to Germany. Prime Minister of Britain Neville Chamberlain made his infamous "Peace in Our Time" speech on returning from his meetings with Hitler. Just six months later Germany invaded and took over the rest of Czechoslovakia.

In 1939, Germany set its sights on the acquisition of Poland. Initially, German demands focused on the return of Western Prussia, known as the "Polish Corridor," which had been ceded to Poland as part of the Treaty of Versailles in 1919. Germany also wanted the return of Danzig, which had been established as an independent Free City after World War I. Although both France and Britain in March 1939 guaranteed to come to Poland's defence if attacked by Germany, once again Neville Chamberlain hoped to negotiate a settlement with Germany which would preclude going to war. With the signing of a non-aggression pact with Russia in August 1939 and a sense that France and Britain would not declare war on Germany, on September 1, Germany invaded Poland. Hitler's gamble this time did not pay off and two days later both Britain and France declared war on Germany. Canada would declare war on Germany seven days later.

The war heated up in 1940 with the fall of France and the Battle of Britain, a key air battle in which Hitler's air force attempted to gain air superiority over the skies of Britain as a precursor to an invasion. The German air force would have likely achieved its goal if it had maintained its focus on destroying the Royal Air Force and associated radar early warning stations and airfields. However, Hitler was to make the first of several strategic blunders when in retaliation for a modest Allied air raid on Berlin in October 1940, he ordered his air force to change its primary targets to London and various English coastal cities. This allowed the British fighter planes to exact a toll on the German bomber force in the ensuing air battle, thereby undermining any German air superiority and ultimately preventing an invasion of Britain.

In 1941 events in Europe continued to develop at a hectic pace as Germany launched "Operation Barbarossa" on June 22, when over 4.4 million Axis soldiers invaded Russia across a broad front of some 1,800 miles. The invasion was an initiative foreshadowed in Hitler's *Mein Kampf* some thirteen years earlier when he discussed creating more living space for Germans in the Soviet Union. Ironically, the French army of six hundred thousand under Napoleon some 129 years earlier had also launched an attack into Russia on June 22 with less than 16 percent of its defeated army returning to France. This latest bloody battle for Russia would continue for several years.

By early 1942, Ron's thoughts turned to playing a more active role in the war. He wanted an opportunity not only to see the world, but also to contribute to the defence of Canada. He was also concerned about the more imminent threat to the birthplace of his parents and paternal grandparents, Robert Hall and Margaret Ann Pyves, who still resided in North Shields, Northumberland. Ron also worried about the safety of his mother's many siblings, including ten sisters and four brothers living in Hastings and St. Leonards in southern England. Although he came from a long line of Master Mariners, with over four generations in the Pyves family in command of both sailing and steam-driven ships, Ron enlisted with the 2nd Battalion of the Canadian Grenadier Guards. Here he would gain some basic military experience.

It was the summer of 1942. The Germans in July launched an attack to capture Stalingrad, located in southwestern Russia on the Volga River, an important line of communication to northern Russia. Symbolically, the capture of Stalingrad (the city named after Stalin) would be a key political coup for Hitler and would also allow access to the oil fields in the Caucasus. For this reason the Russian army was equally determined to defend Stalingrad to the last soldier. Over the ensuing seven months the Germans would sustain over seven hundred thousand casualties in their failed attempt to capture the city now called Volgograd.

On the North African front in June, Rommel was successful in recapturing Tobruk, thereby forcing the British army to fall back to El Alamein, Egypt, on the coast of the Mediteranean Sea, sixty miles west of Alexandria. Tobruk was a key seaport in eastern Libya. It had a natural deep-water harbour, key to army resupply. Tobruk was, however recaptured by the British Eighth Army under General Bernard Montgomery in November 1942.

Some months earlier, on August 19, a raid by mainly Canadian forces on Dieppe, France, was a disaster when almost 60 percent of the attacking force comprised of five thousand Canadian and one thousand British soldiers were killed, wounded, or captured in the near six-hour raid. The objective of "Operation Jubilee" was to assess the German response to a seaborne raid and to demonstrate whether it was possible to capture and hold a major port. This slaughter was a precursor to the D-Day landings in 1944.

The war was heating up when Ron began his first military training at an army camp two miles outside of Saint-Basile-le-Grande in Quebec. Shortly after arriving at the camp by train, he managed to find a break to write a short note home.

> *Dear Mum & Dad, I don't know if you were at the station Sunday morning or not as I didn't see you there. We left the station at 10:30 AM, arriving at St.-Basile-le-Grande about 11:15 AM. After marching from the station to camp we were given a cup of coffee and we ate our sandwiches. Sunday afternoon we spent putting up tents and arranging our kit in them.*
>
> *I think we will be getting plenty of rifle drill tomorrow as we are supposed to be going up to the rifle range Thursday. The rifles are all .300 bore. The S.M. (Sergeant Major) told us that he is going to skip the basic training and give us the real stuff. He thinks we might be using Tommy (Machine) Guns before we leave camp.*
>
> *Well I want to go and watch a softball game between No. 1. & 2 Co.'s. Please write to me soon. Lots of Love, Ronny*

Recruits were billeted six men to a tent, given straw-filled mattresses to sleep on, and rose at 6:00 AM each day. In the morning, the recruits had twenty minutes to fold up their beds and blankets and arrange them outside of the tents for inspection. Nothing could remain inside the tents except the soldiers' rifles for safety reasons. The army issued each cadet a .303-calibre vintage World War I rifle—the U.S. Lee Enfield Eddystone—and Ron became quite proficient at target shooting. However, the routine of camp life only helped confirm Ron's new driving ambition to become a pilot in the Royal Canadian Air Force (RCAF) in Bomber Command.

At this stage of the war, the RCAF had the advantage over other military services in its ability to strike back at the heart of Germany. Besides, the RCAF was an all-volunteer force. Ron would have no part in a land war after listening to the trench warfare experiences his dad had shared with him, including one particular hair-raising close call in which his company had been recalled from the front lines just hours before a German underground mine obliterated almost *all* of the newly arrived replacements.

On February 10, 1943, Ron decided to enlist full time in the RCAF.

At the time of enlistment, he stood 5′ 9 1/2″ tall and was a wiry 130 pounds. Ron had blond hair, piercing blue eyes, and a wry sense of humour. The RCAF soon deemed him physically fit. Though he was quite reserved except amongst his closest friends, he was always a welcome addition at the local dance halls. However, Ron had now begun a nineteen-month journey of intense military training that would ultimately take him over the hostile skies of Germany, France, and Norway. Life was about to change, in more ways than one.

2
Chance Encounter

B y the time Ron joined the Air Force in February 1943, the initiative of the war in both Russia and North Africa had passed from the Germans to the Allies. In Russia the siege of Stalingrad had just been broken and one month later the Germans and the Italians had finally been driven from Africa. This allowed the Allies to consider taking the war across the Mediterranean into Sicily and ultimately into Italy itself in early September 1943. The Canadian First Infantry Division and First Canadian Army Tank Brigade would be key participants in the invasion of Sicily. With the exception of the raid on Dieppe, participation in the invasion of Sicily and Italy represented the first Canadian army broad-scale operation against the enemy since the war had begun almost four years earlier. Ron was anxious to get overseas so he could contribute to the RCAF's efforts.

Ron had been initially assigned to No. 5 Manning Depot in Lachine, Quebec, one of five collection points in Canada involved in the British Commonwealth Air Training Plan (B.C.A.T.P.). The B.C.A.T.P. was designed to train not only pilots but all of the key trades, including air gunners, flight engineers, navigators, bomb aimers, and wireless radio operators required to support air combat operations.

In early April 1943, after completion of his basic training, Ron was reassigned to No. 4 Bombing and Gunnery School in Fingal, Ontario, just southwest of London. When Ron wrote home to his mother in early April, he indicated that the base there *was "a swell looking and neatly kept place and quite a difference from Lachine. The food is really good. All the sweeping and cleaning in barrack rooms and mess halls is done by civilians.*

Life on a flying station is quite different from Manning Depot. There are not so many airmen on the station, as a result things are friendlier and there's not so much discipline.

We're out here as part of our ground duties (Tarmac Duty), wheeling planes in and out of the hangars in readiness for flight, Washing them down etc., making ourselves useful. You can learn quite a bit about aircraft working around the hangar. We can also go up on flights quite often.

I just got back an hour ago from my first flight. It was quite a delightful experience. I was up for about an hour and a quarter on a bombing flight over the target range.

Well I hope I'm not boring you with all this stuff.

I guess it will be quite a while before I get home because the train fare is $14 which isn't chicken feed.

Well so long for now and I'm going to make sure I mail this letter now. Love, Ronny"

A few days later Ron and his close friend Johnny were reassigned to the bombing range where they kept score for the bomb aimers. They were required to work ten consecutive nights and were then given a forty-eight-hour personal leave.

Upon his return to camp, Ron managed to get reassigned to the RCAF No. 6 Initial Training School (I.T.S.), located on Church Street in Toronto. All students here were put through a rigorous training regimen for two months. It included aircraft recognition, principles of flight, armament, navigation, meteorology, and signals. In order to be considered for instruction as a pilot, trainees first had to excel in the classroom. In his letter home on June 21, Ron noted:

Dear Mum, I was very glad to get your letter today – you are doing alright on the typewriter now eh!

We were on the range this afternoon firing .38 calibre revolvers, quite a difference from a rifle. I didn't get one shot on the target. The score didn't matter anyway it was just to show us how to handle a revolver.

*Say mum could you lend me a dollar till payday please, it
has cost me plenty to keep my uniform and laundry clean. Just
take a chance on putting it in an ordinary letter. I'm staying
in all week and studying from about 8:30 in the morning until
lights out at 10:30 PM. I'm just going out Saturdays only. It's
a tough course and I really have to work. Please write soon.
Ronny"*

In July, Ron had an interview with his flight commander who said
he had done very well, so far, and that if he kept it up he shouldn't
have to worry about getting through. However, in a note home on July
15, Ron mentioned that the work had become increasingly harder
and that,

*We had a navigation problem today where there were twen-
ty-five different answers to find. So you can see, it's not all as
easy as adding two and two. If I pass out of here as a pilot I
don't think there's much chance of getting any leave. The Elementary Flight Training schools always have room. If I was
a navigator or bomber I'd get two or three weeks. They always
have to wait for an opening. However I am not kicking.*

*Tell Dad that I'm working on the Browning machine gun
now, learning all of the parts. Your loving son, Ronny*

*P.S. If you ever want to get rid of some cookies I think they
will get here alright.*

Even though Ron was evaluated as a good student overall, his
teachers felt he tried too hard to be successful and appeared
somewhat immature. This was not surprising, given his age—eighteen. At a second interview in late July, after seven weeks of studies, his commander asked if he would like to be a navigator rather
than a pilot. Ron said no, assuring him he had not changed his
mind in the least. He was certain, as he wrote home just before
his courses in Toronto were finished, that he would be moving on
to pilot school.

*Dear Mum, We have four of our final examinations this
week and the last three next week, then we are finished*

one way or another and just hang around for a week or so awaiting posting.

I stayed in this weekend and studied for our exams. I'll be doing the same tonight.

If I get through this course I'll be posted down near Ottawa which will only be about sixty or eighty miles from Montreal.

Well you'll have to excuse this short note Mum; I'll do better next time. So long for now and I hope to see you and dad on the 14th. Ronny

In August, Ron went up before the aircrew selection board who rated him a candidate pilot, subject to the successful completion of pilot training school.

His dream to train as a pilot finally came true in late August 1943, when he enrolled in RCAF No. 10 Elementary Flying Training School, three miles north of Pendleton, Ontario. The Pendleton airport consisted of three short runways that could accommodate the De Havilland Tiger Moths, which were biplanes built in the early 1930s and used by many of the Commonwealth air forces primarily as training aircraft. On August 23, Ron wrote home:

Dear Mum, Well here I am at No. 10 E.F.T.S. (Elementary Flying Training School) now. It's really a lovely station; it's only about a year and a half old. We've a swimming pool here and some tennis courts under way.

I was up for my first flight today. It was really swell. We went up about 2,000 feet and levelled off, and then he let me take over the controls for a while. I flew straight for awhile and made a couple of banks (turns). I'll be up again tomorrow if flying isn't washed out because of bad weather.

It's looking kind of cloudy right now. I came 24th out of 150 at No. 6 Initial Training School. You should see the lovely flying suit, boots, helmet and gloves we were issued with.

The air at nights out here smells just like the Laurentians, really sweet after Toronto. The camp is about twelve miles from the nearest village which consists of a couple of houses and a railway station, something like Nantel.

While at school, he had received a letter from his mother, Laura, in which she informed him of the accidental death of his paternal grandmother, Margaret Pyves. She had been struck by a car in North Shields. In his letter of August 23, Ron continued:

I'm awfully sorry to hear about Gran Pyves's death. But I guess everybody has their day. But it hurts when it hits your own family eh mum. Well so long for now Mum and please write soon, Ronny

On August 27, just four days since his last letter, he sent another home:

Dear Mum, Well I've had five hours of dual instruction so far and I'll be going up for another hour or two this afternoon. I'll admit it is quite a thrill in some of the turns, spins, stalls and dives etc. I'm practicing take offs and landings just now. They are quite hard to get on to.

Well mum I have to go on parade now so so-long for now and give my regards to dad. Your loving son, Ronny

A footnote to the letter noted that he had just returned from a one-hour "flip" (flight) and that he had made a couple of fair landings and takeoffs.

Ron's positive feelings did not last for long. On September 1, Ron wrote:

Dear Mum, Flying is washed out right now for rain so I thought I'd drop you a line. There's a chance that we might get a 48 this weekend, if we do I'll be home Friday night. I hope I get it as it would be swell to see Nantel again.

Don't be surprised if I re-muster as a navigator or bombardier soon. Johnny and I aren't doing so good in flying. It's not easy by any means. The average washout is thirty percent so I may well be caught up in that thirty percent although I hope we won't. All I can do is try my best and wait for results. I'll know one way or the other by the weekend. Love, Ronny

It was unfortunate that Ron's dream was short-lived. After just a little more than fourteen hours of dual flying, it had become painfully obvious to his instructors that he had a significant co-ordination problem that resulted in too many hard and unsafe landings. It was better that Ron's pilot career be short-lived rather than his instructors' lives. His skills and excellent eyesight could be better utilized at the "back of the bus"—as a tail gunner. So in late November 1943, he transferred to RCAF No. 9 Bombing and Gunnery School at Mont Joli, Quebec, near the south shore of the St. Lawrence River.

The first six weeks of training at Mont Joli consisted of all ground training, including time on the Browning machine gun, which fired .303-inch-calibre ammunition. In combat, the ammunition used was usually a mix of 30 percent incendiary, 60 percent armour piercing, and 10 percent tracer bullets to help the gunner see where he was aiming. When the Browning was mounted in the tail section of a bomber such as the Halifax, the air gunner would sit in a powered turret which could rotate 180 degrees. The aircraft version of the Browning machine gun was air cooled, and normally four guns would be employed in the tail section turret. In the Halifax, two Browning machine guns were stacked on top of each other to the right and left of the tail gunner with the control column and firing button located centrally. Ron felt that the Browning was a lovely gun because it fired almost 1,200 rounds per minute. He was anxious to start his air instruction in the rear turrets of both the single-engine Fairey Battle and the twin-engine Bristol Blenheim light bomber, knowing also that his daily pay would be increased to $2.25. Content with training, Ron was now anxious to return home for the holidays and looked forward to family Christmas traditions.

Early in January, with mixed emotions, Ron returned to camp. Shortly after arrival, he went up on his first familiarization flight as a tail gunner. At an elevation of 15,000 feet, Ron quickly realized how cold it could get in the gunner position and appreciated his flying suit more than ever. He also found that flying helped break up the monotony of classroom work, which had become intensive. While at Mont Joli, Ron accumulated a total of eighteen hours of daylight flying. Unlike his experience in pilot training, Ron excelled in air gunnery training, where he placed eighth in a class of eighty-eight students.

On February 26, 1944, Ron transferred to RCAF No. 4 Air Gunnery

Training School in Valleyfield, Quebec. On his leaves between train-ing sessions, he had taken up skiing in the Laurentians, where the invention of the ski rope tow in the early 1930s made it one of the first areas in Canada to offer the sport. It was on one of these leaves up north in March that Ron met Kathleen (Kay) Eason. It was in the most unromantic of circumstances—Kay was brushing her teeth just out-side of her rented cottage entrance when they met. Kay was a striking brunette with shoulder-length hair, a broad smile, and dark brown eyes that seemed to twinkle with mischief and yet with the innocence of an eighteen-year-old. This was a lady Ron just had to meet. And it was an encounter that would eventually provide Ron with the moti-vation and calming influence to survive one of the most challenging and terrifying periods in his life.

Kathleen Emily Eason was born in 1925 in Montreal to Bar-tholomew (Bert) and Kathleen Mary Eason. Kay's father had come to Canada from Brighton, England, to work as a physical education instructor at Bishop's College School in the Eastern Townships. In the First World War, Bert had been stationed at a Royal Air Force training facility in Texas when the war ended. He never made it overseas. Bert then moved to Montreal to work as a chauffeur for the A.D. MacTier family. Kay's mother, Kathleen Mary, from Dundalk in County Louth, Ireland, had migrated to Canada in 1912, where she obtained a job as a lady's maid for the Allan family in Montreal. Bert and Kathleen Mary were married in 1915.

When Kay arrived on the scene, she had three older siblings, which included six-year-old Margaret Violet, five-year-old Rita, and James Anthony, a brother just two years older than her. Kay and her sib-lings grew up in an old converted coach house on Peel Street in a lane just south of Sherbrooke Street. This stretch of street known as the "Golden Mile" housed many of the city's elite. Kay went to Berthelet Public School and then attended Montreal High School. In 1942, Kay, Jimmy, and her parents moved to Dorion Street after both her sisters left home. Unfortunately, in October 1942, just after the move, Kay's mother succumbed to the cancer that she had so valiantly fought. Kay, just seventeen years old at the time, was devastated by the loss.

That same year Kay found work as a stenographer with the firm

Heward Holden. And that's where she worked when she first met Ron. The relationship between the two would soon evolve and mature through the exchange of over 170 letters.

On one occasion just prior to his departure for England, Ron went on a sleigh ride up north with Kay. There were many on board, including one of Kay's other admirers. Partway through the trip Kay made a surprise discovery: her other admirer could no longer be found. Ron eliminated the competition by discreetly pushing him off the slippery straw-covered sleigh when she wasn't looking.

It wasn't long before Ron wrote his first letter to Kay. In fact, it was within days of their first meeting.

> *Dear Kay, I don't know whether you'll appreciate me writing or not, however I'll take a chance on it.*
>
> *How did you like going back to work Monday morning? If you were like me, you didn't enjoy it very much. I got up at four and took the 5:25 bus back to Valleyfield. The first thing in the morning they took us for a four mile run through all of the water they could find. Some fun!*
>
> *I don't mind work after such a swell weekend though. It was the swellest weekend I've spent for a long while. Everything was perfect, the weather, the atmosphere and the company.*
>
> *By the way, I'd like to get to know the company much better. That is if the company agrees—do you? Swell.*
>
> *Kay if you have time to write I'd really appreciate hearing from you. So here's hoping there'll be a letter along soon.*
>
> *Well I haven't got any news right now so I'll close. Love, Ronny*

Ron happily received a quick response from Kay and seven days later sent off another letter. It was March 22.

> *Dear Kay, It was really swell to hear from you. I didn't know whether you would write or not, but anyway took the chance. I had a swell time up north last weekend, went to Morin Heights this time. It's not quite as good as St. Sauveur but we had plenty of fun anyway.*
>
> *I'm expecting to be posted to No. 1 "Y" Depot sometime*

tomorrow, that's at Lachine (on the island of Montreal). I guess you know that eh!

Say Kay, how about letting me have a picture of you, if you have one to spare. That's about all for now as I haven't any real news at the present. Love, Ronny

He did move to No. 1 "Y" Depot the same day and had an opportunity to go out with Kay one last time before heading overseas. With no end to the war in sight, Kay and Ron could expect a separation that might be measured in years.

Ron and Kay visited a number of the downtown clubs. Ron didn't get home until five in the morning with orders to report for duty just two hours later. With Ron and Kay having only gone on three dates— including their first meeting while up north skiing—what would develop in the ensuing months would be an incredible love story fueled by their prolific correspondence. Kay would be Ron's rock despite being some three thousand miles away.

He next wrote to Kay on March 29 while on a train passing through New Brunswick, on his way to Halifax for embarkation to England. In his short note, he remarked:

Dear Kay, I thought I had better not wait too long before writing to you, so here I am. I hope you'll excuse the writing, as I haven't got a pen with me and the train is swaying from side to side, making it hard to write. I hope you had a good time last night. It was swell for me being out with you. I really enjoyed it and I'm looking forward to our next date.

Don't forget to let me have a picture of yourself soon dear. The scenery going by the window right now is really very pretty; I wish you were here to see it. I bought you a little bracelet, last night; I'll send it to you as soon as I can. All my love, Ronny

3
Over There

Ron left Halifax for England on March 30, 1944. With the exception of some troop ships like the *Queen Mary*, which could outrun German submarines, the majority would cross the ocean as part of a larger convoy. The Canadian Navy played a key role in providing convoy escort for both troop ships and merchant vessels. The Navy would in fact become the primary defence force for the Allies in the Northwest Atlantic by war's end. In addition, Canada's Merchant Navy provided hundreds of cargo ships to carry key war material and food supplies to Britain and its Allies.

Many of Ron's fellow passengers found it a rough trip as their ship zigzagged across the Atlantic in convoy. But Ron found his sea legs quite early and enjoyed the passage. All ships changed courses on a frequent basis to avoid possible torpedo attacks by the many German U-boats that lurked not only in the Atlantic, but also in the Gulf of St. Lawrence. In the North Atlantic, German submarines often travelled in "wolf packs," overwhelming escorting warships with their numbers as they simultaneously attacked merchant ships. As many as thirty German U-boats could be involved in one attack. It was only when the Allies were able to provide air cover and reconnaissance over the entire Atlantic that the battle of attrition between German submarines and Allied merchant shipping tipped in favour of the Allies.

Just prior to departure, Ron had given Kay his Air Force ring which needed to be resized. It was a beautiful silver ring with the Air Force motto *Per Ardua Ad Astra* (Through Adversity to the Stars) and a Canadian goose in flight engraved in the middle. Kay accepted the ring, but with the understanding that at this point they were just friends with no formal commitment for the future. For parents, spouses, and family members on the homefront, the most terrifying part of the war was worrying about the possible death or wounding of a loved one. Not knowing from day to day could put a tremendous strain on the mind, only temporarily relieved when the postman delivered good news from overseas. With over ninety-nine thousand Canadians killed or wounded in World War II, by war's end almost every household member was intimately aware of a friend, relative, or neighbour who had received that dreaded notification from the war department. Such anxiety could also be measured in letters sent from the homefront. For instance, in 1943 alone, the post office processed over thirty-one million letters to Canadians serving overseas. With the impact of war on individuals' lives being just too unpredictable, and with Ron expected to be away for a year or longer, it didn't make sense for either party to be tied down, especially since they had just met a few weeks earlier.

Ron's ship anchored at Liverpool on April 7. He took a train to Bournemouth in the south of England, the initial clearing station for all Canadian military personnel. Processing of new arrivals and the wait for an opening at an operational training unit could take up to two months.

By now, planning was in its final stages for the invasion of Europe. "Operation Overlord" would be set for early June. All of southeastern England was being transformed into one massive staging area for the hundreds of thousands of combatants who would be involved in the largest amphibious landing in history. Meanwhile, in Italy, both the American 5th Army and British 8th Army, including the 1st Canadian Armoured Brigade, were pushing the Germans and Italians toward Rome, which would fall to the Allies just two days before D-Day.

While waiting for an assignment, Ron wrote to his parents and Kay frequently. In one note Ron gave his first impressions of England.

Dearest Kay, Well I guess I am quite a long way from you now eh!

This is really a lovely country; I never imagined it could be so beautiful. I haven't done very much in the way of work yet, but I expect it won't be long before I start again. Don't forget dear we have a date for a little less than a year from now and I'll keep it.

Have you had the picture taken yet that I'm hoping you are going to send soon? Please write soon. Goodnight for now dear.

All my love, Ronny

During the wait for a permanent assignment Ron received a letter.

Dear Ronny, Hello there. I hope this letter does not take too long to reach you. It was swell to receive your letter and card, and to know that you had a lot of fun Monday, I enjoyed every second right up to the last one.

I guess you were glad to get off the train as it's always tiring.

How do you like it overseas? You'll be having a lot of thrilling experiences; it would be nice to hear all about them. Tell you what; we'll exchange news, mine from Montreal and yours from there OK?

I brought the ring into the jewellers to have it made smaller, it's awfully nice and needless to say every time I look at it, I think of you and the fun we've had.

About the picture Ronny, I'm having it taken at the "Surprise Studios." I hope the picture doesn't take after the name. I hope you'll send me yours too.

Well Ronny this isn't a very long letter but will write again soon, and hope you will too. Thinking of you, All my love, Kay

Sitting in the sun in the local park after roll call, Ron read over her letter several times. He felt good that he had someone back home with whom he could share his feelings and experiences. Taking out a new pen, he responded:

Dear Kay, I was surprised to receive a letter from you so soon after arriving here, I thought it would be about a month before I started getting any mail over here.

I wish you could see this country; you would really enjoy the scenery. There are all kinds of lovely rock gardens and parks. Maybe someday you'll take a trip over and see it all for yourself.

I'm certainly glad that I was up at St. Sauvier on a certain weekend about a month ago, if I hadn't I would have missed something very important to me—meeting you Kay.

I've been having life pretty easy so far, haven't really done anything yet. This afternoon I lay in the park and took in the sunshine. The little kids here come running up and ask us for chewing gum, candy and money.

I expect we may be getting a leave sometime soon. I hope so as I have quite a few relatives in England to visit. The last time they saw me was about fourteen years ago, so I don't suppose they'll recognize me eh!

We aren't allowed to give any names of towns or cities in our letters as you can well understand.

Well darling I guess that's about all for now but I will write again soon. All my love darling, Ronny

Just prior to the start of a seven-day personal leave he received a number of letters from Kay which included one dated April 14.

Hello Ronny, I hope this letter finds you as happy as me (pay night). Everything always appears brighter on Pay Day; of course the "Canadians" winning the Stanley Cup helped too, they certainly played a good game.

All I need now is to hear from you, I feel just like you said you did when you went to the Base P.O. to see if you had mail and were disappointed, but I'm keeping my fingers crossed it won't be long now until you're able to write.

Talking about spring, you should see Montreal; I wish you could, no kidding Ronny it's just like winter out.

The lawyers in our office are throwing a party on the 13th of May for the stenographers and guests and I wish you were here to be my own very special guest.

Well Ronny I certainly can rave on, if I'm like this at eighteen, goodness knows what a gossip I'll be when I'm sixty. Of course men do their share of gossiping too, I hear.

I'll wish you goodnight for now and hope to hear from you in the very near future, in fact tomorrow I'm hoping it will be. All my love, Kay

At the time, Kay worked as a stenographer for one of the first women lawyers to be called to the Quebec bar, Ms. Constance Short at Heward Holden.

Although Ron had written several letters to Kay since his arrival in England, as of April 22 none of them had yet been received by her.

Hello Ronny, how are you? I'm still a Lady In Waiting—for your first letter I mean. I'm still hoping though.

I wasn't very busy at work this morning and I was tempted to type a letter to you, but resisted temptation and waited till I got home. Now if I can resist all temptations like that it will be O.K.

I got the ring out of the jewellers the other day and they made a swell job of making it smaller, size nine to six, I'll have to admit you win there.

Looking forward to that letter and hoping, I'll say so long, and take care of yourself. Love, Kay

At the start of his leave on April 24, Ron decided to head to London to see the city and visit with his cousin, Lenny Bellringer. Lenny, like Ron, had volunteered for the RCAF as an air gunner. In 1939, before the onset of war, the Greater London area had a population in excess of 8.6 million, representing a third of the population of England and Wales. This population would shrink to under 8 million when young children and families were evacuated to the countryside at the start of the war. London had been a city under siege since September 1940 when German bombers first attacked the capital. The London Blitz, which ultimately resulted in the death of over twenty-two thousand Londoners, had continued until May 1941 when Germany's focus turned to Russia. The extensive damage from the blitz was still evident as Ron travelled about the city. The presence of air raid shelters, anti-aircraft flak batteries, barrage balloons, and the ever-present military were strong reminders that this historic city was still very much at war.

While in London, Ron joined The Beaver Club, an association located near Trafalgar Square which provided welcome refuge for many Canadian military personnel on leave in the city. After his quick two-day stay in London, Ron paid a surprise visit to his grandmother, Ellen Hilder, in Hastings, feeling fortunate to have relatives in England, unlike so many other military personnel. Ron was often up twice a night due to flying bombs but his luck held and nothing came close. Ron also visited St. Peter's Church where his parents were married. But once back on base, Ron checked to see if he had any mail from home and was pleased to receive several letters from Kay. In one of these she confirmed,

Dear Ronny, I received your letter and was glad to hear from you. I would have answered it last night but some of the gang from the office dropped up and knowing how girls are for talking (or do you?) I couldn't make it. It's 7 o'clock in the morning so you can see I really did have good intentions of writing you right away.

It's true that you say we are both a long way off, but letters are a swell way of keeping in touch, until we actually see each other again. Montreal did have some excitement yesterday when a B24 Liberator crashed near Ottawa Street but it was awful and not the kind of news one likes to hear, I guess it's old news to you now.

As it's just about time to get ready for work, I'll say so long but just for a little while as I will write real soon.

Looking forward to hearing from you and seeing you, All my love, Kay

Ron wrote another letter home to his mother, being anxious to re-connect with both his parents after almost seven weeks of no news.

Dear Mum & Dad, Well here I am back again after seven days of leave. I had a really swell time. Your ears must have been burning last week because there sure were a lot of people talking about you mum. I've invited them all over to Canada for a visit so here's hoping they take me up on it.

In case dad is interested, we're flying in Wellingtons here for our training and later on we'll be flying in aircraft with the same name as the port that I left Canada from, you know what.

We were on the range today doing some skeet shooting. That's a lot of fun especially when you are using a 12-gauge shotgun to fire at them with. Whenever a crow flew by we took a pot shot at it too. Most of the crows over here aren't as big as the ones in Canada.

Boy, am I glad I am not an officer over here. They have to pay for everything and through the nose. We get our laundry, shoes repaired and sometimes better food than they do, at least as good anyway. The best rank in the Air Force as far as I'm concerned is a Warrant Officer 1st Class.

Well mum and dad I'll ring off for now and I hope to hear from you soon. Your loving son, Ronny

Although he had received mail from Kay, by May 3 Ron had not received any letters from home and started to become concerned that something had gone wrong. He wrote to Kay on Tuesday, May 9.

Dearest Kay, Boy I'm just about the happiest fellow around here today after receiving two swell letters from you. It's wonderful to hear from you and to know that you have started receiving my letters at last.

I haven't had a single letter from the family yet. I'm sure they must have written, but the letters must be mislaid somewhere. Would you mind phoning my house sometime and ask mum if she's had any mail from me yet?

We are getting paid tomorrow and I promise to get my picture taken the same day. I never can take a decent picture any-

way but I'll take a chance and see how it turns out. I hope you will not be disappointed with the result.

Ron added:

You know Kay I'll never forget you, as you were, the last night I was in Montreal. I was proud to be out with you dear, you were lovely. The next time we go out, we'll go to the same places and do the same things okay, just as if I had never had to leave you.

Well darling I'll leave you until tomorrow and please phone mum will you, she'd love to know that you are hearing from me alright. All my love and kisses, Ronny.

On May 10, Kay sent Ron a letter through the regular mail system.

Dear Ronny, This letter will probably take ages to reach you, as it's not half as fast as the Air Mail forms.

I haven't heard from you for nearly two weeks now, I heard the mail is being held up so I'll just keep my fingers crossed until I have some luck, I will keep right on writing and hope that you're receiving all mine O.K.

(Buzz) Beurling was in our office a few days back, to see one of the lawyers. The poor guy, with everybody peeking around corners to see him. But I bet he loved it just the same. Don't forget to send the picture and above all to keep writing. All my love, Kay

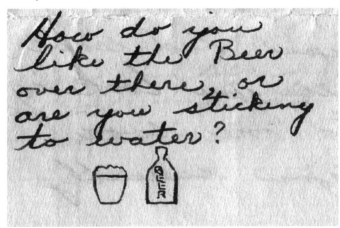

George Frederick "Buzz" Beurling, at the time of his visit to Heward Holden, had become the most celebrated and successful fighter pilot in the RCAF in World War II. He had destroyed thirty-one enemy aircraft during his active combat career while stationed in Malta.

Desperate to make contact, Ron decided to send another letter to his parents. He wrote:

> *Dear Mum & Dad, I've just been down and sent off a telegram to you, I hope you receive it alright. Are you receiving my mail?*
>
> *You'll probably get a phone call from Kay sometime, I asked her to phone you to see if you are getting my mail or not. I'd like you to meet her mum. Invite her down for supper some time if you can. I'm sure you'll like her she's really a swell girl.*
>
> *I just got paid today, boy am I glad. A pound note around here lasts just about the same length of time as a two dollar bill in Montreal, you know how long that is. I haven't done a thing since I came here except go on roll calls twice a day. I'll get fat if I lay around much longer. I saw some kittens today that were only a few hours old, they were hardly more than a handful.*
>
> *Well mum I'll close now and will write again soon. Your loving son, Ronny*

On May 16, Ron was finally struck off strength at Bournemouth and received orders to report for duty at Operational Training Unit (O.T.U.) No. 22, located in Wellesbourne, Warwickshire, just three miles from Stratford-upon-Avon, one of the most beautiful locations in England. Ron was anxious to start his operational training and get in the air as it had been three months since he'd been up.

Ron arrived in Wellesbourne on May 18, 1944. At the start of the O.T.U. program, hundreds of unassigned air personnel were placed in a large hall and instructed to form individual aircrews. This was a critical process, as who you selected could mean the difference between survival and a quick demise—if even one member of the crew rated below average in performance.

Ron was quick to team up with twenty-three-year-old Flying Officer Bob Henry from Saskatoon, and Sergeant Bill Thomson, a youthful twenty-year-old mid-upper gunner from Toronto. Ron was very lucky to be teamed up with Bob, an "above average" pilot, who had already accumulated over nine hundred hours of flying experience. Additional crew members selected included bomb aimer Flying Officer Frank Welsh, twenty-one years old from London, Ontario; wireless operator Flight Sergeant Hal Ward, twenty-three years old also from London; and navigator Flying Officer Al Coleman, twenty years old from Magrath, Alberta. The flight engineer, Sergeant Joe Casavant from Tisdale, Saskatchewan, would not join the crew until they later moved on to the Heavy Conversion Training Unit where they cut their teeth on four-engine planes. At twenty-six, Joe was the oldest crew member and Hal the only married member. With the exception of Bob, who had been a pilot instructor in Canada, Hal had the most flying experience, having logged over eight hundred hours prior to his arrival in England.

As officers, the pilot, bomb aimer, and navigator ate their meals and drank at the bar in the Officers' Mess. Even though the crew would all share the same dangers on future combat missions, as non-commissioned officers, the flight engineer, upper gunner, wireless operator, and Ron had to take their meals and drinks in the Sergeants' Mess. If the crew had to bail out over enemy territory, the officers could also be expected, as prisoners of war, to be detained in facilities which were better than those for non-commissioned officers. But formalities aside, Ron was liking his crewmates and looking forward to training together.

> *I'm now at an Operational Training Station. I got posted away from all the fellows I knew during my course but have met a very nice fellow who was in the same boat so we stuck together. He is an A.G. (Air Gunner) also and we are in the same crew. They are a swell bunch of fellows and I'm sure we'll get along well together as a team. The oldest member of our crew is twenty-six. I'm the youngest at nineteen. Just a baby. ha! ha!*
>
> *I met a fellow here who I used to go to school with, it was quite a surprise as I haven't seen him for about six years.*
>
> *Well mum goodnight for now and I'm hoping to hear from you soon. Your loving son, Ronny*

Letter writing represented the primary means of communication for all the hundreds of thousands of military personnel who tried to remain in contact with their families back home. It came as no surprise that letters sometimes were held up for weeks on end. It was more rare and surprising when a letter would make it from Canada to England in just three or four days.

I know I'm just the happiest fellow around the camp today. What a lovely surprise getting eight letters from you and all at once. Honestly though, I nearly fell over when I checked through the mail and found all those swell letters from you dear.

There are lots of things I would like to tell you dear, about a few exciting times I've had here so far but of course censorship won't allow it as you can no doubt understand. However I'll have plenty to tell you when we do meet again.

I'll be getting a 48-hour pass sometime next week after which I'll be starting to fly again. It's really going to be good to get upstairs again with the clouds; you'd really love it up there Kay that is if you weren't airsick.

There is some really solid boogie coming over the radio right now. Gosh that really makes me think of the good old city again and the swell times we used to have there. I went and saw an old show last night that I've seen before just to hear the music. It was Hello Frisco Hello.

It's funny when you think of the difference in time between this country and Canada. Here I am writing this letter at 8:20 in the evening and it's only 2:20 in the afternoon in Montreal right now.

There is still no sign of any mail from home. I'm beginning to wonder if everything is okay at home. If I don't soon get some I'll send them another cablegram. I received all your mail okay and the family only lives about five miles from you so there is no reason why I shouldn't get theirs okay, is there?

Well Kay I'm going to have to end our little talk now as I haven't got another nickel to put in the phone so I'll call you up again okay? Goodnight darling, all my love and kisses, Ronny

By May 31, with still no news from his parents, Ron became quite concerned, so that morning sent a Canadian Pacific Telegraph through normal commercial channels.

Dear Mum, Have not heard from you yet. Is everything Okay? Please Reply. Ron Pyves

He sent this telegram just an hour before his first training flight. All his training for the next three weeks would be in twin-engine Wellington bombers which were armed with two .303-calibre machine guns in the rear turret. The aircraft, although covered in a canvas skin, had a geodesic structure designed by famous British aircraft designer Barnes Wallace and was, in fact, quite durable. Geodesic structures take advantage of the strength characteristics of both the pyramid and the sphere to create curved surfaces, which can be light and extraordinarily strong so they can withstand high wind speeds. The Wellington bomber was significantly smaller than the four-engine Halifax bomber used on Ron's first combat missions. The Wellington empty weighed in at just over 18,000 pounds versus 38,240 pounds for the Halifax. It was also seven feet shorter and had a wingspan of just over eighty-six feet versus nearly ninety-nine feet for the Halifax.

From mid-May to the end of July Ron flew on forty-eight training missions, which included manoeuvres in night interception, bombing, fighter affiliation, air firing, and cross-country navigation exercises, which provided an additional fifty-one hours of daylight and forty hours of nighttime flying experience. Ron would soon join the over four thousand Bomber Group 6 aircrew engaged in pushing Hitler off the coast of Normandy and back to the Rhine and, in the process, destroying key transportation and manufacturing facilites deep inside Germany.

Finally on June 2, after his return from a test flight in late afternoon, Ron received two letters from friends who informed him that his mother had gone into hospital for a major operation. She was now recovering satisfactorily. Relieved to hear she was all right, he scribbled a note to his parents that very same day.

Dear Mum & Dad, How is everything, back home now and

above all how are you feeling now? I was wondering why I hadn't heard from you and when I got a letter from Leslie and one from Bette saying that you had just come out of the hospital after an operation I nearly fell over.

We just started flying again yesterday for the first time since February. It was so good to get off the deck again. Quite a few of us go up together and stay for a little more than an hour, so after I had finished my part of the exercise I started writing this letter on the navigator's table. So if you find the writing hard to understand it's because we were flying at 3,000 feet at about 150 M.P.H. and it was very bumpy upstairs today.

I was just thinking last year at this time I was in Toronto at No. 6 I.T.S. (Initial Training School) remember? Now I am over here, one thing you sure get around with the Air Force.

Well mum, I'll close now hoping to hear from you soon. Your loving son, Ronny

Ron was in flight on a late afternoon firing exercise on D-Day (June 6). That day he wrote of the invasion and his expectations. Ron was now getting close to his first mission.

Dear Mum & Dad, It was really swell getting your letter today dad. I'll have to confess I didn't recognize the handwriting at first.

I'm really happy that you're feeling much better now mum and I hope by the time you get this letter you are feeling 101% again.

I guess the good news of the start of the invasion has reached Canada today. I only hope that it's not another Dieppe. I'm just waiting for my chance to get a crack at the Germans now and all the boys here feel the same. I suppose after it really gets going they will be fighting for all the same spots you fought for in the past war, eh dad like Vimy Ridge etc.

I was up flying this afternoon only for about an hour and a half though. The Wellingtons are really good kites to fly again in. The other day I lay down in the bomb aimers position and watched the country roll by. It was really swell as the fields look just like a huge patchwork quilt of different shades of yellow, green, and brown. We happened to fly over Stratford, you know Shakespeare's home town, it's really a smartly laid out city.

Well mum, I'm going to say adios for now and I will write again soon. Your loving son, Ronny

As news of D-Day spread, Kay immediately decided to send Ron a quick note by aerogram to share the excitement swirling around the city.

Dear Ronny, Yesterday was a very memorable day, as it was the first news we had received about "D-Day." I'm afraid no one did much work; it just seemed to bring the War so much closer to us.

Over here there's a little war going on all its own, between the sailors and fellows in uniform and Zoot-Suiters, it's really something. I'm afraid the Zoot-Suiters are losing out too. They're going to either have to swap their zoot-suits for a uniform or else at least change their tailor if they can't get in the services.

The new songs out now that I think are the best are "Holiday for Strings," "I'll Be Seeing You," "I'll Get By." Don't you think "I'll Be Seeing You" is sort of a nice title?

I'll close for now but will write again in a very little while. Missing you very much, All my love, Kay

In many parts of North America, many young men were labelled zoot-suiters because they wore a style of clothes that included a long coat or suit jacket with wide lapels and padded shoulders, an anti-uniform symbolizing independence and in some cases, opposition to military involvement. Due to the excessive use of cloth required to outfit a zoot-suiter, technically their clothes contravened the rationing of fabrics and textiles set out by the Canadian Wartime Prices and Trade Board. Many Canadians viewed them as "unpatriotic." Many servicemen also viewed zoot-suiters as slackers avoiding military service. By late May 1944 there were many isolated incidents of violence between zoot-suiters and servicemen in Montreal which culminated in a major disturbance on the evening of Saturday, June 3, when hundreds of sailors sought out zooters at various Montreal night clubs and dance halls. It would take until the early hours of Sunday morning before local police and shore patrolmen were able to regain control of the streets.

Back in England, Ron finally had a day off after flying for six out of seven days in various exercises which included air firing, and circuits and bumps with eight different pilots. The break allowed him to pen another letter to Kay in which he remarked:

Darling, Gosh what a lovely surprise to receive your picture in a letter, it's really swell and I'm looking forward to the big one. I carry your picture with me all the time even when I'm flying. You were up flying with me for two hours this afternoon whether you know it or not. Did you enjoy it dear?

I've really got in with a good crew; they're all a nice bunch of fellows and get along well together. The whole crew is going into town tomorrow to celebrate the fact that we got paid today. You should see the old English Pubs; they are really quaint and go under names like Pied Bull, the Stag's Head, the King's Head, and Chequer Inn etc. Last night I met a couple of Americans who were driving around in a jeep, so I promptly made friends with them and borrowed it for a while. I've never even driven a car before and here I was tearing down the road in a jeep, boy what fun. The cops took a dim view of the fact that I didn't have a driver's licence but I managed to talk them out of taking my number.

On our flip yesterday afternoon, my skipper (F/O Murray) let me take control of the ship! I was flying a Wimpy around for about half an hour, lots of fun but hard work. There's so many instruments and controls in the cockpit, they darn near make you dizzy just to look at them until you get to know what they are all for.

Well history is certainly being made over here now, eh! I guess all the Montreal papers are featuring the invasion news now. I saw the huge fleets of planes going over the night the paratroopers went in. It was really an impressive sight and I

won't forget it in a hurry.
I guess I'll have to close now but will write you again tonight.
So until I see you again stay as lovely as you are dear. All my
love and kisses darling, Ronny

The planes that Ron saw carrying paratroopers over to Normandy on the evening of June 5 were the lead element of what would be a massive invasion of France in the early morning hours of June 6. Over twenty-five thousand Canadian, British, and American paratroopers were dropped behind the German lines with an additional one hundred and sixty thousand troops landing on the shores of Normandy that day. Over five thousand ships were involved in the transportation of the invading forces that were dropped off along fifty miles of Normandy coastline divided into five areas labeled Utah, Omaha, Gold, Juno, and Sword. The First U.S. Army landed on Omaha and Utah beaches while the British Second Army landed on Sword, Juno, and Gold beaches. Many other Allied countries also played a role in the landings, including Free France, Australia, Poland, Greece, Norway, and New Zealand. Five days after D-Day, over three hundred and twenty-five thousand soldiers and fifty-four thousand vehicles had landed on the beaches along with over two hundred million pounds of supplies. It had been an unparalleled logistical operation.

On the night before the landings Allied bombers, including the RCAF, flew over 1,200 sorties targeting German gun emplacements, troops, rail and transportation communication structures, and ammunition stockpiles. The air campaign against German synthetic oil factories also continued to limit the mobility of the German Panzer reserves that depended on adequate fuel supplies to counterattack the Allied invasion.

The majority of Canadian forces, consisting of the Third Canadian Infantry Division and the Second Canadian Armoured Brigade, landed on Juno Beach, with the first wave of assault suffering 50 percent casualties. By the end of the first day of fighting, the Third Canadian Division had made greater progress than any other Allied military force. The objective of the Canadian forces was ultimately to capture Caen in the subsequent weeks and assist elements of the British

Second Army in protecting the left flank of the First U.S. Army, who had the key task of capturing the port of Cherbourg and then breaking out into Brittany.[1] Securing a major port was critical to the Allies, who needed to re-equip the troops with military supplies, food, and ammunition. The goal of the Canadian units once a bridgehead had been secured and Caen captured was to play a defensive role until Cherbourg was in the hands of the Allies. Cherbourg would not fall to the Americans until June 26 and Caen would not be captured by British and Canadian troops until July 9.[2] Nevertheless, by the end of D-Day, over 21,000 Canadian troops would land at Juno Beach with the loss of 335 officers and men killed in action or dying of their wounds. Kay's brother-in-law, Lieutenant William Albert Bennett, participated in the D-Day landing on Gold Beach. He had been seconded to the Dorsetshire Regiment. It would not be until almost two months later that Kay and her sister Rita would learn that William was missing in action. By the end of July, Canadian forces in France would suffer over 10,500 casualties.[3]

Ron had just returned to base from a bombing and cross-country exercise on June 12 when he received his first letter in his mother's handwriting since March 1944. Ron was excited and immediately crafted a response.

Dear Mum, Boy, it was good to get a letter from you again. I guess the last time I got one was at Mont Joli or was it at Valleyfield?

I hope you are feeling much better now mum, whatever you do, take it easy and don't work too hard. It'll be good for you when you can go up to Nantel again. The fresh pine up there is really good for what ails anybody.

Thanks ever so much for the swell parcel which I received yesterday mum. Those shortbreads were perfect, as the rest of my crew readily agreed. The crew was out on a little party last night so the cigars didn't last long either. I'm saving the last one to smoke tonight.

We were on a four-hour cross-country flight this afternoon. It was a nice warm summer afternoon on the ground but where we're flying at 12,000 feet it was no less than fifteen below zero.

Brrr! We're on another one tomorrow and I'm certainly going to put on more clothes than I did today.

I expect we'll be getting a 48-hour pass in about two weeks time, if we do the whole crew is going to London together. We should have a good time there eh!

Well what do you think of the invasion news? It certainly will be a costly project, but lets hope it will put a stop to the war soon. Then once again it'll be an oddity to see a military aircraft flying around overhead or a uniform in the street. Of course there will be plenty of commercial aircraft flying around but that's what we want. I believe that Canada will be the centre of a world-wide airways system.

Well mum, four hours in the air is as hard on you as about ten on the ground so I will close now as I am so tired I can hardly keep my eyes open, but will write again very soon. So I'll say goodnight to the swellest mum and dad anybody could ever want and I'm looking forward to another letter from you soon. Your loving son, Ronny

Kay also wrote to Ron with some big news. She had at last taken the initiative to contact his mother, Laura, which had been at first a little awkward.

Dear Ronny, I phoned your mother on Tuesday and she said that she had sent 4 parcels and 20 letters, so you'll probably be receiving them all O.K. She was sorry that you hadn't received them but gosh all the mail is so darn mixed up.

She asked me down to see her sometime and so I am going on Thursday, she really sounds very friendly and at first I was sort of shy to introduce myself but she received your letter and made me feel at ease. All my love, Kay

Ron participated in a solo cross-country exercise in Wellington XNA, with Flying Officer Bob Henry piloting the aircraft. It had been twelve days since D-Day. Ron practised his air firing and, having been airborne for almost five hours, landed back at Wellesbourne in mid-afternoon. After a late lunch in the Sergeants' Mess, he sat down and wrote a letter to Kay about some of his most recent flying adventures, which included the loss of several crewmates. It was the first time he had experienced the loss of fellow aircrew and it brought to reality the significant risks involved, even in training.

Darling, We are really flying a lot now, we've been up five hours a day for about two weeks now. While we were up today, I saw a few of the many huge fleets of Fortresses that went over Germany today. It was a wonderful sight, the formations with their escorts of fighters moving as one plane, we were about 8,000 feet above them and so had a perfect view. I guess Germany is really taking a pounding now.

One of the crews in our station that was on a cross-country flight with us two days ago crashed into a mountainside and were all killed instantly, it's too bad things like that have to happen but I suppose that's all part of the game when you are flying.

Gosh! Dear you should see the fields of flowers over here right now. It's really something worth seeing. There are huge fields of beautiful red poppies dotted all over the English countryside so thick in places it looks like red paint or blood. Yes I guess it has a good reason to look like blood.

They've started bombing London and the south coast again this time with their ingenious robot planes, but I don't suppose it will take the British long to find a counter measure against them.

The latest letter from mum and dad said that dad had gone up north for the weekend to open up our country house. Did I ever tell you about it dear? It's at Nantel, a little two-house and a railway station village about fifteen or twenty miles up the C.P.R. line from St. Sauveur. It's a lovely little place but too quiet but sometimes people appreciate a quiet place for a change.

Well honey I guess I'll close now but will write again soon. All my love and kisses darling and take care of yourself. Yours always, Ronny

The aircrew that Ron referred to were most likely flying in Wellington HZ715, which had hit a hill at Buttermere, Cumberland, in Scotland.[4] This plane had eight Canadians on board, including three pilots. Five crew members were from Ontario with the remaining crew from Quebec, Alberta, and Saskatchewan. All were buried in the Blacon Cemetery in Chester. In World War II, over three thousand Canadian airmen were lost in training, which represented over 19 percent of all RCAF wartime losses.

On June 20, Ron and the crew had a three-day leave and decided to grab a train to London together. Everyone enjoyed themselves but they had quite a time dodging buzz bombs and once or twice thought that their day had come. Even though there was an interlude of over three years when London was not attacked by German bombers, in June 1944 London once again came under siege from unmanned flying bombs launched from across the English Channel. These early weapons of terror would be responsible for another eight thousand London lives and the destruction of over one million British homes before the continental launch sites were overrun by Allied armies.

There were two versions of unmanned flying bombs launched from sites in France. London of course was the main target. The V-1, about twenty-seven feet long, carried a payload of close to one ton of explosives and travelled at speeds in excess of 300 miles per hour. The V-1 had a range of approximately 160 miles and was propelled by an engine that cut out just before the bomb started its descent. This meant that when the bomb engine's buzzing noise stopped, individuals below knew they only had seconds to seek shelter. These unmanned bombs were designed to terrorize the civilian population— and they did. Hundreds of thousands of Londoners evacuated the city when these "terror" bombs started falling. Notwithstanding the panic and dread, Londoners with their dry sense of humour would label these bombs "doodlebugs." What better way to cope than with a sense of humour.

The V-2, first launched at London in early September, had a similar payload to the V-1 but travelled at a much greater rate than the speed of sound—so there was no warning before impact. The V-2 was the world's first ballistic missile, stood almost forty-six feet high, and if launched vertically could reach an altitude of over fifty miles before it started its deadly descent back to earth. Before these unmanned V-bombs, the most recent major blitz on London had occurred almost three years earlier when four hundred German bombers attacked London on the night of May 10, 1941, and into the early morning hours.

Darling, My crew and I just came back from a three day leave which we spent in London together. We had a very good time, it's quite a city, and of course we didn't do any drinking. I had quite a time dodging doodlebugs which isn't too bad if they don't come too close. Once or twice I thought my day had come but anyway here I am still in one piece. If you were to light a firecracker or if a car backfired near me, I'd probably dive for the sidewalk or under a table, I suppose it takes time to get used to these things.

Well dear I'll have to close for now as we are flying tonight and it takes a long time to get ready for a flight. I'll be writing again very soon dear. Your picture will be with me tonight as it always is.

Goodnight darling, All my love and Kisses, Ronny

That evening Ron and the crew flew on a one-hour fighter affiliation exercise with F/O Kennedy in command of Wellington XNG. It was important that the bomber crews learned how to fly with a fighter escort. Ron took the opportunity to write another letter to Kay just two days later when heavy rain and fog enveloped the local air bases, cancelling all flying. The dreariness that crept over the base permeated right through to his letter.

Darling, It's going to be a happy day when I can have the pleasure of taking you out again and going any where we want, doing what we want and when we want, won't it be swell Kay? In the meantime, I've got a job to do over here and the sooner it's over with the better, so honey, wish me luck. I can probably use some of your good Irish luck soon. Anyway I'm convinced after the events of the past couple of weeks that as long as I carry your picture with me I'm safe and I've really got faith in that. I've stared death in the face four times lately, and got away with it so you can see what I mean.

Well sweetheart, I'll say goodnight for now, Ronny

On July 4, Ron sent a cable to Kay in which he wished her *"Many happy returns of the day"* so he could be sure she would receive his birthday wishes in time for her nineteenth.

Dear Ronny, It was a lovely surprise to receive your cable, I thought it was so nice and luckily I received two letters just the other day so I'm actually darn well treated on my birthday. Now that I am at the ripe old age of nineteen I'm becoming really an authority on life and have come to the conclusion that it's a pretty nice one too, especially because such nice people are in it.

Gosh Ronny I could go on and on but then that's impossible. Take care of yourself. All my love, Kay

With the exception of one particular hair-raising diversion to Ireland on July 7 due to foul weather, Ron felt that overall his training experience had been quite uneventful, as he recounted in a letter on July 10.

Well dear, I've finally visited your homeland. We were on a flight the other night, when we got cut off by bad weather and so we were forced down in Ireland near Belfast. I had to spend the night there and then flew back to base the next day. We landed there without any trouble, but things looked bad for a while, the kite (aircraft) was being tossed around by rough air and lightning was flashing around us, so I still claim your picture is bringing not only me but our whole crew good luck. Whenever we go out anywhere together I always interrupt everything that's going on and propose a toast to Kay.

No Kay I'm not on ops yet but it won't be long now. Don't tell mum that, will you dear because I wrote and told her that I had a long training to do yet and I don't want her worrying for nothing. We are flying about every night now though, it gets very tiring flying all night and sleeping all day, then the same thing over again but I guess I shouldn't kick. Lots of people over here have to put up with much greater hardships than that.

Write again soon won't you dear, yours always, Ronny

While flying in this severe rain storm, Frank Welsh later recalled that it was the first time he experienced the marvel known as St. Elmo's fire. It appeared not only as a greenish purplish glow around the bomber windows but also on the propeller tips, which resulted in a violet halo around each of the four engines. St. Elmo's fire is an electrical weather phenomenon in which a luminous ionized gas is created by an electrical discharge, usually from a grounded object in an electrical field such as a thunderstorm. St. Elmo's fire had originally been associated with ships caught at sea in a thunderstorm, but it can also appear on aircraft in flight.

Ron and his crew were lucky to have survived their foul-weather ordeal—fatal air accidents occurred on a fairly regular basis due to inexperienced aircrew, mechanical malfunctions, unpredictable English weather, and sporadic enemy fighter attacks over air bases. At Wellesbourne alone, over two hundred Canadian aircrew were killed or seriously injured in air training accidents during the war. Many an unfortunate aircrew in training never made it to operational readiness. Ron was almost one; while crawling to his rear turret he slipped off the narrow walkway which led to the back of the aircraft. One of his legs broke through the canvas skin of the Wellington where it dangled precariously outside the plane some several thousand feet above ground. He tenuously hung on to the metal framework to make sure he didn't slip out any further. His fellow crewmates heard his desperate screams for help and after some tense, freezing moments, pulled him safely back into the aircraft. This was just one example of how each member of the crew needed to act together as an attentive, cohesive team to survive. There was clearly no room for mistakes—even one mistake could be the last.

With Ron's last training flight at Wellesbourne scheduled for midnight, he picked up his pen to convey some of his innermost thoughts. It was July 18.

> *Dear Kay, I can tell you something that you probably didn't know about me, that is I am shy, unless of course I've been drinking and if it wasn't for that, I would have told you the night I left you in your porch that I love you dear instead of waiting until now. The reason I told you now Kay is because I'm just about finished my training and will be going on ops*

soon and just in case anything does happen to me I want you to know how I feel about you dear. I'm not a pessimist but you never know in this game which is your last flight.

Well dear I've done my best to explain how things stand, I'm sorry if this letter is a bit mixed but you know when the bug bites you it bites hard, I'm always thinking of you honey day and night, it keeps my morale up.

Well I'll say goodnight for now darling. All my love and kisses as ever, Ronny

Ron graduated from the Wellesbourne training school with an "above average" rating as an air gunner, and moved to his final stage of pre-combat training at No. 1659 Heavy Conversion Unit Training near Topcliffe, a small English village beside the River Swale in North Yorkshire. His first mission was drawing near.

Ron's parents, Edward Lewis Pyves and Laura Hilder, who were married on December 26, 1917, in St. Leonards, England

Ron as an army cadet and while he attended Maisonneuve Public School in Montreal

Ron with his older brother, Edward Lewis Pyves Jr., who would later volunteer for the Navy

Air Force ring that Ron would give to Kathleen Eason in March 1944 just prior to embarking for England

Ron with fellow classmates at No. 9 Bombing and Gunnery School, Mont Joli, Quebec. Ron is in front row on right side.

First picture that Kay sent Ron, which he received shortly after he arrived in England

Ron posing on Serpentine Bridge in Hyde Park located in London, England, while on personal leave in summer 1944

Ron's membership card for the Beaver Club in London, which was a social club and welcome refuge for the many Canadian military personnel on leave in London. Members could have their mail forwarded to the club for pickup.

THE BEAVER CLUB, LONDON, 1940

SPRING GARDENS, S.W.1

MEMBERSHIP CARD

MEMBER:

Ron on a visit with his relatives in Hastings while on personal leave in 1944. From left to right: Ron Pyves, Auntie Pop, Ellen Hilder, cousin Reggie Simmonds, and two other sisters of Laura Hilder unidentified.

F/Lt. Bob Henry, Pilot

F/O Frank Welsh, Bomb Aimer

Warrant Officer Second Class Bill Thomson, Mid-Upper Gunner

F/O Hal Ward, Wireless Operator/Air Gunner

F/O Alan Coleman, Navigator   F/Sgt. Joe Casavant, Flight Engineer

Ron's crewmates, whom he met up with at Wellesbourne, England, while stationed at No. 22 Operational Training Unit, except for Joe Casavant who joined the crew at No. 1659 Heavy Conversion Unit. These six individuals along with Ron, hailing from Quebec, Saskatchewan, Ontario, and Alberta, would end up as one strong cohesive team.

= Somewhere In England =
May 3rd 1944.

Dear Mum & Dad,

Well here I am back again after seven days leave. I had a really swell time. First of all I went up to London to see Lenny, he wasn't there but his wife and mother inlaw were so I spent the weekend with them. Betty is really a very nice girl. By the way she would very much appreciate a couple of pairs of stockings size 10. So I'll pay me for them and you can take it out of my money.

After I left London I went down to Evans I walked in there about 9 o'clock Sunday night, boy were they surprised. They could hardly believe it was me. I spent the last five days of my leave there. It was good to see Aunty Pop, Aunt Bess, Uncle George and Fran. Of course I visited Aunt Kate & Uncle Arthur and met Peter and little Roger. I went out at nights with Reg. Then I saw Aunty Em and George Ballinger. I went out to Olive Vale and saw Aunty Edie, Uncle Arthur and Pearl. Pearl took me over to Cousin Vic's and met her husband. Auntie Ede took me along to an office in your home town and I met Sid's wife Daphne. She a very nice girl. I dropped in to see Uncle Ted, he's really keeping very well. Also Aunty Nell and Uncle George White. Sure was a lot of people talking about you mum. your ears must have been running last week because there

I went up and had a look around the ruins of the old castle and carved my initials on the wall. Aunty Ede did too. We took a look in the door of the caves but couldn't go in as it is easy to understand.

Oh yes here's something, I visited St. Peter's Chapel where you and dad were married and stood on the exact spot where you stood. It's really a beautiful church isn't it.

I'd like to look all around these places again in peacetime. I've invited them all over to Canada for a visit so here's hoping they take me up on it.

Have you been getting my mail okay mum. I hope so. I haven't received any from you as yet but they often take a month to get across. I got one letter from Montreal ten days after it was posted. That wasn't too bad was it.

Well mum I guess I'll close now, give my love to the kids and I'm hoping to hear from you soon.

(I've just received a letter
from Lenny.)

your loving son   xxxx
Ronny   xxxx

4
Heavy Conversion Unit Training

Significant military developments were occurring in Normandy in which the First Canadian Army and Bomber Group 6 would play a key role. After the capture of Caen by both elements of the British and Canadian armies on July 26, 1944, Hitler made a decision to commit six armoured divisions to push the Allies off the coast. The Allies quickly recognized that there was an opportunity to encircle the German armour by bringing the First Canadian Army and the Third U.S. Army together in the Falaise-Argentan area in France.[1] With the American Third Army flanking the Germans by moving northward, and the British and Canadian armies vectoring on Falaise, the German presence in Normandy could be effectively eliminated. The Canadian First Army, which consisted of three Canadian, two British, and one Polish division, opened up their attack on the night of August 7–8 with the objective of capturing the town of Falaise.[2] This initial attack was supported by over one thousand planes from Bomber Command which included 222 RCAF bombers. Their key aiming points were directed to protect the left flank of the Canadian attack.[3] Due to stiff German resistance it would take until August 21 before Falaise was captured and the Falaise-Argentan Gap completely closed. Although a number of German elements were able to escape through the Gap before encirclement was complete, losses to the German army were catastrophic with some 240,000 soldiers killed and wounded and another 210,000 taken prisoners.[4] First Canadian Army casualties alone were 12,659 of which 58.5 percent were Canadian.[5]

Ron realized that Topcliffe represented the final stage of training for the crew before they joined a combat squadron. The seemingly never-ending training was about to end. As Ron unpacked his kit in his new quarters, his stomach ached in anticipation. It would be critical over the next few weeks for the crew to really come together as one if they were to have any chance at surviving their tour of duty.

Despite the fact that Topcliffe was the last stop before an operational combat base, ironically, all the crews here were billeted at a beautiful mansion known as Skellfield House, located some three miles from the air base. Before it was requisitioned for use by the military, Skellfield had been a girls' private school. It was situated on eighty acres along the River Swale in Ripon, North Yorkshire. It even had an outdoor swimming pool. It was from here that Ron wrote to Kay.

> *Darling, You should see where we're living now, in an old mansion about four miles from the camp, it's a huge place. The room I'm in must have been Madame's Boudoir as the walls are covered in a sort of a pink-coloured silk, pretty posh, eh!*
>
> *I saw some swell pictures when I was in London. They were* Going My Way *with Bing Crosby,* Cover Girl *with Rita Hayworth and* Pin Up Girl *with Betty Grable. Have you seen any of them Kay? They are a welcome change from the monotony of murder and war stories.*
>
> *Oh I haven't got your picture yet dear and mine (a small version of a larger photo to follow) is starting on its way now so it should be there soon after this letter. So we'll part for now until the next letter. Goodnight sweetheart. All my love always, Ronny*

Ron and the crew did not fly on any further instructional flights until August 30. They were preoccupied with extensive parachute and dinghy training due to the probability of having to ditch over land or sea. Each stage of training brought Ron closer to the reality of active combat and with each exercise he was learning that he or a member of his crew—or all—might become a prisoner of war or, worse still, be permanently maimed or killed. Unlike other military services, air-crews were caught in the surreal world where one day you would be drinking a pint in a quaint English pub and the next, be high over enemy territory.

The purpose of the Heavy Conversion Unit Training was to allow Ron and the crew to train on four-engine Halifax bombers which would soon carry them into combat over the hostile skies of For-tress Europe. The Handley Page Halifax heavy bomber was oper-ated at one time by all Royal Canadian Air Force squadrons. The first prototype was first flown just weeks after England declared war on Germany. It was a versatile and reliable aircraft that would be used throughout World War II and continued to be used by some air forces until the early 1960s. The Halifax bomber evolved from an earlier twin-engine design which was not produced due to the un-reliability and availability of the designated Vulture engine. Instead, Handley Page moved to a four-engine design initially using Merlin engines. It normally carried a crew of seven with the pilot located in the front cockpit seated on the left, and the flight engineer sitting back-to-back with the pilot. In the front nose cone section of the plane, located at a lower elevation than the cockpit, was the bomb aimer's domain where he would operate the bomb sight and also, when necessary, the single hand-operated Vickers machine gun. The navigator was located directly below the pilot in a curtained area with a small lamp and working table for maps and navigation tools which would allow him to plot out and make course correc-tions inflight. The navigator had a small window which he could use to look port side. On the same level and directly behind the naviga-tor was an area for the wireless operator who could operate both the wireless equipment as well as other navigation aids, including early radar devices. The wireless operator also had a small port-side window. The centre of the mid-upper gunner's turret was located on top of the plane's body, in line with the trailing edge of the plane's wings. Here, the mid-upper gunner would operate two Browning .303 machine guns. At the very end of the Halifax, some seventy-one feet from the front of the aircraft, was the tail gunner, who operated a Boulton Paul Type E Tail Turret armed with four Browning .303 machine guns. The tail gunner would sit on a small leather padded bench, and in an emergency, could rotate his turret ninety degrees and fall backward out of it. The tail gunner's turret was isolated and very difficult to get to when the gunner was fully dressed—with his parachute harness and the multiple layers of clothes required to remain warm in this freezing environment, which could easily reach -40°F.

The Halifax Mark III bomber, in operation by late 1943, had a cruising speed of just over 270 miles per hour and a service ceiling of 24,000 feet. Its normal range was 1,660 miles when fully fuelled up with a bomb load of 5,800 pounds. The plane's maximum takeoff weight was 34 tons and it required a takeoff distance of just over 3,700 feet to clear a 50-foot obstacle at the end of the runway. The Halifax was now powered by four Bristol Hercules 18-cylinder radial engines capable of lifting the aircraft at 750 feet per minute and, unlike the Wellington bomber, it was an all-metal plane. It also had a maximum bomb load capacity of 13,000 pounds. Over 6,000 of these graceful and yet deadly airplanes would be built during the war. Almost 30 percent would be lost in combat.

Ron was now sensing he was even farther apart from Kay and might not see her again. There was now a sense of urgency in his writing.

Hello darling, I've been walking on air all day after receiving two wonderful letters from you dear. I only got them at noon today and I've read them over six times already and they'll certainly be read again before I go to bed.

Things change so fast over here that you are never really finished training.

I'm mailing my (big) picture tomorrow morning dear. I hope you will like it. If I look a little startled, it's because I had it taken in London and just before the photographer clicked the shutter a bomb landed not very far away. We don't get any of them up in this part of the country thank goodness as they disturb your sleep.

I believe I told you that we're living in an old mansion house here didn't I, well we've got a fireplace in our room with a nice

cheery coal fire burning in it right now and best of all your pic-
ture is up on the mantel piece smiling down on me.
     Goodnight sweetheart and I'll be writing again very soon to
my only and very special girl friend. All my love always, Ronny

Toward the end of training, the crew decided to name their normally assigned aircraft in anticipation of combat. Quite often aircrews placed distinctive artwork on the nose of the aircraft for good
luck, accompanied by a slogan or distinguishing name. "Nose art"
helped crews personalize their planes, with the often humorous artwork providing relief in what was otherwise a deadly business. In
this instance, Ron's entire aircrew agreed that since Kay's picture had
already brought them good luck, the nose of their plane (still to be
identified) would carry the figure of a nice young lady along with the
name "Kathleen."

My darling, (Irish blooded) sweetheart, here I am sitting
here with your picture in front of me writing to you and wish-
ing it was you here instead. But I guess I should consider myself
lucky to even have your dear picture.
     Oh, by the way dear, we're naming our aircraft after you; yes
"Kathleen" will be the veteran of a few operational flights over
Germany before we are finished. So you see dear you can't get
away from me even over here.
     Have you been down to see mum and dad lately dear? I'm
really happy that you like them Kay and they are very fond of
you too. Do you think mum is the kind of woman that would
make a good mother-in-law? Have you met my brother and
his wife Edna yet, she's really a nice girl, I'm sure you'd like her.
     Well darling I'll close now and remember that I'll love you
always, Ronny

Kay responded eleven days later.

Dearest Ronny, I've just received three of the nicest letters
dear and I'm so pleased that you're receiving my letters fine.
     Seriously Dear, I know I was just about the proudest girl go-
ing to know that you have named your aircraft "Kathleen," you
must have a first rate bunch of fellows in your crew as you all

seem such good pals, and it's inspiring to be with such wonderful company. Every time you are up there Ronny you'll know you have a stowaway, a pretty persistent one too, because I will be there always.

You must be ready to go on Operational Flights, you're certainly going to be way ahead of me, and you'll have so many thrilling experiences to let me in on. Well dear I'm afraid I'll have to close for now with thoughts of you.

Thanks once more for that news about your aircraft; it just makes me feel all warm and wonderful way down inside. Take care of yourself always dear. God Bless. All my love dear, Kay

***

The crew's unhurried pace of life was about to change. Starting on Wednesday, August 30, Ron and his crewmates were involved in an additional nineteen training flights in just thirteen days. They focused on bombing, air firing, night circuits, fighter affiliation, and cross-country sorties in which Ron accumulated an additional twenty-four hours of daytime and twenty-two hours of nighttime experience. This stage of intensive instruction occurred during a time when bomber losses were heavy and fresh combat crews were desperately needed.

On September 3, upon completion of a bombing exercise in the morning, Ron wrote a short note to Kay. This would be his last letter to her for almost three weeks. He mused about how the momentum of the war was shifting against the Germans.

Dearest Kay, I received a lovely letter from you today dear, your letters always make me so happy. It's awful when you're waiting and hoping for mail and it doesn't come. Next time I go on leave (If I do) I'll keep on writing anyway and take a chance on being caught.

By the way the news is now, I don't think that Germany will last much longer now, do you? I've got a bet that the European war will be over at 2 o'clock in the afternoon of September 7th, 1944. That is only four days from now but there is still a chance.

Anyway, it can't last much longer now. (I hope). I'd welcome a chance to go to India now it's so miserable and cold here. This is the worst summer England has had for seventeen years so they tell me.

There is nothing I look forward to more dear, than that day when you and I will be together again. I'm not over here just for England or Canada, but everything I may be able to do in your bomber is for you dear and you only. Everybody is fighting for their own ideals and it's very clear in my mind what and who my ideal is.

I haven't been doing anything very exciting lately. About all we have been doing is flying, sleeping and then flying again. I go out with the boys down to the Duke once in a while for a couple of beers.

Well dear I guess I'll say adieu for now and part with all my fondest love and kisses for you until my next letter which will be very soon, Ronny

Upon completion of training on September 11, 1944, the crew was given a forty-eight-hour leave before their transfer to 434 Bluenose Squadron, an operational combat unit at Croft-on-Tees in North Yorkshire. Croft was an ancient village located on the banks of the River Tees between North Yorkshire and County Durham. At 54 degrees 28 minutes north, Croft sat on a latitude similar to that of Grand Prairie, Alberta, which is some 290 miles north of Edmonton. If a plane flew in an easterly direction from Croft toward mainland Europe for 412 nautical miles it would strike the city of Kiel, Germany, a key wartime naval base and shipbuilding facility on the Baltic Sea. Besides being the childhood home of Lewis Carroll, author of *Alice's Adventures in Wonderland*, the town was also known for its spa and sulphurous spring water. But by the time Ron and his crewmates arrived there, its most important landmark was now the military aerodrome, operational since 1941.

Prior to his departure from Topcliffe, Ron paid one last visit to the Sergeants' Mess to pick up his mail.

Dearest, Did you hear about our famous earthquake? We

had it just the other night, I was just falling off to sleep but instead pretty nearly toppled out of bed, it was really quite a tremble and I was so intent on getting to Jim (her brother) and he to me except that I was the scared party, that we nearly had an accident as we bumped into each other in the rush. You should have heard all of the French neighbours out on the street talking a mile a minute, everybody was pretty excited and Jim and I were just jealous that we couldn't chime in with them.

Last week I was down to see your Mom and Dad, she had just received a letter from you and was really happy.

I've waited until now till the end of the letter to thank you for your picture I received a few days back, as if I put down on paper all the nice things I could say about it (& you) well I could just sail on and on. It arrived undamaged and must have come across pretty fast. Everyone thinks its swell. Goodnight for now dear and I'll write again soon. God bless. All my love, Kay

Even though Croft was just 130 miles away from Topcliffe, Ron and his crewmates would find that, in many ways, it felt like they had travelled to another world—a world where one's existence was measured in days and weeks instead of years. The country mansion and fireplaces of Topcliffe were now a thing of the past.

5
Combat Ready

By early September, Canadian troops were still clearing out German resistance along the coast of France, including the Port of Calais, which was the closest French port to England and directly across from Dover. Led on the ground by General Sir Bernard Law Montgomery, the Allied Expeditionary Force, which included the British Second Army, had pushed deep into Belgium recapturing Antwerp. And the Allies were starting to move into the Netherlands. The First and Third American Armies had reached the German border with Belgium and were approaching a major German line of defence known as the Siegfried Line in anticipation of pushing deeper into Germany.

One of the key roles of Bomber Group 6 in September was to provide tactical support to the Allied Armies. This included the First Canadian Army, which had taken on the role of recapturing the Port of Calais then held by German troops. During this month, Bomber Group 6 would fly on several missions in support of the Canadian troops on the ground: four to Calais, one to Port of Le Havre at the mouth of the Seine River on the French coast, as well as one to Boulogne, located just south of Calais.

By 1944, RAF Bomber Command was comprised of a number of operational groups including 1, 3, 4, and 5 Groups as well as 8 Group which acted as a Pathfinder Force, and 100 Group which was a Bomber Support Group. RAF Bomber Command was led by Air Marshal Arthur Harris. Each individual Bomber Group was comprised of from ten to seventeen squadrons, each under the command of a squadron leader. Normally a bomber squadron would have from twenty to twenty-five planes, of which fifteen to twenty might be operational at any one time. On the other hand, the American Eighth Tactical Air Force, located in southern England in 1944, was under the separate command of Lieutenant General Jimmy Dolittle who controlled over 1,300 bombers and more than 900 fighter aircraft.

By January 1943, all Canadian Squadrons with the exception of 405 "Vancouver," a Pathfinder Squadron, was under command of RCAF Bomber Group 6 with headquarters at Allerton Park Castle. They were led by Air Vice-Marshal Clifford "Black Mike" McEwen. The fourteen Canadian Squadrons in Bomber Group 6 were dispersed on seven airfields in North Yorkshire, which were the most northerly airfields within Bomber Command. Squadrons 427 "Lion' and 429 "Buffalo" were located at Leeming, with 424 "Tiger" and 433 "Porcupine" at Skipton-on-Swale. Squardons 415 "Swordfish" and 432 "Leaside" were based at East Moor. Tholthorpe hosted 420 "Snowy Owl" and 425 "Alouette" Squadrons with 419 "Moose" and 428 "Ghost" based at Middleton St. George. Squadrons 434 "Bluenose" and 431 "Iroquois" were located at Croft.

Ron and his crewmates were officially posted to 434 Squadron on September 14, 1944. The "Bluenose" Squadron had been formed in June 1943 and was sponsored by the Rotary Club of Halifax, Nova Scotia. The motto was *In excelsis vincimus* (We conquer in the heights). When Ron and his crewmates joined, the 434 Squadron had the unenviable reputation of having the highest combat losses of all Canadian squadrons. In fact, it was labeled the "chop" squadron. Since its formation, it had experienced the loss of fifty-nine aircraft in combat out of a normal complement of twenty-five planes, including the loss of eight aircraft in June 1944 alone.[1] Since Croft was the second most northerly bomber airfield targeting Germany, no doubt some of the higher combat losses could be attributed to the added flying time required to get to and from enemy mainland targets.

The Croft air base had three runways with individual parking spots to accommodate thirty-six aircraft on the tarmac at one time. Ron's squadron consisted of twenty-five Halifax bombers and forty-one crews who were divided into alternating "A" and "B" flights, thereby allowing the planes to be flown on a more frequent basis.[2] Ron and his crewmates were assigned to "A" Flight. The squadron shared the airfield with 431 Iroquois Squadron which had been formed in November 1942, almost seven months before 434. Wing Commander Paul Blackburn was in charge of 434 Squadron.

As was the case at many other air bases, the more experienced aircrew at Croft did not fraternize with fresh combat crews right away—no one wanted to make friends with someone who was likely to be shot down in his first handful of combat missions. A staggering 76 percent of total planes lost from 434 Squadron—between August 1943 and March 1945—occurred during a crew's first ten trips.[3] It wasn't even uncommon that new replacement crews would participate in their first combat missions even before they could unpack their personal belongings. In some instances, a new crew would not return from its very first flight. For instance, nine crews were lost on their first combat missions from 434 Squadron alone.[4] Survival for a crew's first few flights was significantly more uncertain because experience dramatically increased one's chances of survival. The name of the game—to survive your first ten missions—enabled the bomber crew to become a more cohesive, alert, and experienced team. After that there was one objective: to survive the balance of the tour.

Ron and his crewmates were fortunate since they had an opportunity to do some basic orientation exercises prior to embarking on their first combat mission. On September 16, 1944, Ron and the crew, except for pilot Bob Henry, had a short, forty-five minute daylight orientation flight in a four-engine Halifax bomber. Bob was recovering from his first combat mission that took place the previous evening when he flew as second pilot on an attack on Kiel in WL-D (for "Dog"). Most inexperienced pilots were first sent out with a veteran pilot and crew prior to joining their own aircrew. The first pilot on Bob's initiation flight, F/O A. Gibb, had flown WL-D on five previous trips.[5] Bob didn't know it at the time but he would soon inherit WL-D as his primary aircraft for future missions. This particular plane had been pretty beaten up as it had already been flown on twenty-five combat missions since June 1944. Nevertheless, it was in fact common practice to give the less experienced crews the older planes.[6]

For the Kiel trip they had left Croft late in the evening and, after three hours of flying, arrived over the target area where they released their bomb load.[7] Bob was expected to do some of the flying to gain the experience he would need to take his crew safely on their first trip. He landed WL-D back at Croft at 4:00 AM and after debriefing found it hard to sleep.[8] Bob tried to focus on what F/O Gibb had told him about surviving a tour of duty, especially about the importance of never flying in a straight line for more than a few minutes.

Later that day the crew participated in an additional hour of local daylight flying, but this time with Bob Henry at the controls. They were all anxious to hear about his first mission. He offered some details but elected not to share with them how scary it was while on the final run into the target when, regardless of the deadly flak coming up to greet the airplane, they could not take evasive action until *after* the bombs had been released *and*, about a minute after this, the requisite photo was taken to confirm whether the crew had hit its target. This excruciating inability to take evasive action would be something they would experience first-hand soon enough.

The next day Ron's crew experienced over four hours of flight. It was target practice in anticipation of their first of many nighttime bombing missions.[9] The American Air Force, on the other hand, preferred daylight operations. To survive daytime flying, the Americans depended on their more heavily armed B-17 Flying Fortress aircraft and tighter flight formations to combat German fighters who could better make out the bomber streams in daylight. The American planes carried a much larger crew complement of ten, including six gunners and a co-pilot. The RCAF, on the other hand, would normally only carry a crew of seven with one pilot and two gunners.

That night also marked the beginning of a bold American and British initiative code-named "Market Garden." Four Allied divisions, including the 101st and 82nd U.S. Airborne Divisions, the British First

Airborne Division, and a Polish Brigade, would land over thirty-four thousand paratroopers behind enemy lines to seize a number of key bridges in the Netherlands. This would allow the advancing British Second Army to penetrate into northern Germany by outflanking the Siegfried Line of defences. This plan had been conceived by Field Marshall Montgomery to get Allied troops over the Rhine and into the Ruhr industrial district of Germany before winter set in. This initiative was expected to shorten the war.

Three of the key objectives were bridges at Eindhoven, Nijmegen, and Arnhem. Over the next eight days the bridges at both Eindhoven and Nijmegen were secured but the last key crossing at Arnhem continued to be held at one end by the Germans. Progress by advancing ground troops was slowed due the presence of marshes and woods which limited roads capable of supporting armoured vehicles. The British First Airborne Division was ultimately forced to withdraw from the Arnhem area due to a lack of reinforcements and supplies. The weather for most of the battle was not conducive to air operations that would resupply the paratroopers located in advance of the approaching British Second Army. The failure of "Market Garden" assured that the war would continue well into 1945 and that Ron and his fellow crew would be needed in the upcoming months to provide both tactical support to the Allied ground forces and to help destroy key industrial targets, including synthetic fuel and plane production facilities.

***

The incessant training and practice over the last fifteen months was finally over. Within hours Ron and the crew could now be assigned to active combat duty. Although more than anxious to get their first mission over with, everyone hoped that their first assigned target would not take them deep into German territory. If they were lucky, they would get a "soft" target, possibly in France, although in reality all missions were risky.

While Ron waited, he wrote home to his parents during this tense wait to be put on active duty.

Dear Mum & Dad, I guess it's quite a while since you had a letter from me eh! I'm awfully sorry but we've been flying so much I haven't had time to do anything. It's slackened off a bit now so I'll be able to get some letter writing done I hope. I hope that Kay won't be mad because I haven't written for quite a while, but you can explain it to her mum.

We've moved from the Conversion Unit now and we're part of the Bluenose Squadron. After we get our third operation in, we get a week's leave so I think I'll head for Bonnie Scotland and see what's doing up there. The boys say they have a swell time and the people are very nice so I'll go and see for myself.

All the English girls I've met over here so far want to go to Canada. They say they won't know what to do for excitement when the Canadians go home (I wonder).

Mum could you send me a white sweater (flannel) like my Grenadier Guards one only without any crest on it please if possible. I want to put my own squadron crest on it. Well mum I'll say cheerio for now and will write again soon. Your Loving Son, Ronny

After a wait of almost forty-eight hours, in late afternoon of September 19, Ron and his crewmates were put on the active list. They were now on call twenty-four hours a day. Their first mission was imminent. They tried to catch some sleep that evening but it was an impossible task. They each worried about how they might react on their first combat mission and wondered if they were up to the challenge. No one wanted to let his crewmates down. After a restless night, Ron reluctantly wandered over to the mess to try to eat some breakfast. He usually had a nervous stomach at the best of times. Now his gut ached as if it contained a ball of wool soaked in water. He had a difficult time keeping his food down. But he did, and after breakfast Ron and his crewmates wandered over to the main Nissan hut to attend their first briefing. They were joined by the other crews from 434 and 431 Squadrons that were on the battle order that day. Ron and the crew arrived ten minutes early for the 2:00 PM briefing. Al Coleman had already attended an earlier briefing reserved for navigators. Al needed to know the winds and temperatures they would encounter at various heights and at all points along the route and what type of weather they could expect as the night wore on. He would address all of these factors in calculating the courses to fly and at what speeds so the Halifax would arrive at each key turning point at the specified time. An error of more than thirty seconds would be considered poor. He was already preparing their maps when the rest of the crew arrived for briefing.

The briefing room was abuzz with conversation and occasional laughter from the almost two hundred aircrew jammed into the area. The room was stuffy. A musty odour of sweat and damp wool hung in the air.

The intended target would be ceremoniously uncovered on a map at the start of each main briefing. Inexperienced crews could judge from the reaction of the veterans how difficult the target would likely be. In this case, Ron and his crewmates were relieved when Wing Commander Paul Blackburn asked for the target to be revealed and the overall reaction was not overly negative.

The target: gun emplacements and German troops defending the French port of Calais. Both Calais and Cap Gris Nez needed to be neutralized so the recently captured French port at Boulogne could be utilized safely. Access to French ports was critical to enable the Allied armies in France to be resupplied with food and war material.

Calais was a target fairly close to the English mainland. The distance from Croft measured 283 miles. In reality, almost no flight to an enemy target occurred in a direct line. In many instances the total miles flown could be almost double that of the direct route. Most routes were designed to keep the enemy guessing until the last moment. Some routes included several diversionary raids by smaller numbers of aircraft including Mosquito bombers. This time, the crews at briefing were informed that soldiers from the First Canadian Army were on the outskirts of Calais and would try to recapture it over the next few days. With friendly troops on the ground, it would be necessary for the bombing to be as precise as possible.

Most crew members had unique rituals they would perform before final inspection of their planes at departure. These might include writing a letter to a relative or loved one, having a short nap, or simply reading a book or letter from home. Ron elected not to write any letters home until he had survived his first combat mission. After they gathered up their flight gear and emergency supplies, Ron and the crew headed out to the dispersal point at 3:00 PM. Bob, Ron, and the rest of the crew had a quick conversation with the ground crew about the condition of WL-D, now near the end of its life as a combat plane. Most ground crew became quite attached to the aircraft that they worked on around the clock, and to the men who flew them.

Bob and Joe did a quick walk around the plane prior to boarding, first to check that the cover on the pitot tubes had been properly removed so the airspeed could be measured properly once in flight. Bob also checked all of the cowling and plane inspection panels and did a visual inspection of the tires. One final ritual which most crews practised was to pee on the tires for good luck—and because there were limited opportunities to address a full bladder once airborne. Once aboard, the crew checked that the emergency escape hatches were securely fastened while Joe made sure that the fuel tanks had been properly refuelled.[10] The inside of the plane was damp and cool and heavy with the aroma of machine oil. Each crew member checked his respective equipment before the engines were run up to 1,200 RPMs, one at a time, to sufficiently warm them in preparation for takeoff. Testing the aircraft intercom system was one of the final checks. Then Ron made sure his requisitioned service revolver was stuffed into his leather boots in case they had to bail out over enemy territory. Although all crew members could carry firearms, Bill, the mid-upper gunner, was the only other crew member to requisition small arms for personal protection in case they were shot down.[11]

While the engines were warming up, Joe checked the rows of temperature and pressure gauges directly in front of him. Bob raised and lowered the flaps to make sure the hydraulic system functioned properly. Once the four powerful Bristol Hercules radial engines were ready, Bob increased the RPMs of each, one at a time, to 1,500 to test that each magneto was properly generating electrical current. Finally, Bob increased the pressure in the fuel injection system to test the two-speed supercharger that would be used to get maximum thrust in flight.[12]

Ron and the crew had developed in training a tradition of quietly singing their theme song, "Mairsy Doates," over the intercom to confirm that it was working.[13] This was technically against the rules since minimal radio conversation prior to each mission was encouraged, but the crew believed the ritual would bring them good luck. Bob and Joe then went through a checklist confirming that the ground/flight switch had been set to flight, that each fuel pump had sufficient vacuum, and finally that the brake pressure gauge read a minimum of 250 PSI. Bob then taxied the plane from its resting place onto the peripheral track, which led to the main runway where they waited for the green light. Bob and Joe went through a final checklist to confirm that the flaps were down fifteen degrees, that the fuel booster pumps were on, and that the air intake had been set at Cold.[14] All these pre-flight check points kept Bob and Joe focused, something that helped settle their nerves.

A fully loaded Halifax could easily weigh thirty-four tons, which included up to thirteen thousand pounds of bombs. Both the bomb and fuel load would be increased or decreased based on the distance to be flown. With this tremendous weight during takeoff, it sometimes felt like the plane would never achieve liftoff. In the cockpit more than twenty feet in the air, Bob found it challenging to make sure he didn't steer off the tarmac into the ever-present glutinous mud that at best would bog them down. Some planes that had wandered into the mud suffered significant damage to their undercarriages.

Bob's plane was ninth in line for takeoff. He could see just in front of him WL-Q (for "Queen") as it started to accelerate down the runway.[15] The control tower referred to Bob's aircraft as "D" (for Dog) and his communications back to the tower would begin with "Bundock Dog to Big Tree."

With the flash of the green light from the control truck, Bob opened the throttles with the brakes still on to confirm that the engines responded with equal thrust. He then throttled back slightly, released the brakes, then opened the throttles wide, watching the speedometer as it climbed to 110 miles per hour. He could feel the plane shudder as it lifted off the runway. It was 3:54 pm.[16] Bob was relieved when the plane's speed passed the 145 miles per hour marker, leaving less chance of the plane's stalling even with a full load. They were finally on their first combat mission together.

The bomb bay held nine 1,000-pound and four 500-pound bombs.[17] The medium-capacity 1,000-pound bomb or "standard" bomb was first developed in 1943. It was made from cast steel and held approximately 480 pounds of high explosives with the balance of the weight attributed to the bomb shell or outer surface, which was 6 feet long and approximately 1.5 feet in diameter. The high explosive used was usually Amatol, consisting of a mixture of TNT and ammonium nitrate. This combination helped create a maximum energy that resulted in a deadly shock wave. Shell fragments from this bomb could be lethal over several thousand feet.

Halifax WL-D joined a mix of Halifax and Lancaster bombers from Bomber Group 6 which included thirteen other bombers from 434 Squadron.[18] The Canadian bombers were joined by an additional 540 RAF aircraft on this maximum effort which included over four hundred Lancaster bombers and forty Mosquito fighter-bombers; the rest were Halifaxes. Unlike the American Air Force, which flew in very tight formations almost wing tip to wing tip, each RCAF and RAF bomber, although required to follow a prescribed flight path with key turning points, made its own way to the target. With clear skies, Ron and the crew were able to spot other bombers enroute leaving distinctive contrails across the English Channel. The Mosquito fighter-bombers, built mainly from plywood, leveraged their superior speed of over 360 miles per hour to scurry ahead and mark the target. The Mosquito bomber carried a pilot and navigator/radar operator and could handle a 2,000-pound bomb load. Because of its great speed the Mosquito was often used by a Master Bomber to orchestrate the entire bombing operation while flying in circles over the target area.

Ron and Bill, the mid-upper gunner, knew that once airborne their primary roles were to scan the sky for enemy aircraft. To maximize the amount of sky covered, both kept their hydraulically operated turrets in almost constant motion while they strained to see any approaching enemy aircraft—including the dreaded Messerschmitt Me-109. The Me-109 was armed with three .79-inch-calibre cannons and two .51-inch-calibre machine guns that outgunned the .303-inch-calibre Browning machine guns operated by Ron and Bill. With a maximum speed of almost 400 miles per hour, the Me-109 was capable of closing quickly for the kill and was very difficult to hit. Like most "Tail-End Charlies," Ron's predecessors had arranged to have a portion of the plastic bubble on the turret removed to improve visibility. Except at exceptionally low altitudes, most gunners used electrically heated suits and wore multiple pairs of gloves to prevent frostbite.

Ron and Bill were also on the watch for friendly bombers or fighter escorts who might inadvertently wander too close to their ship. Too many bombers had already been lost to mid-air collisions on previous missions. Ron was proud of his excellent vision, although it came at a cost. After hours of scanning the sky, both above and below the plane, his temples throbbed from the constant eye strain. On this mission, the crew carried an extra member, Sgt. R.A.F. Magurn, a mid-upper gunner.[19]

This first bombing operation was conducted at a low altitude of 10,000 feet with clear weather, at least over the target. Even at such low altitudes, the temperature in the turret could easily be -15°F and as low as -40°F at 20,000 feet.

To ensure accurate bombing in the last few minutes running up to the target, Frank adjusted the bombsight to take into account the air temperature and wind speed, as well as the altitude. Frank then took command of Halifax WL-D, guiding Bob with minor course corrections to assure that the target appeared in the crosshairs of the bombing device. He then squeezed the bomb release button informing the crew of "bombs away" while Bob anxiously waited for the photoflash. This was his signal that he could once more take control of the aircraft. Photos were not only taken by all aircraft to confirm that they had released their bombs on target, but to assess any damage done by the bombing. Only at this time could Bob take evasive action to avoid any flak, enemy searchlights, attacking aircraft, or other bombers which might wander into their airspace. Fortunately there was no need to take any drastic evasive action on this mission.

Al, the navigator, then gave Bob the initial course settings for their return journey. The return flight remained uneventful, although all crew maintained vigilance to make sure they were not pounced on by enemy fighters. Even though all Canadian aircraft got out of France safely on this mission, every Bomber Group 6 airfield was mired by poor weather. This meant diversions for all aircraft to alternative southern air bases. Ron's plane diverted to a Royal Air Force training air base at Turweston, two miles east of Brackley, a small English village in south Northamptonshire.[20] More stress was placed on Bob and Al on this first mission since they had to locate and land at an unfamiliar airbase. Yet Bob piloted WL-D to a safe landing at 7:24 PM.[21] They had been airborne for three and a half hours. What Ron found strange was the simultaneous sensation of sweating and being chilled in his flight gear.

Once the plane touched down, Bob raised the flaps and opened the radiator shutters to make sure the engines did not overheat. He then shut down the outer engines as the inner engines were sufficient for taxiing. After having been led to a dispersal point, Bob switched off the last two engines. They had finally come to a full stop. A great, almost palpable sense of relief enveloped WL-Ds entire aircrew as they returned unharmed from their first combat mission.

After a debriefing the crew sought out a place to catch some sleep. The next day they had to wait for the weather to clear before the one-hour morning flight to home base. After lunch, Ron decided to post a letter to Kay to let her know he was now officially on "ops."

> *Dearest Kay, I hope you'll forgive me dear for not writing for quite a while, as we've been flying day and night and have had hardly any time even for sleep.*
>
> *We were over pounding Calais today in France and what a lovely surprise was waiting for me when I got back, three lovely letters from you dear. I felt awfully tired until I saw them there, then I felt as though someone had lifted a ten-ton load off of my shoulders.*
>
> *As you say dear, music cheers you up. It really does me too but nothing like your letters do. After receiving them I want more than ever to get this war over with in a hurry so I can get*

*home to you darling, that's going to be the most wonderful day
I ever want.*

*Yes Kay, I'm on ops now and I like it although it's no fun
at times. It's a very exciting life but full of unexpected events.
But you'll know that wherever I go over Germany or anywhere
at all, your ship "Kathleen" will be right there with me. I only
wish it was in Canada and was you instead. But that day will
come soon dear it's got to for our sake.*

Goodnight darling, All my love Always, Ronny

Ron also received three letters from Kay that day. The first, dated
September 15, read:

*Dear Ronny, I just received your letter dated the 3rd of Sep-
tember, you mentioned that you were going to write if you go
on leave, gosh dear, it's not worth the risk, and I couldn't for-
give myself if you got into hot water.*

*You lost your bet about the war, but here's hoping you aren't
far wrong.*

*So you'd welcome India now, gosh it would be too hot there,
one extreme to the other. I wonder just how much longer the
war will last, but then I'm only one in millions wondering the
same thing and not coming to any opinion.*

I saw a good show the other night, Gaslight, *gosh it was really swell, and Charles Boyer makes a better murderer than
lover I think.*

*You must be doing a tremendous amount of flying, it must
be straight hard work, and it sort of helps a lot when you like
it like you do. They certainly train you fellows into perfection,
and I bet by the time they're finished instructing, you feel pretty
well as if you can take care of yourself, but then something tells
me that you always could.*

*It was announced on the radio this morning that different
parts of Canada have been having Hurricanes, and that quite
possibly Montreal will get it too, slight though. Gosh I certainly
hope so as I wouldn't relish myself under the table. I certainly
have a picturesque imagination haven't I?*

Your mom and dad were so glad to receive your big picture; your mom received it the same time I did mine. It's lovely dear and I think it's so natural too, it's really you, especially the way you smile and that certain gleam in your eyes, but then it's just completely swell.

I'll say goodnight for now Ronny and will be writing tomorrow. All my love, Kay

The next day, the crew was stood down due to poor weather. This provided Ron with the opportunity to scribble a quick note home to his parents after roll call. He wrote,

Dear Mum & Dad, Gosh it was a lovely surprise yesterday getting a letter from you and three from Kay. It was the first mail I'd had for quite a while. I'm trying to write home to you and Kay as often as I can but don't have any time to myself now.

We are on call 24 hours a day now so you have to work some sleep in somewhere when possible. However you know I'll do my best to keep writing as often as possible. Well mum I've got to get going so I'll say cheers and will write soon. Your loving Son, Ronny

The next day, pilot Bob and the crew boarded Halifax WL-D, lifting off mid-morning on a fighter affiliation exercise.[22] For Ron, this included air firing practice. They landed back at base at noon. All said, the crew was quite anxious to complete their second mission. But their anxiety would only heighten as operations were cancelled the next day due to inclement weather. Such interruptions would become a recurring theme over the next several months as winter approached.

***

On September 25 there was a real chill in the air. Ron walked over to the briefing hut to find out about his second mission. The hut was particularly packed on this occasion, with over 240 crew members jammed in. All active bomber crews were briefed on the third of four daylight raids to be conducted on Calais. They were told by the briefing officer that the primary objective was to damage harbour fortifications. This included German troops that defended the port who were being pressed by the Canadian infantry. This attack was coordinated so that as the last bombs fell, two Canadian infantry battalions supported by armour would immediately begin an assault on the German defensive positions located outside the city.[23]

It was not only Al who worked at his maps during briefing. Frank, the bomb aimer, had picked up both a Mercator projection map for plotting radar fixes and a topographical map to use inflight to assist in spotting landfalls that could serve as additional navigational checks for Al.

Frank recalled later what transpired immediately after the briefing:

"After a light breakfast, Ron and most of the crew headed over to the Nissen hut that housed their flight gear. Bob and I had gone over earlier and we were already fully dressed. While taking the time for a cigarette we watched the antics of Ron and Bill, the gunners, as they struggled with their gear. As Ron and Bill would be exposed to the freezing air in their open gun turrets, they pulled on their bulky, electrically heated suits. If that wasn't difficult enough, they also had to pull on an inflatable life-jacket and parachute harness making it almost impossible to move without an effort. Ron was slim, fair and as the youngest member of the crew quick in his reactions and speech while Bill, with a dark complexion, would appear morose but for his flashing smile. Hal, the radio operator, was big, blond and although one of the oldest crew members, quite jovial. In contrast, Joe, the flight engineer, was squat and a former prairie farmer whose demands on life were uncomplicated. Al, the navigator, also from the prairies, had a steady wit and even disposition which would prove to stand the crew in good stead in tight situations.

"Finally, Bob took one final puff and threw down his cigarette and stood up. That was the signal for the crew to get moving. Although to the crew Bob appeared small and almost delicately built, he was a quiet spoken and intense individual, and an excellent pilot. He would prove to be always calm and unruffled even in the direst of circumstances.

"The crew followed Bob out to the truck that would take them to the dispersal area. The planes were widely scattered around the airfield to minimize damage in the event of an air raid. We were accompanied by three other crews in the truck and a chaplain who rode with the crews out to their planes. After leaving the truck at their dispersal point, the ground crew greeted Ron and the crew. They watched as Bob did his final walk around the plane and I checked that the proper fuses had been attached to the bombs. After entering the plane from a door in the fuselage near the tail, each crew member went through their final checklist including checking in with Bob over the intercom. As Bob started up each of the four engines, the racket from the engines became almost mind numbing. It was a noise that we would have to endure for the entire trip. Just before taxiing, I noticed through the Plexiglas nose a dimly lit figure darting under the fuselage giving me the thumbs-up as he pulled the wheel blocks away and the plane lurched forward. Bob could barely see the plane ahead of him with one dim light on its tail as they both moved around on the perimeter track to line-up for takeoff."[24]

Just after 9:40 AM Bob turned Halifax WL-A (for "Able") into the wind and they were ready to roll. The green light was flashed from the control truck parked to his left on the grass. Two minutes later they were airborne in this different Halifax—which to the superstitious was not a good thing.[25] The bomb payload was identical to that of their first attack on Calais—thirteen bombs delivering eleven thousand pounds of high explosives.[26] This time, bombing took place at an elevation of 6,000 feet, significantly increasing the risk of being hit by anti-aircraft fire.

The mainstay of the German anti-aircraft arsenal was the 88-mm artillery gun. It was capable of effectively firing a twenty-pound high-explosive shell up to a height of almost 26,000 feet. Normally a number of 88s would be mounted close together so together they could create a flak barrage. Each gun was capable of firing up to fifteen rounds per minute. The explosive power was capable of taking down a bomber even without a direct hit because the hundreds of fragments from each shell-burst could tear up vulnerable areas of the bomber and injure and kill aircrew. The tail gunner would get a most terrifying view of all this from his vantage point at the end of the bomber. It was a vulnerable place to be.

The target for this mission had been well-marked by the Master Bomber, who arrived over the target area before the main bomber stream. Depending on the amount of visibility, the Master Bomber had at his disposal a number of options which he could call in from other Pathfinder aircraft to assist him. These included coloured high explosives, coloured flares that would float to the ground on parachutes, and sky markers, which were canisters that emitted smoke of various colours and also descended on parachute. For each attack a specific colour would be chosen along with a backup colour so that these target indicators could be differentiated from possible German diversionary fires. The Master Bomber directed the attack of the incoming aircraft and made any adjustments to the bomb release point as needed. On the Calais mission, although the route to the target was fairly clear, cloud cover made for a more difficult bombing task given that the Canadian ground troops were located just a little over a mile from the bombers' aiming points. Frank released the load of nine 1,000-pound and four 500-pound bombs just as the sun reached its zenith.[27] He then returned the flying controls back to Bob. Frank later reported that he had bombed on the red target indicators, which had been dropped by the lead aircraft and were clearly visible. As an early arrival over the target, the crew had difficulty assessing the extent of the damage although Frank had seen several bombs burst in the target area.

Wing Commander Paul Blackburn, piloting WL-C, had personally led his squadron in this attack on Calais.[28] The mission lasted just four hours. There were no losses. A total of 253 planes from Bomber Group 6 had participated, including 18 aircraft from 434 Squadron.[29] The total bomber stream vectored to Calais included 872 aircraft.[30] Although fewer than 300 were able to safely drop their bomb load because of the clouds, over three million pounds of high explosives were dropped on the target.

Now that Ron and his crewmates were on active duty, the pace and pressure of combat missions started to accelerate, with another trip scheduled for the next day. On September 26, he penned a quick note to Kay before the next mission.

Dearest Kay, Here I am again to bother you for a while. You mean more to me than I could ever hope to express in writing. I want you to know that dear. I think you already do just in case any thing should happen to prevent me from telling you personally dear.

I'm writing this letter at 5:30 AM in the morning, quite an early hour for me eh! You "Kathleen" and I are going out again very soon, so I thought I would write to you first. This will only be a short letter as I haven't got much time but I'll write again tonight.

Well darling I have to leave you now until tonight. All my love sweetheart, Ronny

Ron posted the letter in the Sergeants' Mess and headed over to join the crew at the main briefing scheduled for 6:00 AM. It was a cold, damp morning—even colder than the day before. There was a hint of winter in the air. When he opened the door to the operational hut, he was hit by the familiar blast of warm, humid air emanating from all the bodies gathered in the hut.

The men were not surprised to discover that they were scheduled to return to Calais for another go, to soften up the port's defences in anticipation of further attacks by the Canadian Army. After briefing, they grabbed a truck out to their dispersal point and quickly completed their pre-flight checks. Flying Officer Bob Henry, piloting Halifax WL-C, then held the second spot in queue for takeoff. WL-C soared skyward, lifting off at 8:43 AM in the wake of WL-E, which had just taken off one minute before them.[31] It was just three hours since Ron wrote his letter. He and the crew were now on their third combat mission in just seven days. Behind them, the last 434 Squadron bomber lifted off just twenty-eight minutes after the first.[32]

The crew was greeted by clear and sunny weather over Calais. This assisted Frank to achieve a direct hit on the docks. Ron later indicated in his log book that it was a "good show." On this trip, WL-C's bomb load, identical to their previous mission, screamed downward toward the target from an elevation of 7,000 feet.[33] To Frank the bombing appeared to be fairly concentrated, but smoke obscured his view, making a more accurate assessment difficult. He felt that the Master Bomber had not accurately marked the target. This mission to Calais, although slightly smaller in size than the previous mission, still involved 164 RCAF planes, including 16 bombers from 434 Squadron. For the third effort in a row there were no Canadian bomber losses.[34]

The Canadian bombers rained down over 1.7 million pounds of high explosives on the German positions while Canadian troops, now in their second day, aggressively attacked the German-held strongholds.[35] Intelligence estimated that over 7,000 German troops had been defending the Calais area. By day's end, German positions were driven in to their inner line of defences within the city with almost 1,600 soldiers taken prisoner.[36]

Ron and the crew arrived safely back at Croft, touching down at 12:53 PM.[37] It was Navigator Al Coleman's birthday so, after debriefing, the crew decided to make a quick trip into Darlington to celebrate. They returned to Croft by early evening knowing they were on the battle order for another trip slated early the next day.

Three trips with no Canadian losses could create a false sense of security, especially for the more inexperienced aircrews. A recent track record of no losses in Bomber Group 6 did not match the aircraft loss rate of 1 to 2 percent per bombing mission over the previous six months. With a loss rate of 2 percent on each mission, only 55 percent of aircrews could expect to survive thirty operations. As the war progressed, the decline in bomber loss rates was offset by an increase in the required number of trips necessary to complete a tour of duty from a minimum of thirty trips in 1944 to thirty-five trips in 1945. This change effectively kept the probability of survival for each crew member at approximately 50 percent. At home, most men in their early twenties could expect to live another fifty years. Here, at Croft, this 50 percent survival rate put them on life's wheel of fortune nearly every day. Before this, from March 1943 through March 1944, the average loss rate in Bomber Group 6 was higher than 5 percent which meant that only about one in five aircrews survived thirty operations. In 434 Squadron, for the first 280 individual crew members who went into combat, only 84 escaped unscathed in completing their first tour of duty without being killed or wounded.[38]

It was against this backdrop that Ron and his crewmates awakened at 4:00 AM. It was September 27. They quickly dressed before their walk over to the mess for a pre-flight breakfast. Even at this time of year, the crew could feel the dampness and chill in the air as they cut across grass bent heavy with dew and glistening in the bright moonlight. The moisture gathered on their boots, which they would luckily be able to change before takeoff. After breakfast, they headed over to the main briefing hut to find out where this daylight "maximum effort" mission would take them.

The briefing hut was packed with forty-two bomber crews from 431 and 434 Squadrons. The room pulsed with the movement and chatter of the almost three hundred aircrew packed inside. One could hear a pin drop when the commanding officer unveiled the route. Unlike the last three trips, today's target, Sterkrade, would take them into Germany to a synthetic oil plant located south of Oberhausen. This was a much more dangerous mission than Calais. The crew changed into their flight gear after the briefing then headed out to their familiar friend, Halifax WL-D. It was just as well that Ron and his crewmates were not aware that four bombers from 434 Squadron were lost on an attack on Sterkrade just three months earlier.[39]

After the pre-flight checks, Bob and Joe worked to get the four engines running. They then moved into line for takeoff following closely in the wake of WL-W (for "William"), which had just lifted off a minute earlier.[40] For the second time in four missions, the regular crew had an additional crew member, Sgt. R. McGee, a mid-upper gunner. Squadron 434 provided twenty-one Halifax bombers to this mission, the most it would provide on the same mission for the balance of the war.[41] A total of 143 aircraft were targeted to Sterkrade, while an additional 96 aircraft from Bomber Group 6 vectored to another synthetic oil plant at Bottrop about six miles north of Essen.[42] A mix of Halifaxes and Lancasters from Bomber Group 6 were joined by additional planes from Bomber Group 8, including a small force of Mosquitoes. Altogether they would deliver a total attacking force of 171 aircraft to Sterkrade and 175 to Bottrop.[43] The intent was to immobilize the German air defences by reducing their key supplies of aviation fuel.

Bombing conducted at this much higher elevation—16,000 to 21,000 feet—brought new challenges, including significant cloud cover over the target. Unlike the previous three bomb loads of 11,000 pounds each, the load on this trip consisted of sixteen 500-pound bombs, which delivered a total punch of 8,000 pounds of high explosives.[44] While on final approach at just over 16,000 feet, through intermittent breaks in the heavy clouds, Bob could see giant puffs of black smoke thrown off by the bursting flak and an occasional bomber as it intermittently appeared through the cloud cover below. Suddenly WL-D was hit by flak, which rattled off the Halifax's exterior, frightening the inexperienced crew. The flak could easily have created large gaps or structural damage or penetrated the plane's exterior, killing the crew. Luckily though, no significant damage occurred. Frank then released the bomb load just minutes before 10:00 PM with Bob turning the plane for home once the standard photo had been taken.[45] Fortunately no enemy fighters were sighted. After a long, stressful flight through freezing exterior air temperatures and the constant possibility of being attacked by enemy aircraft, Ron and his crewmates arrived safely back at home base. They had just completed a flight of five hours and twenty-five minutes.[46] This made WL-D one of the slowest planes to complete the mission, with twelve of the twenty-one planes from 434 Squadron arriving earlier.[47] At the debriefing session, Frank reported that the target did not seem to be well marked and that he had bombed about 150 feet to the right of the red target indicators. Although miraculously no planes from Bomber Group 6 were lost for the fourth consecutive mission, sadly one pilot from 432 Squadron sustained serious injuries from flak and died the next day.[48]

While Bomber Group 6 aircraft were targeted to synthetic oil plants in Germany, the battle for Calais continued. A flight of 341 RAF bombers was directed to bomb the western outskirts of Calais to further assist the Canadian Army.[49] Another attack consisting of 494 aircraft, including planes from Bomber Group 6, was carried out the following morning on the eastern and northern approaches to the city. The attacks were a success, resulting in the German garrison commander requesting a truce by the end of the day.[50]

Now that Ron had flown for seventeen hours of active combat in just eight days, the stress of little sleep and consecutive flying missions started to take its toll. That afternoon, Ron took time to write home to his parents.

Dear Mum and Dad, Here I am getting a letter off to you while I have a little spare time, that's something we don't get much of now.

I've got four operational trips in now over enemy territory. Life on a squadron is much better than on any other station but awfully tiring, both mentally and physically but I like it. I sort of feel at last after all of this training, that I'm actually doing something to help get this war over with soon.

The town near our camp has its street lights on again. It makes quite a difference in the look of the place. The only trouble is you can't see where you're going; the lights blind you after being so used to the blackout.

We're due to go on a week's leave on Nov 5th so I hope we get some decent weather then. I don't know whether to go up to Scotland or back down to London. Oh well, time will tell.

Well mum I think I'll close for now as my eyes are just about doing the same. Cheerio for now. Your Loving Son, Ronny

For Bob Henry, September 27 turned out to be quite eventful. His older brother Jack had just been posted to 431 Squadron. Jack, like Bob, was also a pilot and would be expected to fly on some of the same missions. Although at this point Bob had only flown on five combat missions, to Jack he was an experienced combat pilot. As expected, Jack and Bob spent most of the afternoon catching up and talking shop.

A new target was unveiled at the morning briefing session the next day: Cap Gris Nez on the French coast just south of Calais. The objective was to provide support for the Allied army that was attempting to push the Germans out of the coastal area to secure key ports.

This attack would contribute significantly to the eventual capture of Cap Gris Nez by Canadian land forces later that day, and also to the capture of batteries which included guns capable of both defending the harbour of Boulogne and reaching the English coast at Dover and Folkstone.[51]

This trip got a late start. Once again the boys were in Halifax WL-D, which now felt like a second home. Nestled in the bomb bay were nine 1,000-pound and four 500-pound bombs.[52] WL-D was joined by another 213 planes, rising from other Bomber Group 6 Yorkshire air bases, including Linton-on-Ouse, Tholthorpe, Skipton-on-Swale, and Eastmoor. Significant cloud coverage over the target area made accurate bombing a challenge. Many crews were sent home by the Master Bomber without releasing their bomb loads. It was the Master Bomber's responsibility to decide whether to bomb close to Allied troops. As WL-D approached the target, Bob and Frank both noticed at the last moment that they had forgotten to open the bomb bay doors, which forced them to abort the run.[53] This error meant that they had to circle around against the bomber stream so they could run up to the target again. Such a move presented serious risk of a head-on collision with remaining incoming aircraft.

Frank released the bomb load at 8,000 feet while aiming on the green target indicators.[54] It would be no exaggeration to say that the "bombs away" signal brought a tremendous sense of relief to the entire crew after the frustration of having to make that second risky run. An aborted bombing run might also not count as a completed mission which could thus extend one's tour of duty. Afterward Frank noted that the bombing operation appeared well concentrated and a number of bomb bursts could be seen. Ron and his emotionally exhausted crewmates returned safely to Croft at 9:30 PM.[55] Although a bit unsettled by the mishap, they were now able to laugh about it. Even with the complications they still managed to land back at Croft ahead of ten of the sixteen planes from 434 Squadron.[56] This was the result of Al Coleman's excellent navigation.

While Ron and the crew were airborne on that harrowing flight over Cap Gris Nez, Kay was safely at home, snuggled on the living room couch in her house on Dorion Street. She wrote:

> *Dearest Ronny, Last evening your Mom phoned and explained that you haven't had much time to write being on operations and all and not to worry if I haven't heard from you recently dear, so just imagine how wonderful it was this morning to be surprised with a letter, you just can't picture how happy I was, and such a beautiful letter too. Each letter only adds to my thoughts of how lucky we were to meet each other like we did, as even if we weren't together long that's not what finally counts, it's all the future that surely will lie ahead that matters.*
>
> *You say you've been on "ops" now for awhile, bombing Calais for one. I'm proud of you Ronny as you must know I am, not because you're on "ops" or because you're doing your part, but because you're everything that one can be proud of.*
>
> *When you mention the ship "Kathleen" I feel very proud and you can't blame me, gosh dear I only wish that I was right there, beside you, I can't think of anything nicer.*
>
> *Goodnight for now my dear and remember how much I'm looking forward to our next meeting. God Bless, All my love always, Kay*

The crew had now survived their first five combat missions—a significant accomplishment considering that 55 percent of the planes lost from 434 Squadron had gone missing over the first five trips.[57] And in a little more than twelve hours the crew would once again be airborne.

6
Cat and Mouse

The air war over Germany included not only the cat-and-mouse game between bomber and enemy fighter, each trying to survive in skies that were saturated with flak and searchlights, but also a war based on technology to enhance each side's ability to either locate the land target or each other. Although most of this technology was based on some variation of radar or radio waves, sometimes something as simple as strips of metal foil, known by the British as "window," could neutralize, at least in the short term, the most sophisticated German radar.

By September 1944, most Canadian bombers had been equipped with H2S, the first radar technology deployed to map ground surface. The H2S device consisted of a centrally located cathode within a vacuum tube, which generated a stream of negative electrons. A magnetic field caused the electrons to spiral outward within the vacuum tube creating a high-frequency radio field, which could be captured by a radio antenna and transmitted toward the ground. The shorter the resultant radio waves the greater the capability of the H2S device to discern smaller objects in its path. The H2S also had a receiver that displayed the resulting image of the ground surface below. Though refined over time, this technology would continue to be used on British combat planes some fifty years later.

This new radar enabled the navigator for the first time to identify targets on the ground even in heavily overcast skies, or at night with little to no moonlight. Targets with distinct ground features, such as those next to lakes or rivers, were infinitely easier to pick out accurately than a specific factory or building complex within a large industrialized city.

With Halifax WL-E (for "Easy") equipped with the new H2S radar, Bob departed Croft midday on September 29 for an extensive cross-country training exercise. This provided Al, the navigator, and Frank, the bomb aimer, the opportunity to become familiar with the new device. Although they conducted the exercise mainly over the English countryside, mid-upper gunner Bill Thomson and Ron had to remain vigilant. No one could ever assume that an enemy fighter attack was not imminent. After almost three hours, Bob Henry touched down at Croft mid-afternoon.

This daytime training flight segued into a well-deserved weekend pass for the entire crew. Now that they had completed five trips in just nine days, the station commander recognized the need for a little crew decompression. Given the shortness of leave, the crew elected to check out the local pubs in Darlington, a small market town due north of Croft and a place where Bill first met Edna Weeks, whom he would later marry.

Altogether that September, 434 Squadron had flown on twelve different operations, putting a total of 192 aircraft into the skies over enemy territory. Luckily there was no combat with enemy aircraft. For the first time in five months 434 Squadron did not sustain the loss of any aircraft. Due to the screening of aircrew that had finished their tour of duty, the number of crews now available for active duty declined slightly from forty-one to thirty-seven.[1]

Ron and the crew left Croft late in the evening of October 1. They were flying for the first time in Halifax WL-F (for "Fox"). Though the Germans in Calais had finally surrendered that afternoon, Ron and the crew had a long, chilly flight ahead of them which would last over four hours.[2] Their objective was to practise a "bulls eye" run on the city of Bristol in southwestern England, 214 nautical miles southwest of Croft. Due to its location next to the Severn River estuary, Bristol had been selected as an ideal city for Al to practise his navigation and Frank to practise his bomb aiming with the new H2S unit.

After having successfully located Bristol, the tired crew returned to Croft in the early morning hours of October 2. They headed to their respective metal Nissen hut dormitories, which were each heated by a single pot-bellied coal stove.The metal Nissen huts were cold and drafty. But the officers had help in theirs: a batman to assist with chores. The military batman, usually of junior rank, was a holdover from the previous century, when each officer had one to help maintain his weapons and uniforms. However, this position would be eliminated in most post–World War II military services.

On Monday, October 4, the crew rose in the dead of night, struggling with the mind-numbing cold that seemed to seep into every joint of their aching bodies. The fire in the coal stove had dwindled to cold ash in just four short hours. It seemed like only minutes since "lights out," but now they had to attend the 2:00 AM briefing for their early morning flight. Ron didn't classify himself as a morning person and hated to get up before daylight. It had been almost a week since their last bombing mission over France (inclement weather had delayed flying), and one could not expect the RCAF to give anybody a break, especially rookies.

They walked on the now well-worn pathway to the briefing hut. Already close to two hundred were jammed inside, anxious to get on with the war. With the exception of the squadron leaders and several support staff, most crew members were seated on collapsible fold-up chairs that some said were left over from the First World War. They were placed in rows as if at a school assembly. Dozens of animated conversations were in progress when the shout of "Attention!" coincided with the arrival of the Station Commander. Amidst the dying background chatter, interspersed with nervous laughter, the crews were told "at ease." The Station Commander then started the briefing with a few words of encouragement before the navigation officer unveiled the day's target. This ritual unveiling was now accompanied by a number of surprised gasps. The operation was an early daylight raid on the newly built German submarine pens in Bergen, Norway. Norway, which had tried to remain neutral at the beginning of the war, was invaded by Germany in 1940 on the pretense that Norwegians needed protection from possible invasion by France and England. In reality, the Germans wanted access to Norwegian ports and its supply of iron ore from neutral Sweden, which would have been at risk if Norway had decided to support the Allies. The Norwegian King and government officials escaped to England and set up a "government-in-exile." Four Norwegian Air Force Squadrons and dozens of Norwegian ships would go on to serve the Allies during the war.

Since D-Day, when the Germans were displaced from their submarine pens on the French coast, Bergen, the second largest city in Norway after Oslo, had taken on greater strategic importance. At this stage of the war, German U-boats continued to wreak havoc with Allied shipping convoys which brought food and military supplies to England. U-boat pens were thus a top-priority target. The German submarine pens in different stages of construction were located in fairly mountainous surroundings, making this a challenging target. The combat mission would also be the first for Jack Henry, Bob's brother, who would be flying as second pilot in SE-U with F/L H.M. Smith as first pilot.[3] Lucky for Jack, F/L Smith was a very experienced combat pilot who was about to be promoted to Squadron Leader.

On nervous stomachs, Ron and his crewmates hastily downed a full breakfast with real eggs, a dish reserved for combat crew. Then they were off, catching their transport bus out to the tarmac. Here Halifax WL-C (for "Charlie") waited for them. They had flown this kite earlier and although WL-C had first been placed into combat less than a month earlier, it had already survived twelve trips over enemy territory. This would be the crew's sixth combat mission out of the required thirty needed to complete their tour.

After climbing aboard, the normal equipment checks were conducted by Bob and the crew. As each motor turned over with a sputter, the whine of the inertia starters and the smell of oil all but overwhelmed their senses. Bob then taxied WL-C onto the runway and with the brakes firmly on, opened the throttles on the engines, meeting their voracious thirst for more fuel. With the flash of the green light, Bob released the brakes and thirty-four tons of airplane, bombs, and crew hurtled down the runway gobbling up almost four thousand feet of it before liftoff was achieved at 8:43 AM.[4] They were the twelfth of fifteen fully armed bombers from 434 Squadron to become airborne.[5]

Bob started the aircraft into an aggressive climb to clear the approaching local mountains, which reached over 2,000 feet. They then joined the bomber stream. The crew could see a continuous ribbon of aircraft stretching out for miles. It included an additional 127 planes from seven other Canadian bomber squadrons, along with their sister Squadron 431.[6] Bob was unusually nervous thinking about his brother Jack.

Frank later recalled that all crews were instructed to fly at an elevation of 500 feet above the North Sea to escape German radar and to climb to 10,000 feet once they were near the Norwegian coast. Once over water, they flew all the way in heavy cloud. None of the crew could see any other aircraft. Bob started WL-C's climb at ten miles out from the coast, breaking through the clouds into a beautiful blue sky. Based on Al Coleman's excellent navigational skills, they were now situated right in the middle of the bomber stream, a comfort for all the crew. Luckily they were accompanied all the way by several Hawker Hurricane escort fighters each armed with four 20-mm cannons. This might have accounted for the lack of enemy aircraft.

Most aircraft on this raid carried 4,000-pound blockbuster bombs designed to penetrate the thick, concrete shells, which protected the submarine pens. WL-C, however, was an exception. Its bomb load consisted of nine 1,000-pound bombs and two 500-pound bombs designed to create additional havoc once the 4,000-pounders had done their job breaking open the pen exteriors.[7] When dropped on a built-up area, the 4,000-pound bomb could flatten an entire city block.

The crews encountered considerable flak over the target, which lit up the sky like a deadly New Year's Eve fireworks display. The raid itself was directed by two pilots, each in the role of Master Bomber, who had the code names "Tweedledee" and "Tweedledum." Sadly, "Tweedledum," an Australian pilot with the RAF, along with his navigator, were shot down over the target area.[8]

Altogether, over one million pounds of explosives and incendiaries were released on this mission, with many hitting the dock and harbour areas.[9] Frank noted in his log that he had released his deadly load at an elevation of 14,000 feet, a good height for precision bombing. Frank felt that the surprise attack was concentrated, effective, and deadly since he was able to visually identify the target. On the return leg, black billowing smoke from the target area could be seen from a distance of one hundred miles.[10]

All planes from 434 and 431 Squadrons returned safely, with Bob piloting his Halifax back to base after midnight, having flown over one thousand miles. Jack Henry's plane landed right on the heels of WL-D, three minutes later.[11] Bob was impressed that his plane achieved the second-shortest flight time to and from the target with an average ground speed of 154 miles per hour. One aircraft from 419 Squadron, based at Middleton St. George, crash-landed while trying to make an emergency landing. Several bombs were hung up in its bomb bay.[12] Unreleased bombs were a common menace during the war and, unfortunately, none of the seven members from the crash survived.

Ron and his crew were granted a seven-day leave following the Bergen raid. This time the crew was anxious to explore beyond the local villages and decided to go up to Edinburgh. While there, Ron met an old friend from Quebec at a local dance hall called "Palais de Dance," a name that struck Ron as peculiarly un-Scottish. Since the crew had rapidly run out of money, they returned a day early to rest up before the next operations. Scraping together the last of their loose change, Bill and Ron decided to visit a town near camp to get the latest hit records for their recently acquired juke box.

While the crew was on leave, the air war had continued unabated with 431 and 434 Squadrons involved in attacks on Dortmund on October 6 and Bochum on October 9. Five more planes from Bomber Group 6 were lost over this period.[13] Jack Henry flew on his second combat mission as a second pilot while his brother was on leave and wished Bob had been at Croft to provide moral support.[14] Fortunately, all planes from Croft made it safely back to base. Jack had learned just prior to his second trip that he had been promoted to Flight Lieutenant.

A Victory Bond campaign had also been launched at all Canadian air bases while Ron and the crew were on leave. Squadron 434 had a target of $25,000. Funds raised were invested by the Canadian government to help fund the cost of war and combat inflation by removing money from circulation. By the end of the campaign, the target had been greatly exceeded, with a total contribution of over $42,000 by the aircrews.[15] This amazing accomplishment amounted to almost $1,000 per crew, equivalent to $12,600 in today's currency.

While Ron was on leave, Kay continued to write as often as she could. On Monday, October 9, which was a chilly day in Montreal, she was happy to return to her warm home and write:

Dearest Ronny, How are you dear? I just came home a few minutes ago from Thanksgiving Weekend at Violet & Rita's place along the Lakeshore. It's pretty cold and bleak out today, you know the kind of weather that just seems to penetrate right through you, and makes you feel just a little bit depressed and darn lonely too, well all I can say is that seeing your wonderful letter waiting for me in the porch just made everything so different, it was just as if you were waiting there for me, and the house didn't even seem empty when I came in, as Dad and Jim are still away.

You mentioned writing your letter at 5:30 in the morning; I guess that's early even for the Air Force. You certainly are doing a lot of flying time, and I shouldn't kick, as boy I can just imagine how really cold it must be flying at high altitudes as you must.

Don't forget Ronny any snaps you have will be welcomed, I've sent some over that we took up in Terrebonne on our last weekend, I hope you get them O.K.

Well Ronny as I've just about run out of news for now anyway, I'll say Goodnight for now dear. All my love, Kay

The following day most of the crews that had been grounded due to continuing bad weather were involved in various training activities in the morning. On Thursday, October 12, sixteen crews were put on the battle order but just after briefing, the mission was cancelled due to bad weather.[16] With some free time, Ron decided to send off another aerogram to his parents.

Dear Mum & Dad, Well every thing's going on pretty much the same as usual around here. We haven't done much flying for a few days now.

We've got some pictures developed that Bill and I took in London during the summer but they took three weeks to get done. Bill sent the negatives home to his mother in Toronto, she'll send you two copies of each picture for you and one for Kay. We figured it would be a lot faster that way.

Did I tell you I got your Xmas card about a week ago mum? I got a lovely birthday card from Kay a couple of days ago.

How are you and dad feeling mum? Have you seen my little Kay lately? In your past letter you were doctoring up a cold for her, I hope it's all gone by now. Come to think of it I've got a pretty bad cold myself right now. All the time we were flying steadily I was alright, but as soon as we stopped to go on leave I got a cold.

Well I'll say goodnight for now with love to all at home. Your Loving Son, Ronny

While Ron wrote this letter a sense of solitude was settling over the base, which would soon be shattered by a beehive of activity. An unprecedented effort had been planned for October 14, including two combat missions scheduled for the same day. It was "Operation Hurricane," a massive campaign to prove the might of the Allied air force. The American Eighth Air Force would provide over 1,200 B-17 and B-25 heavy bombers that would attack between two massive RAF/RCAF bombing runs. The target was built-up areas of Duisburg, an industrial city located at the junction of the Rhine and Ruhr Rivers. The region produced large quantities of steel, key to the production of German weaponry. Duisburg was also the largest inland port in Europe and had a major railway junction located just fifty miles from the British and American front lines. The city was a popular target for Allied bombers and thus heavily protected by flak units. Elements of the RAF and RCAF from November 1940 to February 1945 would fly over 6,500 sorties against the city, losing 231 bombers in the process.

Ron and the crew had to crawl out of their warm beds at 2:00 AM to attend the first of two briefings scheduled for the day. After downing an early morning breakfast, the crew took transportation to the airfield and was welcomed by a frost-covered aircraft that looked surreal in the moonlight. Frank walked around the aircraft to conduct his usual check of the bomb bay to confirm that the plane had been properly armed—this time there were seven 1,000-pound bombs and six 500-pounders.[17]

After pre-flight checks were completed Joe, the flight engineer, assisted Bob in coaxing the four giant Hercules to life. They were again in Halifax WL-D, except that this was a newer plane (Serial No. MZ435). The original had been retired. Fortunately they had been able to put the lucky Kathleen nose art on this plane as well. With the roar of so many engines starting up across the airfield it was hard to imagine how anyone in close proximity to the runway could remain asleep. Their normal wait in the runway queue was one or two minutes, but for this flight they had to wait six minutes after WL-G lifted off directly in front of them.[18] Bob did not like to wait long for clearance and welcomed the green light. He could sense the rush of air as they lifted off the tarmac.

Bob soon joined the bomber stream comprising 257 aircraft from Bomber Group 6, which included 18 aircraft from 434 Squadron.[19] An additional 755 bombers from the Royal Air Force were also simultaneously targeted to Duisburg on this massive daylight raid.[20] The bomber stream had a heavy fighter escort. The 434 Squadron crews experienced clouds rising as high as 12,000 feet over the target. The black spray of flak above the clouds was so thick that Bob felt like he could land on it. WL-D was hit by several shell fragments which punched several holes in the outer skin but fortunately none of the crew was hit. There was so much flak on the final approach to Duisburg that three of the 434 Squadron bombers on this mission would need to be replaced for the second wave of attack later that day.

Luckily there were no enemy aircraft seen in the target area. Frank visually identified the target and quickly released the bomb load at an elevation of 19,500 feet.[21] They were anxious to depart the target area. Within a minute Frank could see several large, orange-coloured explosions lighting up the target area. Once the automatic

Crew: F/O R. Henry (1ˢᵗ Pilot), F/O A. Coleman (NAV), F/O F. Welsh (B/A), P/O H. Ward (WOP/AG), Sgt. A. Thomson (MU/AG), Sgt. R. Pyves (R/AG), Sgt. J. Casavant (F/E)

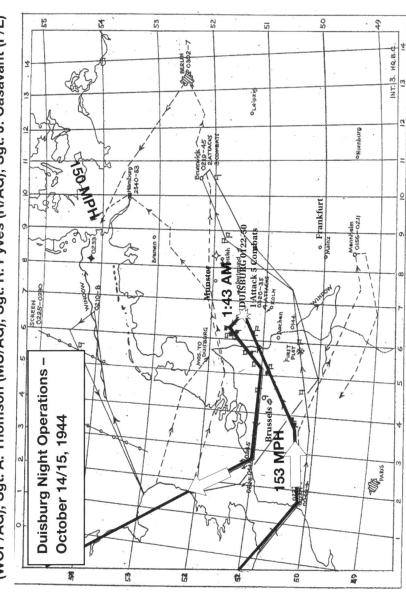

Duisburg Night Operations –
October 14/15, 1944

Outbound: 508 Miles, Inbound: 438 Miles, Total Distance Flown: 946 Miles

434 Squadron: WL-D (MZ435), Bomb Load: 7 x 1,000, 6 x 500 pounds

Source: *Night Raid Report No. 741*, Bomber Command, 1944. Reproduced with the permission of the Minister of Public Works and Government Services Canada, 2009.

photoflash was complete, Bob quickly banked the aircraft to port to start the return leg of their trip. At the same time, Joe checked to make sure that all bombs had been safely released before he closed the bomb-bay doors.

This first attack on Duisburg took almost six hours of incessant flying to complete. On the return flight they were passed by hundreds of American bombers heading for the same target. Upon their return to Croft just before noon, battered and dead tired, Bob Henry and the crew were debriefed and immediately started to mentally prepare for the second mission scheduled to start in less than twelve hours. Ron and the crew could barely stay awake and desperately sought an opportunity to get some sleep. This initial Duisburg mission resulted in fourteen lost bombers, including four planes from Bomber Group 6.[22] Sergeant Bill Thomson had been promoted to Flight Sergeant immediately following this first Duisburg mission. Although pleased that his promotion had finally come through, Bill worried that it wouldn't matter if they didn't make it through the rest of the day.

Halifax WL-D had been refueled and patched up after countless hours of cold and heavy outdoor work by the ground crews. This included work by the armourers to place 10,000 pounds of bombs in the bomb bay. Less then eleven hours since their first run to Duisburg, WL-D lifted off from Croft at 10:23 PM.[23] Once in the air Bob circled close to the base to gain altitude before heading off on a southeasterly course. Tragically, one bomber, WL-C from 434 Squadron, flown by Flight Lieutenant D. Wood, crashed just after takeoff, with only two of the crew surviving.[24] Just ten days earlier, Ron and his crewmates had flown in WL-C to Bergen and just that morning, it had been flown by Wing Commander A. Blackburn in the attack on Duisburg.[25] The lost crew was on its eighth trip and marked the first loss for 434 Squadron since Ron began flying combat missions. The accident occurred just after takeoff when an engine caught fire, causing the entire wing to fall off.[26] This incident was particularly unsettling for Ron and the crew who took off just minutes *after* WL-C. All said, whether a crew got the chop was sometimes just a matter of chance.

Bob guided his plane into the bomber stream of 239 Halifax and Lancaster bombers from all fourteen Canadian squadrons, including seventeen bombers from 434 Squadron.[27] An additional 435 bombers were also vectored to Duisburg from RAF bases located south of Bomber Group 6.[28] When WL-D crossed the English coastline, Ron could clearly see the White Cliffs of Dover in the moonlight, calmly rising some 300 feet above the turbulent ocean. When they were 150 miles out from their target, Bob banked to port on a flight path that would take them just south of Brussels and straight into Duisburg. The bomber stream approached Duisburg at a flying altitude of between 17,000 and 21,000 feet.[29]

Visibility over the target was good with scattered clouds. Local defence included several fighters. Frank released the bomb load of ten thousand pounds of high explosives at the top of the bomber stream just before 2:00 AM, bombing on the centre of the green target indicators released earlier by the Pathfinder Force.[30] The crew could see lots of smoke and explosions in the target area. Immediately after bomb release, as the plane jumped upward when relieved of its bomb load, Bob banked steeply to port and, after traveling twenty-four miles through what seemed initially like a tunnel of flak, turned once more to port, setting his ship on its homeward journey. Ron observed that the attack appeared very concentrated and, once again, their plane was hit by flak as they headed out of the target area.[31] This time their luck ran out as serious damage was sustained to the plane's hydraulic system. Joe, the flight engineer, informed Bob that both the brakes and the ailerons had been incapacitated. The ailerons were normally used to slow the plane down on landing.

Glow from fires in Duisburg lit up the horizon for almost two hundred miles as the plane headed back to base. The three-hour return journey gave the crew too much time to think about the uncertain landing they would have to make. Once over Croft, Bob was cleared for an emergency landing only after most of the other returning planes had already touched down safely. This was done in case they crashed and obstructed the runway, or damaged other planes. With no brakes, Bob reduced the plane's momentum to almost stalling speed to minimize the length of runway needed to land the plane. Bob was glad he and the crew had urinated on the tires before the mission as they'd need all the luck they could get. As WL-D glided down for touchdown the crew held their collective breath hoping that the fire truck and emergency vehicles rapidly pursuing them would not be required. One of Ron's fears was getting stuck in the rear turret if the plane caught fire. Their luck held and, absolutely sapped of all energy and emotion, the crew safely touched down at 4:35 AM.[32] They all breathed a sigh of relief as the four Hercules motors were shut down without further incident. Suddenly it seemed so quiet. No other returning bombers landed for what seemed like an eternity as the emergency crews made certain that WL-D did not pose a fire hazard to other returning aircraft. By now the entire crew had been airborne for just under twelve of the last twenty-two hours and had flown over two thousand miles, putting an unbearable strain on both man and machine. After debriefing and the usual hot coffee, both Ron and Bill, trying to look chipper, were photographed by the press. The photo appeared in a short caption in the *Montreal Herald* on December 15, 1944, almost two months after the mission. The same photo, but with only Bill in it, appeared in Bill's hometown *Toronto Star.*

The fight was not done that night, though. A second wave of 330 RAF bombers struck Duisburg just two hours after Ron and the crew had left the target area.[33] Duisburg suffered significant damage over this period. On the night raid, an additional six planes were lost, which included one Canadian plane from Bomber Group 6.[34]

Ron and his crewmates were taken off the duty roster for forty-eight hours for a well-deserved rest during which time the aircraft could be repaired as well. They had now beat the deadly odds by safely completing their first eight missions. But they were far from home and would have to face this night madness twenty-two more times if they were to complete their tour of duty.

While they were on the return leg of their second trip to Duisburg, Kay wrote just her third letter to Ron that month from the home front, to a young man who was now in many ways a world apart.

> *Dearest Ronny, Hello Dear, I hope everything is fine with you and that you are receiving my letters fine too. It's strange Ronny but letters are just like a tonic, they make one feel so swell, and well that's the way I feel when I find one of your letters waiting for me.*

You mentioned that you and the crew were flying day and night, gosh you must be just about dog-tired with all that intensive flying and I understand that you won't be able to write so often. You say that you like to be on ops, and that it's exciting, I think it would be too damn exciting but one thing you know always, and that's that you're doing an important job and doing it successfully, of that you can be proud, as I always will be (proud) of you.

You must be anxiously awaiting that well-earned leave and I don't blame you.

Gosh Ronny it's gradually getting colder & colder now, soon it will be skiing weather all over again. It was beautiful up North last winter wasn't it? I think somehow that one would have to go pretty far to see a spot with everything combined like up North.

The lights are all on again in Montreal and it makes quite a difference on St. Catherine Street.

Well dear as I've just about ran out of news for now, I'll say goodnight to you for now. Take care of yourself always for me. God Bless, All my love, Kay

This letter would take about ten days to get to England.

While October was shaping up to be a challenging month for Ron and his crewmates, especially after the double run into Duisburg, it was also challenging for the Canadian forces on the ground. As most supplies were still coming through D-Day beaches, it was becoming increasingly difficult to resupply all Allied armies, including the First Canadian Army as they pressed farther into France, Belgium, and the Netherlands. Although the Port of Antwerp had been captured almost intact on September 5, 1944, the harbour could not be safely utilized by Allied shipping until all land approaches to Antwerp were cleared of German forces which still manned coastal gun batteries. This included South Bevland Peninsula and Walcheren Island, a German stronghold at the mouth of the Scheldt Estuary, which inbound shipping to Antwerp would need to pass. Something had to be done, so on October 2, the Allies advanced north from Antwerp. The troops were comprised of elements of the Second and Third Canadian Divisions and Fourth Canadian Armoured Division, supported by the British Fifty-Second Division and First Polish Armoured Division. It would take them to November 8 to secure the Scheldt Estuary.[35] Military supplies began moving through the Port of Antwerp at the end of November.

Bomber Command flew on nine additional missions in October in support of the First Canadian Army. The crews attacked River Scheldt gun batteries and the sea wall on Walcheren Island in a successful effort to flood out and disrupt German defences. Eight bombers were lost in the efforts.[36] On the ground the First Canadian Army suffered almost thirteen thousand casualties with over six thousand Canadians killed or wounded.[37] It had been a bloodbath.

7
A Lucky Fellow

The Squadron stood down on October 16 to allow both the crews and aircraft to recover from intense operations. They had just delivered three blows to the enemy—two to Duisburg on October 14–15 and one to Wilhelmshaven in northern Germany on the coast of the North Sea on October 15–16. Next day, with enough visibility to make a safe takeoff, the crew departed Croft mid-morning in Halifax WL-F (for "Fox").[1] Their own bomber was still undergoing extensive maintenance and repairs. The crew was now exhausted and the last thing Frank and Al wanted was another cross-country radar exercise. No matter—after two hours of cross-country flying, they finally returned to base to catch up on their sleep.

Four planned combat missions were cancelled due to inclement weather over the next five days. Stress created from cancelled missions took almost as much toll on aircrew. This on-again off-again routine worked on the nerves of all aircrew who just wanted to finish their tour of duty and get home to family and friends. Aircrew had to get mentally and emotionally prepared for combat, and knew a cancellation would require that they do it all over again.

Nevertheless, Ron could now take advantage of the lull in the fighting to drop Kay a quick line.

Dearest Kay, Whenever we're on an op and things start looking grim I can feel your presence beside me and I don't worry any more. You can't imagine how much that just knowing you are thinking of me, helps me along. I consider myself the luckiest fellow going to have met you Kay and gosh, how you've grown into my heart since, just as if I've known you forever.

Thanks ever so much for the cigarettes dear, they came exactly at the right moment just as I was running out of Canadian cigs. The English ones aren't worth smoking.

Well darling I've got to go and get dressed for a little job we've got to do so until next time remember how much I love you Kay. All my Love Always, Ronny

On the morning of October 23, the crew was finally briefed on their next night bombing mission that would actually get off the ground. The target was the Krupp Steel Works in Essen on the Rhine River. Essen had been a key German steel production area given the nearby abundance of coal required to fuel the large blast furnaces. The Krupp Steel Works had started in the early 1800s and had since the First World War been associated with the production of military equipment, including artillery and other armaments. Over time, the steel works had grown into a vast complex that covered hundreds of acres.

Both 431 and 434 Squadrons were briefed by Squadron Leader W.A. Bentley, with the Croft Station Commanding Officer R.S. Turnbull and Wing Commander Paul Blackburn also in attendance. Paul Blackburn would lead this mission.[2] A public relations photo was taken of this briefing, with Ron appearing quite pensive and gaunt, which is not a surprise given all the recent last-minute cancellations. Bob also felt apprehensive about this upcoming ninth mission as it would be the first trip in which his brother Jack would be flying as first pilot, and Bob knew, inexperience killed airmen. Just as the sun was disappearing below the horizon, Ron, Bob, and the rest of the crew raced down the runway in Halifax WL-D with a full bomb load.

The crew anticipated a long and treacherous flight to one of the most heavily defended areas of Germany, the Ruhr Valley. The Ruhr was the industrial heartland of Germany. The large veins of coal running through the valley had been the lifeblood of German industry for over one hundred years. In fact, the area had been fought over by France and Germany in three major conflicts starting in 1870 with

Crew: F/O R. Henry (1st Pilot), F/O A. Coleman (NAV), F/O F. Welsh (B/A), P/O H. Ward (WOP/AG), Sgt. A. Thomson (MU/AG), Sgt. R. Pyves (R/AG), Sgt. J. Casavant (F/E)

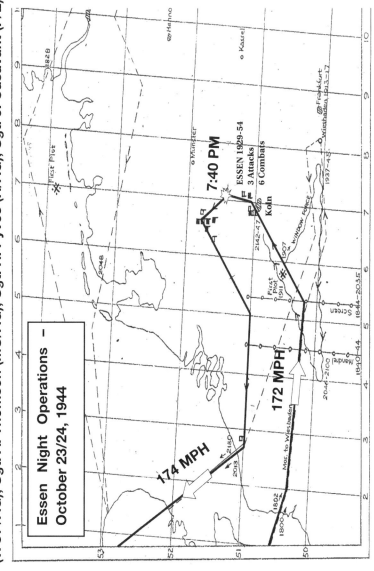

Essen Night Operations –
October 23/24, 1944

7:40 PM

ESSEN 1929-54
3 Attacks
6 Combats

Koln

172 MPH

174 MPH

Outbound: 538 Miles, Inbound: 456 Miles, Total Distance Flown: 994 Miles

434 Squadron: WL-D (MZ435), Bomb Load: 1 x 2,000, 5 x 1,000, 6 x 500 pounds

Source: *Night Raid Report No. 748*, Bomber Command, 1944. Reproduced with the permission of the Minister of Public Works and Government Services Canada, 2009.

the Franco-Prussian War. The region of Alsace in France had large deposits of iron ore while the Ruhr had an abundant supply of coal. Each country had a resource that the other needed to cost-effectively produce steel. In peacetime the availability of coal and iron ore was not a considerable issue, but in times of conflict could become problematic. With the German occupation of France in 1940, Alsace iron ore was readily available to keep the German blast furnaces operating smoothly. The Ruhr thus became a strategic target for Bomber Command. Over time Ron and the crew would visit almost all major cities located in the Ruhr.

Immediately after takeoff, Bob began a steady climb while circling the field until at 10,000 feet he momentarily levelled off to allow the crew to put on their oxygen masks. He then turned southeast to join the bomber stream. Jack, in SE-H (for "How"), lifted off fifteen minutes later. Like 434 Squadron whose plane identification always started with WL, 431 Squadron plane identifications always started with the letters SE.

All fourteen Canadian bomber squadrons participated in this raid with 272 aircraft from Bomber Group 6 joined by an additional 783 Royal Air Force bombers, which included crews from many Commonwealth countries.[3] Squadron 434 had been able to deliver a maximum effort, putting twenty bombers into the air with an additional fifteen bombers coming from 431 Squadron.[4] After crossing the French coast, WL-D headed due west and forty-five minutes later turned to port on a northeast setting. Thirty minutes on, Bob made another steep turn to port for his final run into the target. Ron could feel his stomach muscles tighten as he anticipated an attack by enemy fighter planes desperate to stop the deadly raid. When they arrived at the target area there was significant cloud cover—reaching as high as 15,000 feet. The bombers were therefore instructed by the Master Bomber to drop their loads on the coloured sky markers.[5] The markers would act as an aiming point for each bombardier as he released his bombs. Although *any* presence of flak could be terrifying, on this mission the flak was light to moderate even though enemy fighters were active in the area. The Krupp Steel Works sustained heavy damage with over two hundred buildings partially or completely destroyed.[6] WL-D delivered a mixed bomb load of one 2,000-pound, five 1,000-pound, and six 500-pound bombs released at 7:40 PM from an elevation of 19,500 feet.[7] This was the first time that the boys in WL-D had dropped a 2,000-pound bomb, which through a combination of blast and fragmentation could be deadly up to 3,000 feet from the centre of the explosion. Frank and the rest of the crew observed a number of bomb bursts through the clouds. Frank, as bomb aimer, concluded that the overall attack had been scattered due to the need to bomb on sky markers. Concentrated bombing was preferred because the resulting conflagration was more difficult to contain by local emergency firefighters and other rescue crew on the ground.

Once out of the target area, Bob banked to port, flying for ten minutes in a northwest direction before heading for the French coast where he made one final turn, banking to starboard, which set them on a flight path that would take them directly to Croft some 262 miles ahead. Halifax WL-D touched down after almost six hours in the air. One Canadian plane from 419 Squadron was lost but all planes from 434 Squadron returned safely to base, although one plane sustained serious damage.[8] It had been hit by an unexploded 1,000-pound bomb dropped from above by another bomber. This was a reminder that it wasn't just the enemy that airmen had to worry about. And Ron and the crew would soon have their own first-hand experience of this kind of danger. Altogether, severe icing, mechanical failure, inclement weather, misdirected bombs, and even friendly fire could result in the same "missing in action" outcome.

After debriefing, the crew packed up for the night and was relieved to learn they were not required to fly the next day. Bob, on the other hand, stayed up to get a first-hand report on his brother's first solo mission as pilot.

On Wednesday, October 25, the crew rose early and was briefed for their tenth combat mission. This would be a milestone, and would complete one-third of their tour of duty. More important, if they survived this tenth mission, they had a much higher probability of surviving the balance of tour. For 434 Squadron, less than 20 percent of planes lost on operations occurred after a crew's tenth mission.[9]

The target was a synthetic oil plant at Homberg, not far from Duisburg. Located in the Ruhr Valley, this target was not greeted with a lot of enthusiasm—it was a dangerous mission that would keep them in the air and vulnerable for at least five hours. Right after the main briefing, Bob met with his brother and reminded the rookie to be vigilant and not fly in a straight line too long. Not only would this tactic make it more difficult for the enemy to single out his plane for an attack, it would not signal to the enemy that here was a rookie pilot, ripe for the picking.

After the briefing and the usual pre-trip mental preparations to remain calm and focused, the crew again boarded their home away from home, Halifax WL-D. As Bob taxied onto the runway he could see ten bombers already lined up for takeoff in front of him. WL-D was given permission to take off from Croft just after 1:00 PM and merged with the bomber stream that included nineteen planes from 434 Squadron and five bombers from 431 Squadron, including SE-M (for "Mike") flown by Jack, inbound to Homberg.[10] This would be the last time Bob and Jack would fly on the same mission for over a month.

Compared to their previous mission, which involved 1,055 RAF and Canadian planes, this would be primarily a Canadian effort with 198 Halifax bombers from Bomber Group 6 and an additional 32 Lancasters from Bomber Group 8.[11] The Lancaster bomber was in many ways similar to the Halifax in terms of armament, wingspan, length, and height. But the key difference was with modifications in the bomb bay: the Lancaster could carry a 22,000 "Grand Slam" bomb. In normal conditions it carried only a little-heavier bomb load than the Halifax.

Due to heavy cloud cover reaching as high as 8,000 feet, H2S blind-bombing was employed over the target area. On this trip, WL-D was carrying 10,000 pounds of high explosives.[12] Bob approached the target at 17,500 feet and Frank released WL-D's bomb load at 3:50 PM.[13] None of the crew could see the result due to heavy cloud coverage. All planes made it safely back to base, with the crew of WL-D touching down at 6:27 PM.[14] Bob was relieved to hear that Jack's plane had already landed five minutes before them. Almost two million pounds of high explosives were dropped over the target area that day.[15] Frank felt good about this mission, reporting that it had been a "pretty good prang."

That evening while Ron and the crew settled down in their hut, thousands of miles across the ocean Kay sat down at the kitchen table to pen Ron a short note.

Dearest Ronny, That woman's back again, how are you dear? Gosh Ronny is this ever a nice night to be home, it's just pouring in buckets outside and it's a pleasure to be inside. How would you like to come over and keep me company, gosh I wish you would.

Jim is going downtown to see the show Mr. Skiffington. *It's a swell picture but not worth getting soaked for, then again it is.*

I sincerely hope that "Kathleen" is behaving herself at all times Ronny, I always feel very proud of that dear.

Well Ronny I'll say goodnight for now, take care of yourself dear. All my love Always, Kay

Ron and his crewmates were not on operations the next day due to inclement weather. Instead they were required to provide assistance in the bomb dump area, restocking the bomb inventory, a task not relished by the crews as it was heavy and dangerous work.[16] Next day the crew were once again assigned to an H2S blind-bombing exercise in Halifax WL-D, a task that lasted a little more than one hour in the air. A late evening operation that was to involve eighteen aircraft and crew from the squadron was cancelled late that afternoon.[17]

Ron and the crew listened to records on his portable juke box in late evening. They huddled around the coal stove to drive out the penetrating English chill which had become all too frequent. The hissing of the wet wood that they had piled on the hot coals to supplement their meagre fuel supply was soothing, a familiar sound that reminded Ron of his parent's cottage on the shores of Lake Nantel.

In Montreal, Kay had finished her work for the week and decided to send Ron another aerogram. It was the start of another weekend without him.

My dearest Ronny, Hello dear, how is everything? I received your postcards yesterday, are the castles in Scotland actually as huge and immense as that? It's hard to imagine isn't it, when you think of a crowded city like Montreal and two-thirds of its three-story flats, but then that is one of the few things I don't think is logical. You sure must have had a nice time on leave.

Just think dear, it will soon be your birthday, I will be thinking of you especially on the 5th, if it's possible to think of you any more than I do now dear. You know Ronny there's a nice popular song, I think it's just about one of the nicest songs I've heard.

An hour never passes, but I think of you.
An hour never passes, but I miss you too.
Ev'ry day from dawning till the moonlight's glow,
You're beside me Darling, ev'rywhere I go.
An hour never passes, a clock never chimes,
But I keep recalling, those old happy times.
Without my prayer for you in each lonely sigh,
An hour never passes by.[18]

Maybe it's because they are so true. Gosh Ronny it certainly won't be long here before it's snowing, it has been so darn cold lately, or maybe it's just because I'm later putting on my Winter Coat this year.

Well dear I'll say goodnight for now Ronny. God Bless and take care of you always. All my love, Kay

Ron lay wide awake in bed that night thinking he just had to survive so he could get back to Montreal and Kay.

Next morning the crew, minus wireless operator Hal Ward, who from time to time experienced ear problems, was briefed on an upcoming daylight raid scheduled for early afternoon. This would be their eleventh mission. Flight Lieutenant C. Brady, a very experienced officer and at the time the signals leader for 434 Squadron, replaced Hal on this trip.[19] The crew learned at main briefing that the target would be Cologne. Located on both banks of the Rhine, Cologne was one of the largest cities in Germany. The city had been the recipient of many earlier bomber command attacks, which included in 1942 the first 1,000-bomber raid which destroyed over six hundred acres of the city. Miraculously, its most famous landmark—the Cologne

Crew: F/O R. Henry (1st Pilot), F/O A. Coleman (NAV), F/O S. McDougall (B/A), P/O H. Ward (WOP/AG), Sgt. A. Thomson (MU/AG), Sgt. R. Pyves (R/AG), Sgt. J. Casavant (F/E)

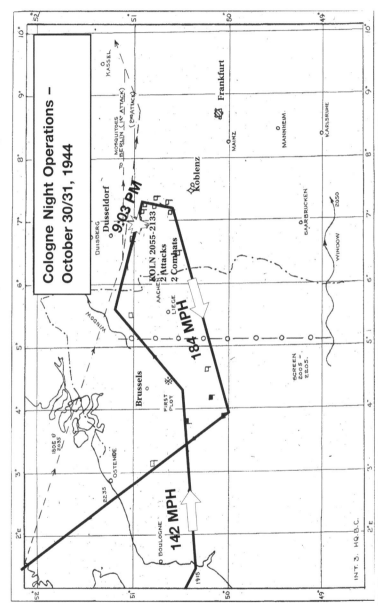

Cologne Night Operations –
October 30/31, 1944

Outbound: 519 Miles, Inbound: 428 Miles, Total Distance Flown: 947 Miles

434 Squadron: WL-D (MZ435), Bomb Load: 1 x 2,000, 6 x 1,000, 5 x 500 pounds

Source: *Night Raid Report No. 755*, Bomber Command, 1944. Reproduced with the permission of the Minister of Public Works and Government Services Canada, 2009.

Cathedral with its twin tours reaching five hundred feet—survived even though it was hit dozens of times.

With Bob Henry at the controls, Halifax WL-D joined 733 other planes including 231 from Bomber Group 6.[20] Squadron 434 contributed a force of twenty bombers to this effort, with Bob's plane in sixteenth position for takeoff.[21] Skies over Cologne varied from clear to almost completely overcast with some clouds topping out at 10,000 feet. The flak would later be described at debriefing as moderate yet accurate. Although there was a full moon there was poor visibility over the primary target. For the first time WL-D had to bomb a secondary target, dropping one 2,000-pound and twelve 500-pound bombs on target indicators at an elevation of 19,500 feet.[22] All said, almost 1.6 million pounds of explosives and over a quarter million pounds of incendiaries were dropped on the primary target.[23] Significant damage was inflicted, including the destruction of thousands of housing flats and over a dozen industrial complexes and railway facilities. Only one Canadian plane (from 419 Squadron) was lost over Cologne, although another from 434 Squadron, flown by Sergeant Fred Hart, crashed on landing.[24] An engine caught fire while Fred was returning to base and he was able to keep his plane in the air until all his crew had bailed out safely. Fred won a Distinguished Flying Cross (DFC) for his heroism. Fred flew on many of the same missions as Ron and on occasion had piloted WL-D with his own crew. Ironically, Fred was a close friend of Kay's.

On the return flight, Bob diverted his aircraft to Wombleton, a Canadian training air base thirty miles southeast of Croft. The following morning the crew made a short fifteen-minute flight back to Croft where there was a 7:00 AM briefing scheduled for the next day. However, that mission was aborted due to bad weather over the target.[25]

Taking advantage of some free time in the morning, Ron collected his mail, which included a letter from Kay written just eight days earlier.

Dearest Ronny, I bet you had a grand time on leave in Scotland, gosh that was a good one about the French name for the dance hall. You say Ronny, you've lost ten pounds over the last three weeks, gosh you certainly had better start drinking more milk and eating more too. Maybe it's the tenseness and that of flying and going on ops so much and it will take time to get accustomed to the life you have to lead.

I was down to visit your Mom just the other night. The way she feeds me, I must be putting on the ten pounds you've lost. Your dad came home later as he was out on parade.

It's really quite cold in Montreal now and even though it's not November yet, you can feel the tang of winter everywhere.

Take care of yourself always dear. God Bless, All my love, Kay

By noon the aborted operation had been reinstated: the crews had a return ticket to Cologne. They would be targeting areas where the bombs would disrupt the industrial work force. Like most trips, the path to the target was indirect and involved four key turning points.[26] Ron and the crew (minus Frank who was replaced by F/O S. McDougall) boarded Halifax WL-D and were airborne at 5:23 PM.[27] Ron watched the moonlight become obscured by clouds as they flew toward enemy territory. A total of 905 Bomber Command aircraft were dispatched, which included 243 planes from Bomber Group 6.[28] Nineteen aircraft from 434 Squadron participated, although one plane, WL-W, had to turn back prematurely due to icing problems.[29] Once at the target, F/O S. McDougall had to deal with significant cloud cover that reached as high as 8,000 feet. Bob approached the target area at an elevation of 19,500 feet, and F/O S. McDougall accurately released the bomb load on sky markers, confident they were on target.[30] With satisfaction he observed two large, orange-coloured explosions one minute after bomb release.

The Canadian bombers experienced moderate flak, with some searchlights and several fighters. One of the great fears was to be "coned" by a master searchlight controlled by German radar. Once the searchlight locked onto an individual plane, it not only blinded the pilot and gunners trying to spot enemy aircraft, it would be almost impossible to shake off, and all the while it would be attracting enemy fighter craft to the party. Being coned was the last thing Ron needed as he tried to protect the plane from fighter attack.

Just a few minutes after bomb release, Bob made a sharp turn to starboard and held this direction for five minutes to clear the immediate target area. He then banked once again to starboard to set WL-D on a southwesterly course. After maintaining this direction for another thirty-six minutes, Al instructed Bob to make a ninety-degree turn to starboard placing WL-D on a northwesterly course toward home. Due to bad weather at Croft, Hal, the wireless operator, received a call ordering them to divert to Fulbeck, a Royal Air Force base located east of Nottingham.[31] Bob made a smooth landing having flown for six hours. This flight was their second-longest to date: they had traveled 947 miles at an average speed of 158 miles per hour. Fortunately no planes were lost on this mission. Next day, they flew back to base. Shortly after landing, Flight Sergeant Hal Ward learned that his commission to Flight Officer had been approved.

Although the sortie had gone off without a hitch, the constant fear and stress of the unknown and the possibility of attack, mechanical failure, or human error was felt acutely by each and every crew member. Over time the stress could become too much to handle. Ron just hoped he would be able to finish his tour before his state of mind became an issue.

By the end of October, 434 Squadron had seen six crews screened from operations and ten new crews arrive. Combat crews were "screened" from operations when they had completed the required thirty missions on their first tour of duty or after twenty missions if they were on their second tour. Most would be given a thirty-day leave after which they might be assigned to a training or other non-combat role unless they volunteered to serve for an additional tour. Forty-three crews were now available in 434 Squadron to man the twenty-eight Halifax bombers.[32]

Over the last month the crew of Halifax WL-D had flown on seven of 434's nine combat missions. They were very fortunate that the losses in Bomber Group 6 for this period had been exceptionally low with a loss rate of 0.8 percent, or nineteen aircraft and crews lost in 2,384 sorties flown.[33] Included in the nineteen planes lost was WL-C from 434 Squadron. Unfortunately, this rate of attrition would become much higher in the months to come as the bombers needed to penetrate deeper into German territory to reach their assigned targets.

Crew: F/O R. Henry (1st Pilot), F/O A. Coleman (NAV), F/O F. Welsh (B/A), P/O H. Ward (WOP/AG), Sgt. A. Thomson (MU/AG), Sgt. R. Pyves (R/AG), Sgt. J. Casavant (F/E)

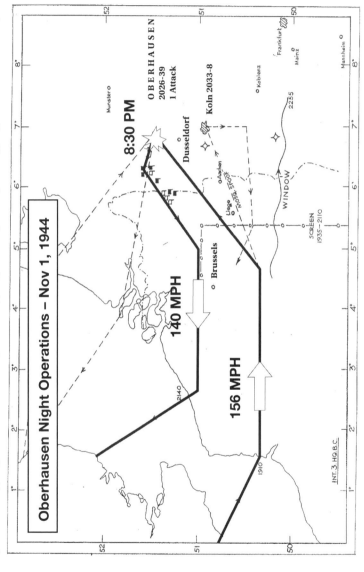

Oberhausen Night Operations – Nov 1, 1944

8:30 PM

140 MPH

156 MPH

OBERHAUSEN
2026-39
1 Attack

Koln 2033-8

Outbound: 534 Miles, Inbound: 257 Miles, Total Distance Flown: 791 Miles
434 Squadron: WL-D (MZ435), Bomb Load: 1 x 2,000, 1,080 x 4 pounds

Source: *Night Raid Report No. 757*, Bomber Command, 1944. Reproduced with the permission of the Minister of Public Works and Government Services Canada, 2009.

8
Lucky Number Thirteen

November got off to a quick start when Ron and the crew attended a briefing before their thirteenth mission. It was scheduled for early evening November 1, 1944. For the superstitious, trip thirteen added additional stress to this upcoming flight.

The target was Oberhausen in the Ruhr Valley, located very close to Duisburg. Once again they were targeting both steel and coal works. As the target was unveiled, groans could be heard from the crews all too familiar with the heavily defended Ruhr area. The men were informed they could expect a full moon, which would assist German fighters locate their prey. Diversionary Mosquito bombing raids were planned for both Cologne and Berlin to draw off any enemy fighters from the main bomber stream.

"Kathleen" was waiting patiently on the tarmac for the crew to complete their pre-flight checks. Frank, in his walk around, confirmed that WL-D's bomb bay held one 2,000-pound bomb and twelve canisters that each held ninety 4-pound incendiary bombs designed to start fires.[1] This was the first trip where the crew would be dropping a mix of high-explosive and incendiary bombs. The mix was designed so that the high-explosive bomb would first rip open roofs and blow out windows of buildings in the target area. The incendiary bombs would then penetrate deep into the buildings where there were lots of combustible materials. A greater supply of oxygen would now be available through the broken windows and destroyed roofs, helping feed the thousands of small fires created by the incendiary bombs. Eventually all the small fires would merge to create one huge conflagration. Although individual incendiary bombs could be put out with a pail of sand, the sheer number dropped made it almost impossible for fire wardens and firefighters to get to all fires in time. Some of these fire bombs were also booby trapped to discourage individuals from trying to put them out—because they could explode at any time.

Bob released the brakes and WL-D started to roll down the runway in the wake of WL-X, which had taken off one minute before them. Bob began his climb to join the bomber stream of 251 Canadian bombers, which included seventeen other aircraft from 434 Squadron.[2] An additional twenty-seven Lancasters and twelve Mosquitos from Bomber Group 8 merged with the Canadian bomber stream.[3] Squadron 431 crews were converting to Avro Lancasters, and for ten crews this would be their first trip in the newly acquired aircraft. Bob followed the bomber stream southward and at the French coast turned to port, heading due east for forty-five minutes. He then banked forty-five degrees to port to set the plane on a direct flight path to the target. Forty minutes later Frank was frustrated to see that heavy stratocumulus clouds up to 7,000 feet obscured the target. This forced him to use H2S radar and aim on sky markers. Frank directed Bob to approach the target at an elevation of 16,500 feet, and the bomb load was released at 11:30 PM.[4] Shortly afterward Frank observed two large bursts of orange flames that looked like oil tanks exploding.[5] Heavy flak and German night fighters defended the target area. The German fighters were out in full force, and as the bomber stream departed, one enemy aircraft was seen falling toward the ground and exploding on impact.[6] But no matter—the German fighters tenaciously followed the bombers all the way to the coast.

After the bombing run, Bob banked the aircraft steeply, reversing directions, and headed almost due west. Just as they started for home, one of WL-D's engines stopped working. Joe quickly turned off the master fuel switch for the failed engine and feathered the engine so that the propeller would not spin and create air drag which would slow them down even further. Bob maintained their altitude, but to do so, he had to continually make adjustments using the elevator controls. They continued this slower pace on the three remaining engines, which made them more vulnerable to enemy fighters. At this point, they were still over four hundred miles from Croft.

Flying ahead of Ron and the crew in the returning bomber stream was WL-U from 434 Squadron. It was flown by Flying Officer J. Bagley. It was his sixteenth mission. They were initially attacked from the port quarter by a German fighter who neutralized their starboard outer engine. A second attack came from the same direction but did not result in any hits.[7] The third attack was fatal, hitting the starboard inner engine which burst into flame.[8] The pilot ordered the crew to bale out. W/O L. Gobel and F/O R. Halfnight were the only survivors and were quickly taken prisoner on the ground.[9] Also flying ahead of WL-D was a plane from 431 Squadron flown by F/O D.D. Connor, in SE-P. It was on his thirtieth and last mission but his first combat mission in a Lancaster. It too was shot down with two crew killed including the pilot; four crew members became POWs and Sergeant J. Campbell evaded capture.[10]

Joe, sweating profusely, nursed the three remaining engines to maximize their output but without overstraining them. Joe knew that the loss of just one additional engine could be catastrophic because the loss of speed and elevation would make them easy prey from both night fighters and flak. Ron and Bill both strained to locate any specks that might be moving toward them in the surrounding sky. They were backlit by the full moon—clear targets. Twenty-five miles beyond Oberhausen, Bob turned onto a southwesterly flight path, which he maintained for half an hour before turning to starboard, flying due west for another thirty-six minutes. To the crew it seemed an eternity. At the final turning point, Bob set WL-D on to a northwesterly flight path for the final leg. They would have another thirty-five minutes to think about the emergency landing ahead before they reached the airfield at Woodbridge. This RAF base, equipped with a significantly longer runway than normal, could accommodate distressed bombers that might require the extra length to make a safe landing. The diversion would also shorten their return flight by over 170 miles, which would improve their chances.

After almost two and a half hours of plodding along, the air gunners' eyes throbbed with pain from the necessity to maintain an above-normal level of vigilance. Then Bob finally sighted the base at Woodbridge near the Suffolk coast. As he maneuvered for touchdown, he found that the brakes didn't work, not a surprise because he knew they had lost hydraulic pressure. Nevertheless Bob guided "Kathleen" to a safe return at 10:20 PM, having flown almost eight hundred miles.[11] The crew had survived its thirteenth mission. A U.S. Liberator came in just after WL-D with one of its twin rudders shot off.[12] WL-S also landed at Woodbridge. Its wireless operator had been fatally injured by flak and three additional members of the crew were wounded.[13] Six aircraft were lost on this mission. Eight aircrew from Croft had been killed. An additional six were taken prisoner.[14] The overall aircraft loss rate of 2.5 percent on this mission was the highest since Ron started flying with 434 Squadron in early September.

After the debriefing each member of the crew received a substantial ration of dark navy rum with coffee. The crew then settled down as best they could for the night and awoke the next morning to learn that their aircraft could be flown back to base but would require further repairs there. At 1:00 PM the next day Bob coaxed "Kathleen" into the air and landed back at Croft without incident an hour later.[15]

Ron wrote to Kay the next day, and for the first time a degree of pessimism began to seep into the correspondence.

> Well dear, I've got my thirteenth op over with, and it was kind of a shaky trip, I'm glad it's over with.
>
> When you stop to think about how much fun people could be having and really have a chance to enjoy life, instead we go around killing each other off by the thousands. It's hard to understand, just like being in the middle of a bad dream. It'll be a happy day, when I and everybody else can wake up and find that it's all over with, and that we're back home with the people we love.

On a happier note, in the same letter Ron told her,

"That's a lovely song you sent the words of dear, it fits exactly the way I feel about you. We've only got a couple of records for our own juke box so far as we haven't had time to get off camp and get any more. We've got "G.I. Jive" and "Milkman Keep Those Bottles Quiet."

The trouble is though; I get kind of sentimental listening to pieces of music like "Star Eyes" and "How Many Times Do I Have To Tell You" and wish I had never seen this place. Of course it's not only the place but the people as well who you love and can't see or talk to because they are so many thousands of miles away.

I'll say goodnight for now darling and the only news that I really want to hear from Montreal is that you're well and safe, that's all that matters to me Kay. All my love always darling, Ronny

Because the crew had just returned to base and there was no operational Halifax available, Ron and the crew were lucky to miss a trip to Düsseldorf. This sortie involved 222 bombers from Bomber Group 6, including seventeen bombers from 434 Squadron.[16] The mission resulted in a further loss of six Canadian planes, or 2.7 percent of the sorties flown, although this time none were lost from 431 or 434 Squadron.[17] The entire squadron stood down from operations the following day, although some crews were involved in ongoing training.

Early on the afternoon of November 4, just as the weak warmth of the sun peaked for the day, "Kathleen's" crew gathered for another mission briefing. The target: built-up areas of Bochum, ten miles to the west of Duisburg. Bochum had been identified because of its steel and arms industries. Between the briefing and scheduled departure Ron penned a quick letter home to his parents.

Dear Mum & Dad, How is everything at home? I guess it's starting to get quite cold now eh!

It would really be swell if you could send a record over of your voices and get Kay on it too. I don't think it would break if you packed it carefully. It would be worth a try anyway, don't you think?

Well we've got thirteen operational trips over with now. That is pretty fast going as we haven't been on the squadron quite two months yet. My promotion to Flight Sergeant will be through in about a week's time.

Well I'll say Cheerio for now. Love, Ronny

Although the Allies were making progress on both the Western and Eastern Fronts with Germany on the defensive, it was expected that the war would continue into 1945. Canadian forces had liberated Belgium, American forces were forty miles west of Cologne, Germany, and the Russians were fighting in East Prussia, Yugoslavia, and Hungary. In desperation, Hitler ordered conscription of all men from sixteen to sixty years of age. After the successful execution of "Operation Overlord," Bomber Command priorities shifted from transportation and communications targets to key tactical targets including synthetic oil plants and steel works, although Air Chief Marshal "Bomber" Harris preferred whenever possible to resume the bombing of German city centres to weaken German moral and disrupt industrial workforces.

Unlike the recent Oberhausen initiative, Bomber Command's attack on Bochum would be a much larger raid with 749 planes dispatched, including 214 bombers from all fourteen Canadian squadrons.[18] Once more, Ron and the crew were fortunate to fly in the familiar WL-D, which had brought them back unharmed from ten previous missions.

WL-D had once again been armed with a deadly mix of high explosives and incendiaries. "Kathleen" lifted off in the dark and joined the bomber stream that led due south for 160 miles. Bob then made a sharp turn to port heading across the English Channel where they reached landfall just north of Rotterdam, skirting the city's defences.[19] Once safely past Rotterdam, Bob, with assistance from Al, turned slightly to starboard for a straight run in to the target. The trip, at least for the first two legs of the inbound journey, was uneventful. Hal would later recall that as the bomber stream was south of Nejmegen in the Netherlands the crew noticed an eerie, spectacular sight in the

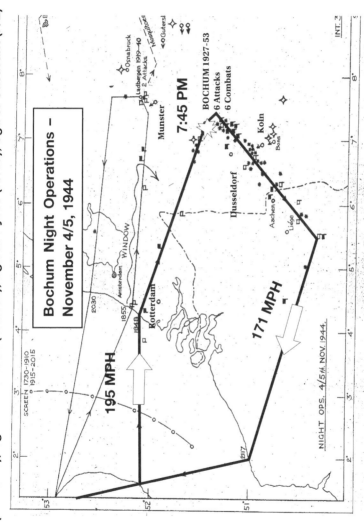

Crew: F/O R. Henry (1st Pilot), F/O A. Coleman (NAV), F/O F. Welsh (B/A), P/O H. Morris (WOP/AG), Sgt. A. Thomson (MU/AG), Sgt. R. Pyves (R/AG), Sgt. J. Casavant (F/E)

Bochum Night Operations – November 4/5, 1944

195 MPH

171 MPH

7:45 PM

BOCHUM 1927-53
6 Attacks
6 Combats

Outbound: 383 Miles, Inbound: 490 Miles, Total Distance Flown: 873 Miles

434 Squadron: WL-D (KB830), Bomb Load: 1 x 4,000, 6 x 500, 5 x 250 pounds

Source: *Night Raid Report No. 760*, Bomber Command, 1944. Reproduced with the permission of the Minister of Public Works and Government Services Canada, 2009.

moonlight—hundreds of wooden gliders as far as the eye could see were being towed by Dakota transport aircraft.[20] The Dakota twin-engine plane was used to tow gliders and carry paratroopers and was a variant of the Douglas Aircraft DC-3, originally built for commercial aviation. It normally had a crew of three and could carry twenty-eight paratroopers as well as pull a stealthy glider.

The bombers experienced significant enemy aircraft activity on both the approach and return leg from Bochum, with the crews from at least four 434 Squadron planes later reporting direct attacks by German fighter planes. These enemy aircraft included a single-engine Focke-Wulf Fw190 capable of speeds in excess of 400 miles per hour, the deadly Messerschmitt Me 109, as well the Junkers Ju-188 high-performance bomber armed with a 20-mm cannon and three .51-inch-calibre machine guns.[21]

The cloud cover over the target ranged from clear to broken, with the clouds topping out at about 4,000 feet. A significant number of searchlights were reported, which in combination with moderate flak and roving hunters, made for a gut-wrenching mission for Ron and the crew. Less than two hours after takeoff, Frank released his witches' brew of high explosives and incendiaries 17,000 feet above the target area.[22]

When Frank called out "bombs away" and Bob confirmed that the requisite photo had been taken, Frank shouted his now favourite line, "Let's get the hell out of here!" This was Bob's cue to take evasive action to avoid the flak and probing search lights. Bob quickly turned the plane toward home. Once he reached the French coast he made one final course correction that set the plane on a path that would take them back to Croft some 240 miles away. Having travelled almost four hundred miles in just under two hours, with moderate tailwinds on the way to the target, WL-D managed an average ground speed of 195 miles per hour which was fast compared to most other trips. On the return trip, their average ground speed was just over 170 miles per hour due to strong headwinds, but to Bob's satisfaction, WL-D still outpaced all other 434 Squadron bombers with a total flight time of four hours and forty-eight minutes.

Frank observed that it had been a very good, well-concentrated attack with many resultant orange-coloured fires. Although over four hundred industrial buildings were destroyed, it came at a high cost: twenty-eight planes were lost, including five planes from Bomber Group 6. [23] This represented a loss rate of 3.7 percent overall. In fact, the number of Canadian planes lost in just the first three missions in early November almost equaled that for the entire month of October. If this rate of attrition continued, the prospect of survival for Ron and his crewmates did not look good, even with half their required tour almost complete.

Gale force winds blew across the base as WL-D arrived back at Croft. It made for a tricky landing. Bob was lucky to touch down just before one of the bombers in the landing queue behind WL-D blew a tire. The balance of the squadron were then required to divert to Middleton St. George.[24] After landing, a quick inspection of the plane revealed significant surface damage with a low probability that "Kathleen" would be available for operations over the next few days. On this mission the crew had flown a total of 873 miles even though Bochum was just 315 miles from Croft.

The crew was stood down the next day due to a lack of aircraft. Having just seen eighteen Canadian planes lost in the last seventy-two hours, Bill, the upper gunner, would later recall how he and Ron made a pact: that the next time they flew over neutral territory, one individual would provide a code word which the other would respond to, and both would bail out together, with the expectation of being interred in neutral Sweden until the end of the war. They would need to wait for the right opportunity. Bill and Ron knew that they might be abandoning their crewmates and leaving them defenceless with no tail or upper gunner, so the gravity of such a plan reflects how utterly concerned they were about not surviving the war and their strong instinct for survival. But Bill noted that in the end it was all scared, youthful talk, and there was no way that they could bring themselves to abandon their fellow crewmates.

While Ron and Bill considered how they might survive, Kay penned a short letter providing Ron with an update on the homefront:

Dearest Ronny, Well at last we have a wee bit of snow in Montreal today, I don't know if that's good or bad.

How are you dear? I haven't heard from you for about a week or so, but I know that you must be pretty busy on Operations. From the news, I gather that the RCAF is keeping you fellows pretty well occupied. Gosh Ronny you'll soon be able to write a book on your experiences. It would seem to me dear that when you're up there in the sky that it must be a truly great experience, and so many thoughts and impressions must pass through your mind. I think of your flying always and always like to think that it's possible for you to know that you're in my heart and thoughts ever.

It will soon be your birthday Ronny, won't it be wonderful when you won't be home just to celebrate your birthday, but to celebrate that and everyday for good.

I was down to see your Mom just the other night dear and she's fine, we just about covered every topic thinkable.

I guess Tuesday is going to be a big day, in the States especially, being Election Day. I bet the Radio will be pretty busy that day alright.

Do you feel any different since you've been overseas; I've often wondered what a fellow's impressions & reactions would be, and just how much they are bound to change.

Well dear I'll say goodnight to you for now and hope to hear from you soon. All my love, Kay

The next night the crew was briefed just after sunrise. They then headed out to their designated plane, which, regrettably, was not "Kathleen." Bob would be piloting an unfamiliar plane, Halifax WL-G (for "George").[25] This was to be another maximum effort, with 738 bombers vectored to Gelsenkirchen in the Ruhr to target both built-up areas as well as the Nordstern oil plant.[26] The ground crew at Croft were able to make sixteen aircraft available from 434 Squadron for this mission.[27] Included in the bomber stream were 215 planes from Bomber Group 6 on their first daylight raid since Cologne. Both rear and mid-upper gunners maintained their vigilance in continuously scanning the sky for potential enemy aircraft—they both knew that their chance of being spotted in daytime would be higher.

There was broken cloud coverage over Gelsenkirchen reaching as high as 11,000 feet. This was well below the bomber stream, which approached the target at elevations of 19,000 to 21,000 feet.[28] WL-G was at 19,500 feet.[29] Although partly obscured, Frank managed to release the mix of 2,000-, 1,000- and 500-pound bombs on the green target indicators that marked the target.[30] Compared to their previous mission where bombing was scattered, Frank could see three good-sized fires with some smoke rising from this target area.

The local air defence included slight to moderate flak. Several Me-262 jets capable of speeds well in excess of 500 miles per hour were also sighted, although not by Ron and the crew. The presence of attacking jet fighters had become a more common occurrence at this stage in the air war. The Me-262 was armed with two 30-mm cannons as well as two air-to-air rockets. Despite the specter of German jets, Halifax WL-G touched down at Croft at twilight after a fairly uneventful trip. The loss of two Canadian planes from 408 and 432 Squadrons on this mission, although tragic, was more in line with the loss percentages incurred by Bomber Group 6 in October.[31]

Ron and the crew had now completed half of their required thirty combat missions. The crew now anticipated a well-deserved seven-day leave. They all hoped no further combat assignments would come before that.

It would take several days and two test flights before Bob and Joe were satisfied that "Kathleen" was again combat ready. But things were changing. The crew attended the first of many lectures to prepare them for conversion to the Lancaster Bomber. At the same time the base held an auction to raise money for the Red Cross Prisoners of War Fund with sundry articles left by members of the two recently lost crews. Only non-personal items such as soap and razor blades were auctioned off.[32] The crew continued to attend various lectures on the Lancaster for the next five days as inclement weather prevented flying.[33] On the morning of November 16, Ron and his crewmates were lucky that they were not one of the fifteen aircrews required to participate in an attack on Julich, an army co-operation effort.[34] Thankfully, all planes returned safely. Ron rose early the next day knowing that he and the rest of the crew were finally on personal leave. Not even the wet weather could dampen Ron's relief.

Just prior to departure from Croft, Ron strolled over to the Sergeants' Mess where he was excited to receive another letter from Kay.

Dearest Ronny, I received a grand letter from you yesterday morning dear, and was really so very glad to hear from you as I hadn't for a little while.

As you say Ronny, war is a strange thing to fathom and understand, you wonder just what it is that's wrong in this world. Some people hardly have it touch them and for others, it's the ruining factor in their lives. I only hope that it will end soon.

Well I see that you've got started with a couple of records for the phonograph, good ones too. I don't know if you've got them over there, but the most popular ones here right now are "I Dream of You," "I Walk Alone," and "Dance With the Dolly," gosh there's actually so darn many that just as you learn the words to a tune of a few, a lot more come out. "How Blue the Night" is a lovely one.

I was surprised to learn that you've completed 13 ops, it's funny but I've always found "thirteen" my lucky number, I guess I'm just not a very superstitious Irishman.

It certainly won't be long before your birthday, it would have been wonderful if you could have been here for it. I'll be thinking of you dear and hoping and praying for the time when we'll be able to celebrate so many things together.

I was just talking to your Mom on the phone and she asked me down next Sunday, as Edna was having a little evening for Eddy's birthday, it's going to be a surprise.

I'll be thinking of you especially on your birthday dear, and hope that it will be your first and last one so very far away. All my love always, Kay

The personal leave would offer a welcome respite from the war in the air. But with the Germans on the run and with only fifteen missions left to complete his tour of duty, Ron had little idea that his marksmanship was about to be tested.

Souvenir three-penny bracelet that Ron sent Kay from London
in November 1944, and referred to in the letter below

Nov, 29, 1944

Dearest Kay,

I received your swell letter yesterday. I just got back from my leave a few days ago and the first thing I did was to go to the mess and see if there was any mail from you dear. When there isn't any it makes me lose interest in everything but darling when there is a letter there for me from you it makes all the difference in the world. You know Kay you mean everything to me dear. There is a swell tune they sing on our radio now = "I'll be around" and Kay next time you listen to it think of what it means to me (and I could to you). I was in London for three days on my leave and then down to my relations in Hastings. All in all it was a pretty nice leave. It was a welcome change from army. I bought you a souvenir in London and sent it by registered mail as a little extra Christmas present for you dear with all my love. I've already told mum what to buy you for Xmas but don't ask her because she won't tell you (I hope).

Lancaster WL-D flown by Bob Henry with "Kathleen" nose art clearly depicted on front of aircraft - named in honour of Kathleen Emily Eason, who had met Ron Pyves just weeks prior to his embarkation for England

Photograph taken just after WL-C flown by Bob Henry has dropped their bomb load of nine 1,000-pound and four 500-pound bombs on the Port of Calais in France at 10:23 a.m. at an elevation of 7,000 feet. This was the third mission for Ron Pyves and most of the crew. At this time the Port of Calais was defended by over 7,000 German troops who were under siege by Canadian infantry. **Source: Library and Archives Canada/National Defence collation/Accession 2008-0377- PL-2157**

Photo taken of Ron while on leave in London just after a bomb had exploded nearby

Ron on leave in London overlooking Westminster, which houses the House of Commons

From left to right, in front row: Ron Pyves (R/AG), Al Coleman (Nav). In back row: Bill Thomson (M/UG), Frank Welsh (B/A), Joe Casavant (F/E). Note how muddy the fields are all around the runway.

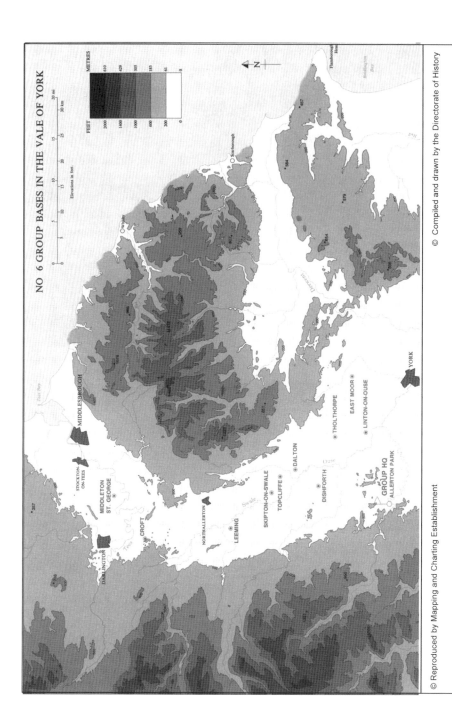

© Reproduced by Mapping and Charting Establishment

© Compiled and drawn by the Directorate of History

© Government of Canada. Reproduced with the permission of the Minister of Public Works and Government Services Canada (2011)

Photograph taken of Ron Pyves (R/AG) and Bill Thomson (M/UG) after they had just completed their second trip to Duisburg, Germany within 24 hours on October 14/15, 1944. Photo appeared in the *Montreal Herald* on December 15, 1944.

434 and 431 Squadron being briefed by S/L W.A. Bentley before the raid to Essen on the night of October 23, 1944. Ron Pyves is located in fourth row on right. Source: Library and Archives Canada/National Defence collection/ Accession 2008-0377- PL-33941

Ron Pyves in rear turret armed with four .303 Browning machine guns, each capable of firing 1,200 rounds per minute

Bill Thomson, the mid-upper gunner, next to his gun turret, which is armed with two Browning .303 machine guns

Interior view of a Halifax Boulton Paul Type E rear tur-
ret showing the rear gunner's seat and control column.
It provided quite cramp quarters for the rear gunner
and was a position isolated from the rest of the crew.
Photo courtesy of the National Airforce Museum of
Canada, CFB-8 Wing Trenton, ON.

Frank Welsh, Bomb Aimer, in secondhand Ford, which
he purchased while stationed at Croft-on-Tees. Frank
and the crew would sometimes use his car to visit the
local pubs in Darlington when off duty.

9
Fighter Attack

The target was Neuss, on the west bank of the Rhine River five miles southwest of Düsseldorf. The objective was to disrupt German communications. Targeting German cities in the well-defended Ruhr Valley was definitely not a welcome assignment. In fact Ron felt a gnawing ache in the pit of his stomach knowing that the target would be well-defended by massive concentrations of enemy search lights and flak barrages, and a protective umbrella of fighter aircraft.

Two weeks had passed since the crew last flew Halifax WL-D. Once aboard, the crew immediately recognized the smell of oil that permeated every part, a familiar perfume unique to "Kathleen." WL-D had been armed with 10,000 pounds of high explosives.[1] All the crew were nervous as they tried to get back into the combat routine, knowing once again that each trip might be their last. Pilot Officer H. Morris stood in on this trip as the wireless operator due to Hal's recurring ear problems.[2] Bob's brother Jack would also participate in SE-D (for "Dog"). It would only be his seventh trip.[3]

WL-D left the runway just at sunset with Jack's plane departing ten minutes later. Nineteen planes from 434 Squadron and seventeen from 431 rose from Croft like birds of prey.[4] They were joined by aircraft from twelve other Canadian bomber squadrons and aircraft from Bomber Groups 1 and 8, with a total of 290 planes merging into one continuous bomber stream.[5] After climbing to 19,000 feet, Bob

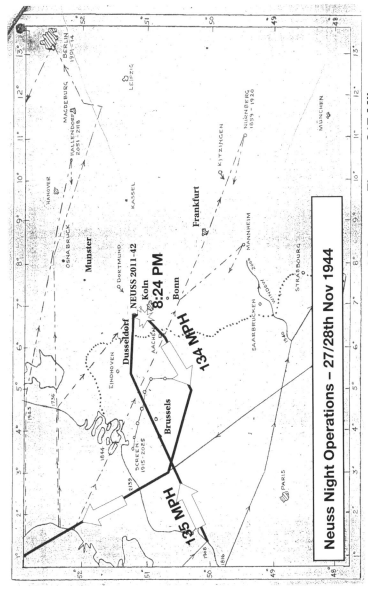

Crew: F/O R. Henry (1ˢᵗ Pilot), F/O A. Coleman (NAV), F/O F. Welsh (B/A), P/O H. Morris (WOP/AG), Sgt. A. Thomson (MU/AG), Sgt. R. Pyves (R/AG), Sgt. J. Casavant (F/E)

Neuss Night Operations – 27/28th Nov 1944

Outbound: 507 Miles, Inbound: 310 Miles, Total Distance Flown: 817 Miles

434 Squadron: WL-D (MZ435), Bomb Load: 1 x 2,000, 65 x 1,000, 6 x 500 pounds

Source: *Night Raid Report No. 776*, Bomber Command, 1944. Reproduced with the permission of the Minister of Public Works and Government Services Canada, 2009.

joined the stream and headed south. Once they reached the English coastline, Bob banked to port, heading across the Channel into France. The skies were overcast over Neuss with the clouds topping out at 6,000 feet. Visibility was poor. Bob approached the target area at an elevation of 19,000 feet.[6] Using sky markers as the aiming point, Frank dropped his load, plummeting to the hidden target below.[7] Almost immediately Frank could see fires and very large explosions through the clouds. The crew experienced moderate to heavy flak on their final approach to the target. Though they had completed fifteen earlier missions, they were still not comfortable with the black, menacing clouds of smoke reaching up toward them.

Bob turned the plane on a course due south from Neuss as soon as they had cleared the target and, five minutes later, he banked the plane forty-five degrees to starboard, which set them in a southwesterly direction. Ten minutes later, Bob set WL-D on a course almost due west. Just seconds after Bob made this last turn, they were attacked from behind by an Me-109 fighter plane travelling almost two and a half times faster than WL-D. The enemy pilot was intent on knocking out Ron to make it more difficult for the bomber crew to defend itself from subsequent attack. The enemy fighter was first spotted by Ron nine hundred feet from his position and closing fast on the same level as the bomber.[8] With no lights on, Ron found it difficult to pick out the approaching fighter against the dark sky. He quickly yelled to Bob to "corkscrew to port," which he did immediately.[9] It was only the intense and instinctive need to shoot down the attacker that prevented Ron from throwing up from nervousness. Bob's corkscrew involved a steep dive following a downward spiral to gain airspeed and make it more difficult for the Messerschmitt to hit the plane. He then reversed the dive into another corkscrew while climbing in altitude to keep the fighter pilot off balance.

Everything happened in a flash and for Ron it felt like a bad dream. With their adrenalin flowing, Ron's and Bill's primary objective was to discourage the Me-109 pilot from pressing home his attack. If they got lucky, they might damage or destroy the attacking aircraft. Ron desperately tried to get the fighter in his gun sights. He fired off two short bursts, sending 250 rounds of ammunition from his four Browning machine guns.[10] Suddenly Ron's guns jammed. And while Bob continued diving, Ron managed to clear the stoppages despite the sweat pouring down from his forehead. Bob was able to shake loose from the pursuing Me-109, which did not get the chance to open fire due to the vigilance of the crew and Bob's quick actions. But the crew could not afford to relax in case another aircraft should suddenly burst out of the skies. Some German fighters teamed up in pairs, with one acting as a decoy while the other went in for the kill.

After almost three unbearable hours with the gunners straining every nerve and eye muscle, the crew finally arrived over Yorkshire, but due to bad weather over Croft were diverted to Methwold, a Royal Air Force bomber base equipped with concrete runways. They touched down at 10:43 PM, making them not surprisingly the slowest bomber from 434 Squadron.[11] SE-D touched down six minutes later and when Bob met up with Jack in the debriefing hut, he was still wound up from the fighter attack.[12] No planes were lost on this effort. The Me-109 attack was reported at intelligence debriefing but no claim was made because there was no damage to the fighter.

When the crew returned to Croft late the next day Ron decided to write Kay.

> *Dear Kay, I received your swell letter yesterday. I just got back from my leave a few days ago, and the first thing I did was to go to the mess and see if there was any mail from you dear. When there isn't any, it makes me lose interest in everything, but darling when there is a letter there for me from you, it makes all the difference in the world.*
>
> *We haven't been doing much flying for quite a while now, but I guess we'll be getting back into our old stride again now. I've got 16 ops done now. If my luck holds out for another fourteen, and I'm sure it will, I'll be finished. My luck's just got to hold out. Love, Ronny*

Bob and the crew took up Halifax WL-Z (for "Zebra") mid-morning next day.[13] After almost two hours in the air they were unexpectedly recalled to base. The station commander decided at the last minute to include them on the duty roster for a mission that very day. It was a familiar target—the marshalling yards in Duisburg, a target they had seen several times already. This time the crew had almost no time to prepare and rest up before the sortie. Although this mission had been unexpected, they were thankful that they would be flying Halifax WL-D. At a little after 4:00 PM, Bob revved up the four engines, released the brakes, and they were once more on their way skyward. It would be their last mission of the month, and they would join another 242 aircraft from Bomber Group 6 and an additional 343 planes from RAF Bomber Command on this maximum effort.[14] Squadron 434 contributed nineteen aircraft for this mission with an additional seventeen coming from 431 Squadron.[15]

Flight Lieutenant C. Brady, who had flown with Ron and the crew on October 28, replaced Hal Ward in WL-D.[16] There was also another crew change. For the first time in seventeen missions, Bob would not have Joe, the flight engineer, to rely on as he had become too sick with the flu. Flight Officer F. Boleman, a very capable flight engineer, was the replacement.[17] For the fifth time in the crew's last seven trips, both Bob and Jack participated in the same mission.[18] After taking off in the late afternoon chill and gaining sufficient altitude, Bob set the bomber on a southeasterly direction before crossing the English Channel and penetrating deep into Germany, flying south of Eindhoven and then heading due east to their target.

Crews experienced moderate to heavy flak on the final approach, with few searchlights seen. Then, suddenly, a master searchlight coned WL-D, putting the Halifax into a column of brilliant light.[19] Then another searchlight quickly locked onto the plane. Bob knew he only had seconds to start evasive action or WL-D would attract Luftwaffe like moths to a candle. He put the plane into a steep corkscrew dive to port. For Ron, it felt like his stomach had dropped out of his body as the plane plummeted toward earth. Ron grabbed hold of his guns and pushed off to prevent being slammed against them and the plastic bubble, which was all that stood between him and open sky. With Ron in the extreme end of the plane, he experienced the greatest sensation of falling as he had no perspective of the ground below. In the meantime the rest of the crew hung on for dear life. Everything that was loose in the plane, including all of Al's papers and

Crew: F/O R. Henry (1st Pilot), F/O A. Coleman (NAV), F/O F. Welsh (B/A), F/L C. Brady (WOP/AG), Sgt. A. Thomson (MU/AG), Sgt. R. Pyves (R/AG), F/O F. Boleman (F/E)

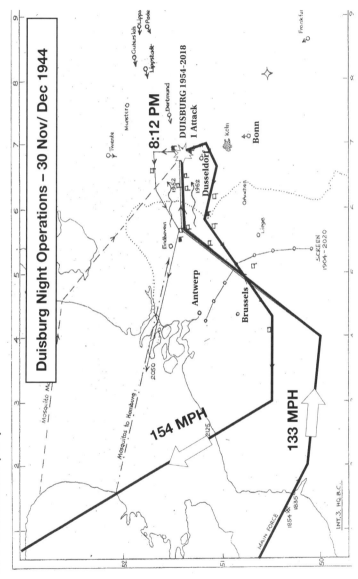

Duisburg Night Operations – 30 Nov/ Dec 1944

8:12 PM
DUISBURG 1954-2018
1 Attack

154 MPH

133 MPH

Outbound: 528 Miles, Inbound: 479 Miles, Total Distance Flown: 1,007 Miles

434 Squadron: WL-D (MZ435), Bomb Load: 16 x 500 pounds

Source: *Night Raid Report No. 779*, Bomber Command, 1944. Reproduced with the permission of the Minister of Public Works and Government Services Canada, 2009.

instruments, were flying around the cabin. Frank was nearly put out of commission as a previously wall-mounted fire extinguisher flew past his head and bounced off the bombsight, smashing the glass cover.[20] Having lost the searchlights, Bob, with almost super-human strength and assistance from Officer Boleman, pulled back on the controls to pull the ship out of its death spiral. While in this extreme dive, it would have been almost impossible for the crew to eject from the plane if they had to.

"Kathleen" had dropped several thousand feet before Bob managed to pull the plane level. Bob and Al, the navigator, worked feverishly to quickly get back on course for the run into the target. With a severely damaged bombsight, Frank had to improvise and used his thumb and index finger to line up the red and yellow sky markers that indicated the target.[21] He then released his load of sixteen 500-pound bombs at an elevation of 19,000 feet. [22] It was just after 8:00 PM. Despite the fact that there were significant stratocumulus clouds with tops as high as 8,000 feet, the attack had been fairly concentrated. The glow of the fires seen through the clouds below provided strong indication that it had been a successful attack.

As soon as the photoflash bounced off the clouds below, Bob made a hard bank to starboard to set them on their inbound journey. They passed twenty miles south of Brussels to avoid the city's flak defences. There were numerous enemy fighter attacks involving Allied bombers and German Ju-88s, Me-110s, and Me-109s on the homeward leg, although the crew of "Kathleen" did not experience any direct confrontations.[23] After seven hours and five minutes of flying—their longest combat mission to date—and having flown just over one thousand miles, Bob managed a safe touchdown back at Croft. They had spent nine of the last fourteen hours in the air. After the ordeal, it was not surprising WL-D was the slowest of all 434 Squadron aircraft to make the return trip. Jack had already landed in SE-D thirteen minutes earlier.[24]

This was one trip that would remain ingrained in the memories of Ron and the rest of the aircrew for a very long time. But they were lucky; two Canadian bombers from 429 Squadron were lost, with one of these aircraft colliding in mid-air with an RAF bomber.[25]

For the entire month of November, Bomber Group 6 experienced a loss of twenty-six bombers versus nineteen in October, even though the Group flew almost seventeen percent fewer missions in November.[26] The November loss rate, now at 1.3 percent, excluding aborted/returned flights, ranked a lot higher than the 0.8 percent loss rate in October.

In November, 434 Squadron had flown on nine different operations involving 151 bombers, with Ron and his crewmates participating in five despite the leave in mid-November.[27] At the end of November, 434 Squadron had 26 Halifax bombers and 41 combat-ready crews on the roster.[28] In just over two months at Croft, Ron had accumulated just over eighty-eight hours of combat flying on seventeen different missions, including targets in France, Norway, and Germany.[29] He received a well-deserved promotion to Flight Sergeant effective November 11, 1944.[30]

10
Birthday over Germany

December 1944 would be a trying time for Ron. This would be the first year he would not be home to celebrate the Christmas season, his birthday (December 5), or his parents' wedding anniversary (Boxing Day). Ron longed for civilian life so he could once more grasp control of his own fate. Having just met Kay, he was even more anxious to get home, alive.

Flying was scrubbed on the first day of December, but the next day Ron and the crew were back at the incessant exercises, practicing H2S bombing in Halifax WL-D. In total, they made nine practice runs to fine-tune Frank's bomb-aiming skills.[1] After two hours of practice, the wireless operator received a "return to base" signal.[2] WL-D was one of nine bombers recalled from training that was slated for that evening's mission.

At the mid-afternoon briefing they discovered that this time they would visit a new target in Germany: Hagen, situated ten miles south of Dortmund in the Ruhr. The objective was to destroy communications facilities and a U-boat factory. At this stage in the war, German submarines continued to take a tremendous toll on Allied Atlantic shipping convoys that originated from Canada and the U.S. These convoys delivered key military supplies and much needed food to both England and Russia. As late as November 1944, German U-boats were still active in the Gulf of St. Lawrence.

Crew: F/O R. Henry (1st Pilot), F/O A. Coleman (NAV), F/O F. Welsh (B/A), P/O H. Morris (WOP/AG), Sgt. A. Thomson (MU/AG), Sgt. R. Pyves (R/AG), Sgt. J. Casavant (F/E)

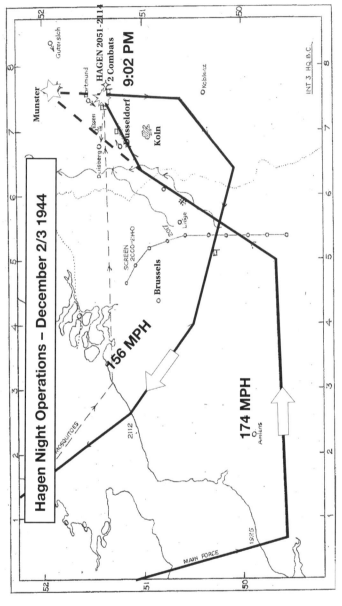

Hagen Night Operations – December 2/3 1944

Outbound: 647 Miles, Inbound: 514 Miles, Total Distance Flown: 1,161 Miles

434 Squadron: WL-D (MZ435), Bomb Load: 1 x 2,000, 7 x 1,000 pounds

Source: *Night Raid Report No. 781*, Bomber Command, 1944. Reproduced with the permission of the Minister of Public Works and Government Services Canada, 2009.

This new mission had been planned as a combined RAF and RCAF initiative, with fourteen Canadian Squadrons contributing 190 planes, including sixteen bombers from 434 Squadron and sixteen from 431.[3] An additional 314 planes from the RAF, with crews from other Commonwealth nations such as New Zealand and Australia, also participated in the attack.[4] The ground crew did a superb job refueling "Kathleen" in enough time to allow for an early evening departure. WL-D would carry one 2,000-pound and seven 1,000-pound bombs. Pilot Officer H. Morris replaced Hal, the regular wireless operator.[5] Bob needed to focus on the mission in front of him, despite the fact that once again his brother in SE-G was also on the duty roster and would leave Croft some sixteen minutes after WL-D.[6] This would put SE-G almost fifty miles behind Bob in the bomber stream and 1,000 feet lower in altitude.

While ascending to 18,000 feet to join the stream, Bob experienced some icing on the plane but managed to continue on. Two planes from 428 Squadron were not as lucky with the ice—four crew members were unable to bail out before the planes crash-landed.[7]

Although the distance from Croft to Hagen was a little less than 260 miles, the actual indirect route would cover just under 650 miles. Once Bob had built up sufficient altitude, he set his aircraft in a southeasterly direction until it had crossed the coast of France. He then turned to port in an easterly direction south of Amiens. It would take Bob another one and a half hours to make his final run into the target. Bob was not aware that strong crosswinds had blown WL-D off its planned flight path. They ended up twenty-two miles north of the target, placing them just north of Essen. Here they were attacked with no warning by a single-engine enemy aircraft.[8] Given that they had strayed from the main bomber stream and were flying alone, it wasn't surprising, considering how vulnerable they were.

Ron first noticed the single-engine fighter about 1,200 feet dead astern but just below him.[9] It was rapidly closing in for the kill. Ron knew intuitively that immediate action was necessary. He shouted into the intercom to warn the pilot. Bob took immediate evasive action, putting the plane into a steep corkscrew dive to port.[10] This was only the second time that Ron had experienced an attack by enemy aircraft. And no training could adequately simulate the rush of adrenalin experienced when an airman's life was really on the line.

Ron's greatest fear was that his guns might jam again. Fortunately, they didn't. As Bob started his dive, he was aware that he shouldn't push the bomber past its maximum designed speed of 360 miles per hour, except as a last resort. As Bob pointed the nose into the dive, Ron fired two hundred rounds at the attacking fighter.[11] He used deflection shooting to anticipate where the enemy aircraft would be as it closed in on them. While Ron engaged the fighter, Bill, the mid-upper gunner, kept a watchful eye for the possibility of a second enemy aircraft which might approach from a different direction. Suddenly the German broke away at a range of less than one thousand feet without having fired a shot.[12] Neither Bill nor Ron was successful in damaging the enemy aircraft.[13] But after seeing those initial bursts of fire from the Brownings trained in on him, the German pilot must have decided to find easier prey. With the immediate emergency over, the crew experienced a sick feeling of relief thinking about how close they had come to disaster. Ron noticed that his hands were shaking and no matter what he did he couldn't stop his fingers from trembling. Two fighter attacks in the last three missions were almost too much to bear. Some aircrews went through their entire tour of duty without seeing aerial combat.

But they weren't finished with the mission. With help from Al, Bob altered course for the run in to Hagen. After a little over three and a half hours of flying, they finally approached the target area at an elevation of 17,000 feet. There were significant clouds below yet the moon provided good visibility above. Just minutes after the scare Frank released the bombs over the target using GEE.[14] GEE was a radio navigation system that could pick up radio impulses from different radio transmission stations in England and, through triangulation, assist in determining the location of the bomber relative to the ground below. This system had proven itself very useful when the target couldn't be fixed visually. In fact, photos taken by the Canadian aircraft over the target confirmed that the U-boat factory had been completely destroyed.[15]

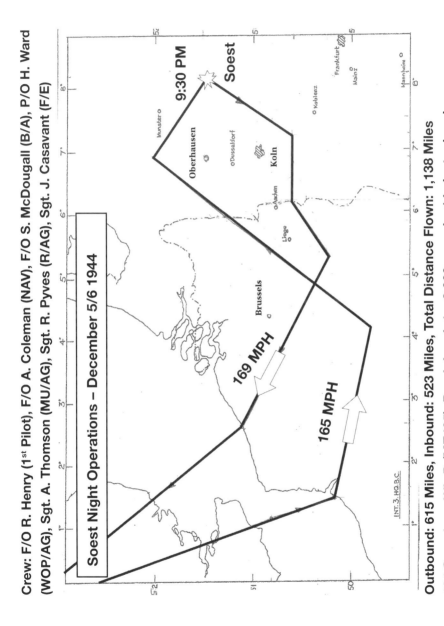

Crew: F/O R. Henry (1st Pilot), F/O A. Coleman (NAV), F/O S. McDougall (B/A), P/O H. Ward (WOP/AG), Sgt. A. Thomson (MU/AG), Sgt. R. Pyves (R/AG), Sgt. J. Casavant (F/E)

Soest Night Operations – December 5/6 1944

9:30 PM

Soest

169 MPH

165 MPH

Münster
Oberhausen
Düsseldorf
Köln
Aachen
Liège
Brussels
Frankfurt
Mainz
Mannheim
Koblenz

INT. 3, HQ.B.C.

Outbound: 615 Miles, Inbound: 523 Miles, Total Distance Flown: 1,138 Miles

434 Squadron: WL-D (MZ435), Bomb Load: 1 x 2,000 pounds, 14 cluster bombs

Source: *Night Raid Report No. 784*, Bomber Command, 1944. Reproduced with the permission of the Minister of Public Works and Government Services Canada, 2009.

Bob then turned the aircraft onto the new co-ordinates provided by Al for the first leg of the return flight. They had already been airborne for almost four hours, and with the recent close call with the Luftwaffe, the last three hours back to Croft seemed like an eternity. The crew strained their eyes in the darkness, anticipating a further attack. As they crossed the French coastline two hours later, Al had Bob turn 45 degrees to starboard, which set them on a flight path directly to Croft some 180 miles away.

Bob guided "Kathleen" to a safe return having flown almost 1,200 miles. It was early Sunday morning December 3. Despite the aerial attack and evasive action, WL-D managed to be the third fastest aircraft of the thirty-two planes that had departed from Croft.[16] Upon landing, the crew did a quick walk around and noticed significant flak damage to the plane's fuselage—it would be unlikely that "Kathleen" would be available for further missions within the next day or two.

The strong coffee at the intelligence debriefing provided a quick pickup. The crew had logged nine hours and fifteen minutes of flying since Saturday morning. Here they learned that one aircraft from 433 Squadron stationed at Skipton-on-Swale was lost over the target.[17]

After a twenty-four-hour break, the crew was assigned to H2S bombing exercises over the English countryside. They completed six practice runs by noon. As the next day would be Ron's birthday the entire crew decided to visit the Slater's Arms pub in Darlington to celebrate. Ron and Bill often helped out at the Slater's Arms on leave.[18] After several pints, they could feel the tension easing as the alcohol took effect. The camaraderie and the roaring fire next to their table created a warmth that reminded Ron of home. But it wouldn't last long. Tomorrow would be a long day and Ron and the crew had to return to base early. They all retired except for Bob, who anxiously waited to greet his brother Jack who had left in the late afternoon for a mission over Karlsruhe, Germany. Jack would not return safely to Croft until midnight.[19]

The crews assembled for another briefing early the next afternoon to learn where they would be flying that evening. The target: Soest, thirty miles east of Dortmund in western Germany. Groans filled the room as the men knew this would be another long and uncertain trip over enemy territory.

After briefing, Ron went down to the Sergeants' Mess and was delighted to find that he had received a cablegram from Kay, which congratulated him on his twentieth birthday. This was one good luck charm he would take on this upcoming mission.

After the traditional walk around their favourite aircraft (which was now covered in frost this frigid winter evening), the crew boarded and set off for Soest. The target was key transportation facilities, including the local railway yards.[20] Bob's brother Jack piloted SE-D which lifted off just two minutes before them.[21] This would be a combined RAF and RCAF effort with all fourteen squadrons from Bomber Group 6 participating. Each Canadian squadron put up on average fourteen planes.[22] Squadron 434 contributed sixteen aircraft just like it had on the Hagen mission.[23] In total, 474 aircraft would bomb the target.[24]

Just after takeoff Bob pointed WL-D in a southeasterly direction which brought them across the French coastline just north of Dieppe. As they continued across occupied France and Germany, Ron strained to see if there were any enemy fighters lurking in the endless stream of clouds that swirled around his turret. From time to time Ron could see the bright moonlight breaking through the cloud cover, throwing off his night vision. He wondered what Kay was doing back home and whether she would also be looking at the same moon this cold winter night. Ron was broken from such thoughts when Bob announced they were within sixty miles of the target and would be on their final bombing approach within the next twenty minutes. The tension built as the crew saw flashes of light on the horizon. At this point, Ron checked his guns to make sure he was ready to greet any uninvited guests. He knew that his vigilance might be all that stood between the crew and certain death.

The bomber stream approached the final target at elevations from 17,000 to 19,000 feet.[25] Al, the navigator, noted that visibility was excellent with occasional clouds rising as high as 10,000 feet. Frank welcomed the opportunity to visually bomb the target, this time aiming at the red target indicators on the ground. It was a very concentrated attack, with WL-D dropping one 2,000-pound bomb and twelve cluster bombs. Frank could see many large fires below. The air defence consisted of moderate flak with a few searchlights and several German fighters in the vicinity. Over 1.7 million pounds of explosives and incendiaries were dropped on the target.[26] Photos taken on the mission and later that month confirmed that a significant portion of the railway yards had been destroyed.[27]

As Bob headed south on the return leg, large fires created by the bombing strike could be seen for a distance of over sixty miles.[28] The crew continued to keep a vigilant lookout for possible enemy aircraft. As they approached their first turning point, Bob banked the plane to starboard, heading due west for forty-two miles before shifting to a southwesterly course to avoid coming too close to Liege. Just minutes later Bob banked the aircraft to port so they would pass south of Brussels and dart for the coastline, which they reached two hours after leaving the target. The crew began to relax a bit now that they were headed across the North Sea but knew that they could put themselves at significant risk if they completely let their guard down. As Ron looked down at the North Sea he shivered to think what would happen if they had to ditch in the near-freezing water below. WL-D still had another 260 miles to cover before they arrived back at Croft. Bob managed a safe landing, having been airborne just under seven hours. Jack, in SE-D, had landed with no incidents just eighteen minutes before, and waited for his brother at the debriefing hut.[29]

The results from this attack were gained at great sacrifice, with a total of four Canadian planes lost and twenty-two lives taken.[30] Included were two Halifax bombers from 428 and 426 Squadrons that collided in mid-air, as well as another aircraft from 426 Squadron shot down by an Me-109.[31] Closer to home, one bomber from 434 Bluenose Squadron, flown by Flying Officer T. Kowachuk on his third combat mission, was lost along with his entire crew.[32] Ron and his crewmates were unaware of this loss until debriefing, even though the downed bomber had taken off just two minutes after them.[33]

The loss rate on this one mission, which excluded early returns, reached almost 2.2 percent. Ron and his crewmates were now acting like real veterans who tried not to dwell on each loss. Otherwise they would not be able to keep going, mission after mission.

They now knew the reason experienced crews were hesitant to make friends with rookies who were more likely to be killed in their first few missions.

In his letter to Kathleen later that month Ron wrote:

Dearest Kay, I just about fell over when I received three cablegrams for my birthday and yours came right on the 5th. The night of the 5th I celebrated the event by bombing a German city. I think that was a pretty good way to spend the day, don't you?

All my love always, Darling. Love, Ronny

It would be one birthday Ron would remember for the rest of his life. It was also the day Flight Lieutenant C. Brady, who had flown with the crew on two previous missions, was screened from operations. He had just completed twenty-one trips on his second tour.[34]

Even with the recent losses, there would be no let-up in the air war over Germany. Another major effort was planned the following day. The target: railway yards at Osnabruck, on the Hase River, fifty miles due north of Soest. Prior to the early afternoon briefing Ron slipped over to the Sergeants' Mess and picked up two additional cables from his parents and brother wishing him a happy birthday. Ron and the crew were then bussed in late afternoon to where Halifax WL-D had been fueled up. It was now ready to go with an 8,000-pound bomb load. This would be the fifteenth and last trip for the crew in "Kathleen" as they were scheduled to convert to the Canadian-built Avro Lancasters in the upcoming week.[35] These new Lancaster bombers were produced at the Victory Aircraft Limited manufacturing plant in Malton, Ontario, and were ferried to England on a regular basis.

The attack on Osnabruck was a combined Royal Air Force and Canadian effort. There were a total of 453 planes, including 199 from Bomber Group 6.[36] For the third time this month, 434 Squadron contributed 16 bombers to the mission.[37] Jack was also scheduled for this trip. It would be his eleventh, and the eighth time he would be flying on the same mission as Bob.[38] The brothers found it unnerving to fly the same mission but this was beyond their control.

Bob guided "Kathleen" down the runway and achieved liftoff just after sunset, joining aircraft from other Canadian air bases, including Eastmoor, Linton-on-Ouse, Tholthorpe, Leeming, Skipton-on-Swale, and Middleton St. George. The airplanes approached the target at heights ranging from 16,000 to 21,000 feet with the Lancasters normally positioned at higher altitudes than the Halifaxes.[39] Osnabruck had become overcast, with some clouds reaching as high as the bomber stream. Visibility was poor. Frank was forced to use GEE to make sure that the sixteen 500-pound bombs found their mark.[40]

The air defence over Osnabruck was formidable, with active search lights, moderate to heavy flak, and very active fighter activity.[41] Here Ron and the crew had their first sighting of a German Me-262 jet fighter, which could exceed speeds of 550 miles per hour. Fortunately it couldn't remain airborne long due to its high rate of fuel consumption. Ron didn't want to think about what it would be like trying to shoot down one of these. Frank released the bombs on target at an elevation of 18,500 feet. With the photos taken, Bob turned "Kathleen" for home. He did not want to linger in what had now become a cauldron of fire from the rising flak. The glow of many fires could be seen as they left the target area.

A few minutes after completing the bomb run, Ron caught sight of a Lancaster moving in and out of the clouds, just behind and above them. Its bomb-bay doors were still open.[42] Sitting in the bay was a 4,000-pound "cookie" which had not released over the target. Blood quickly drained from Ron's face, as he anticipated the destructive power of this 4,000-pounder if it should shake lose and hit them. Ron quickly warned Bob over the intercom, having some difficulty getting his words out under the circumstances. Bob took immediate evasive action. He pushed the four Hercules engines to their limits to widen the gap with the trailing Lancaster and simultaneously started into a dive to gain speed quickly.[43] Suddenly Ron saw the hung-up bomb tumble out of the plane's bomb bay. Just seconds later he saw a large explosion and a cloud of black smoke as the bomb hit another Halifax below it.[44] The shock wave from the explosion pushed their plane violently upward. And in an instant, the bomber and its crew disappeared. Ron and Hal had seen the giant cloud of black smoke and were stunned. It could have easily been them. Pilot Bob took only one comfort—he knew it wasn't his brother's plane; Jack had been piloting a Lancaster.

Halifax WL-D carried the shaken crew safely back to Croft after nearly seven hours of flight. Jack had already landed some thirty minutes before them, achieving the fastest return trip of all planes at Croft.[45] For the second consecutive evening, Bomber Group 6 had suffered the loss of an additional four bombers from 419, 424, 429, and 422 Squadrons.[46] Photos confirmed that the railway yards and a key munitions plant in Osnabruck had suffered significant damage.

After taxiing back to the now-standard parking spot and disembarking, Ron and the crew paid their final respects to "Kathleen," the plane that had faithfully taken them over enemy territory on thirteen missions—and returned them safely every time. Having to change aircraft for the balance of operations did not bode well for the crew, and especially Ron, who had been fortunate to have had WL-D named after Kay. But now 434 Squadron was converting to Lancasters.

Those Halifax aircraft, which were still in good operational shape, were transferred to other squadrons. WL-D was transferred to 420 Squadron and renamed PT-M (for "Mike"). There it remained in service for the balance of the war, and continued to bring its crews safely back from each mission.[47]

11
Goodbye Halifax

The crew had mixed emotions about switching from the reliable Halifax. They had flown it in twenty successful combat missions. In fact, it was the only plane that they had ever flown in combat. However, moving to the Lancaster gave them at least one advantage: they would be pulled out of active duty for almost two weeks, a welcome respite from the stress and frantic pace of active duty. Although the Halifax was sometimes positioned as the "poor cousin" to the Lancaster, it was a very durable and flexible aircraft. It saw service in Bomber Command as well as Coastal Command, and all in all, over six thousand Halifaxes were produced in the war years. The Halifax also had one more escape hatch than the Lancaster, so a crew's odds of survival if their plane was shot down was 29 percent in a Halifax versus 11 percent for a Lancaster, a significant difference.[1]

Ron had his first opportunity to check out the Lancaster on December 9 with Flight Lieutenant Tonellier piloting WL-A (for "Able").[2] It did not have a new plane smell since it, like most of the 434 Squadron Lancaster bombers, had already been flown in combat by 419 Squadron.[3] For Ron the rear turret was an improvement. The hard, clear plastic Perspex forming the rear part of it was larger, thereby offering greater visibility. Even a one- to two-second delay in identifying an incoming enemy fighter could mean the difference between life and death. The Lancaster also had a Frazer-Nash 120 turret in the rear with each pair of Browning machine guns arranged side by side rather than stacked on top of each other as was the case in the Halifax. In Canadian-built Lancasters like WL-D, the mid-upper gunner operated a Martin turret, which offered excellent visibility and was armed with two .50-inch-calibre Browning machine guns. Even with these changes, the Lancaster would remain undergunned until the rear Frazer-Nash was replaced in some squadrons by a Rose Rice turret armed with two .50-calibre machine guns. Just thirty minutes after landing, Bob took the crew up for an additional two hours of local flying before returning to Croft in WL-A. Bob liked the Lancaster because Joe, his flight engineer, was now located directly across from him in the cockpit on his right. It made it easier to work together—especially in an emergency. Al, the navigator, was now located directly behind Bob in a curtained area. Behind Al was Hal, the wireless operator, who had his own work area. These were the only three positions that had changed from the Halifax. The crew's confidence soared over the next four days as they accumulated almost thirteen hours of flying experience in the Lancaster.[4]

With Christmas fast approaching and snow on the ground at Croft, Kay sent Ron an aerogram hoping it would get to him before the holidays.

> *Dearest Ronny, Hello dear, I hope this letter reaches you in time to send you my love at Christmas Ronny, but if I'm too late I hope you had a merry one.*
>
> *You know Ronny, you've been away nearly a year, only it seems like ages. It will be so darn wonderful when this War is won, and things go back to normal once more, only I guess though people everywhere are just going to have to concentrate on Peace a little harder this time.*
>
> *I hope you like the record we sent you Ronny, I was nervous alright, I did so want to say so many things to you, and then I just didn't know how to start.*
>
> *Every time Ronny I think of all the fun we had in the short time we had together, I think of how lucky we met even as late as we did. Gosh dear, one of the thousand little reasons I liked you Ronny, besides the most important you being you, is that you have a really lovable sense of humour and I think that's pretty wonderful.*
>
> *Well dear I'll say goodnight for now dearest, Merry Christmas, All my love always, Kay*

On December 17, after a four-day break from flight operations, the crew was bussed midday over to Middleton St. George to pick up Lancaster WL-H (for "How").[5] The return flight to Croft took just ten minutes. The ground crew checked out the new arrival and then Bob and the crew once again took WL-H up for a short fighter affiliation exercise, landing back at Croft just in time for lunch.

With most of the afternoon free, Ron took the opportunity to pick up his mail and write home to Kay.

> *Darling, I've got a little bad news for you, they took "Kathleen" away from us and we're flying Canadian-built Lancasters now. I hated to see our old kite go, after taking us through so much hell and 15 ops but I suppose we'll get used to the new one in time. I've got 20 ops done now, just 10 more to go. Gosh! Am I ever keeping my fingers crossed now.*
>
> *We won't be flying again until after New Year as we're going on seven days leave starting the 20ᵗʰ. I know I've got countless things I want to tell you and something to ask you of which your answer will mean everything to me. All my love always darling, Ronny*

The crew's leave officially began on December 20, so everyone was anxious to avoid any further combat before then. They got lucky. On December 18, 434 Squadron received orders to make eleven aircraft available for an attack on Duisburg.[6] The crew were not on the active roll for this mission, but Bob's brother did participate in SE-D.[7] Because returning aircraft had to be diverted due to inclement weather, only a limited number of planes were available for the next operation scheduled for December 19ᵗʰ, which ended up being cancelled due to very heavy fog.[8] In the end the boys didn't have to fly over Germany before their personal leave.

Ron made his way through heavy fog to the Sergeants' Mess and was quite excited to pick up a letter from Kay written just seven days earlier. It was one day before his leave. In it she shared some exciting news.

> *Rita received some pretty hopeful news from Ottawa about Bill; they think he's a Prisoner of War, although they can't*

confirm it. I hope she receives some good news for Christmas,
which would be the present she's waiting for.

Wish all your crew and Bill a Merry Christmas Ronny, for
me, but I'm sending you a special one that's tucked way down
in my heart. All my love, God Bless, Kay

***

Ron and Bill headed toward the Darlington train station where they waited almost two hours in the cold and chilly fog before finding space on a train to London. They arrived at King's Cross Station, and spent two days checking out the sights. Ron was continually amazed at the spirit of the people who regularly went about their daily lives despite the renewed attacks by flying bombs. Early in the war most of the bomb damage had been concentrated in London's East End, which contained the many docks vital for the handling of military and food supplies. As the war progressed and with the indiscriminate nature of the V-1 and V-2 targeting systems, other parts of the capital, including Central London, fell victim to Germany's latest "Vengeance" weapons. As Ron wandered around London, he was struck by the contrasting beauty of St. Paul's Cathedral, Westminster Abbey, and the Parliament Buildings, which stood amidst piles of rubble that were once entire city blocks.

Ron and Bill were drawn to the West End with its many theatres and night clubs. Here was a sea of servicemen from across the globe, released from the stress of combat. One such serviceman was Private Tom Edgerton, from Plymouth, but now stationed in London as a signalman. Tom was just eighteen and worked in an underground bunker in Whitehall. He helped manage a wireless network using radio and Morse code linked to key command centres throughout England. Except for a rare excursion to the West End, Tom would normally commute to Whitehall by tube and was rarely outside. So rarely in fact that the military made available a sunray treatment room deep inside the bunker for Tom and his comrades, a precursor to modern-day sun tanning salons. In 1941, when Tom was in the "boy's service" at age fifteen in North Yorkshire, he was called to the

Commandant's Office and informed that his parents, two sisters, and a brother had all been killed by a German bombing attack on Plymouth. Tom was typical of many Londoners who, despite personal tragedies, continued to contribute stalwartly to the war effort.[9]

Ron did some last-minute Christmas shopping for his relatives who lived in Hastings. Although wartime, there was still excitement in the air and one could sense that people were in the holiday spirit even if there were still significant shortages of many food and luxury items. On December 22, Ron and Bill boarded a train for Hastings that was packed with holiday-goers and military personnel anxious to spend time with loved ones.

Although against military rules, on Christmas day Ron took the chance and posted a letter to Kay using the public mail system. In this clandestine note he wrote,

> *My Dearest Kay, I'm on leave right now down in Hastings at my Grandmother's house. They've been treating me really swell, but somehow all I can find myself doing is thinking of you, Kay and wondering what you're doing right now at home in Montreal. If I could only be with you right now dear, just you and I, that's all I'd ask dear, we'd have the best celebration ever.*
>
> *You know dear it doesn't seem like Christmas at all over here without any snow and a very small Xmas tree. I think they are the mainstay of the holiday spirit, don't you dear?*
>
> *Oh well, just 10 more ops and then maybe I'll be able to get home and say all the things I've been wanting to say to you for a long time.*
>
> *Well darling I'll say Au Revoir for now until I get back to camp, which will be in a couple of days time. All my Love and Kisses Sweetheart, Ronny*

With Christmas over Ron and Bill returned to Croft via London, and arrived back at base late on December 27. The reality of war quickly set back in. They had missed four combat missions, in which their squadron participated, including missions to Duisburg, Cologne, Düsseldorf, with all but Cologne located in the Ruhr.[10] Upon their return, Ron and the crew were on the Scholven/Buer mission

Crew: F/O R. Henry (1st Pilot), F/O A. Coleman (NAV), F/O F. Welsh (B/A), F/O O. H. Ward (WOP/AG), Sgt. A. Thomson (MU/AG), Sgt. R. Pyves (R/AG), Sgt. J. Casavant (F/E)

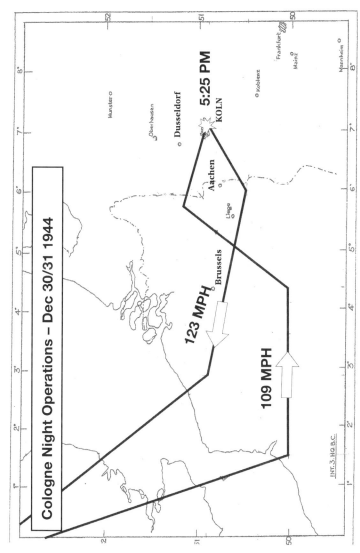

Cologne Night Operations – Dec 30/31 1944

123 MPH

109 MPH

5:25 PM

KOLN

Dusseldorf

Aachen

Brussels

Liege

Munster

Oberhausen

Koblenz

Frankfurt

Mainz

Mannheim

INT. 3. HQ.B.C.

Outbound: 547 Miles, Inbound: 454 Miles, Total Distance Flown: 1,001 Miles
434 Squadron: WL-D (KB830), Bomb Load: 1 x 4,000 pounds, 6 x 1,000, 6 x 500 pounds

Source: *Night Raid Report No. 804*, Bomber Command, 1944. Reproduced with the permission of the Minister of Public Works and Government Services Canada, 2009.

as spare crew but luckily in the end were not required.[11] A total of ten Canadian planes were lost on these bombing efforts, including one Halifax—WL-U from 434 Bluenose Squadron flown by Flight Lieutenant J. Parrot—lost during the attack on Duisburg on their sixth mission.[12] This was the fourth bomber lost from 434 Squadron since Ron began combat in September. The losses included one plane crashing on takeoff and one plane lost in landing. In total, twenty-five crew members had been killed and two taken prisoner out of approximately 290 aircrew in 434 Squadron alone.[13] All these losses had been sustained in an eight-week period, from October 15 to December 18.

Ron and his crewmates would face one final trip to Germany before 1944 was complete. It was December 30 and they would be flying in Lancaster WL-D (for "Dog"), their old call signal. Frank missed this trip with substitute bomb aimer Flight Officer S. McDougall filling in for him.[14] Everyone felt anxious as they prepared for takeoff. The crew had not flown on a combat mission for three weeks and it would be the first in a Lancaster. They departed Croft and just missed sunset as they climbed to clear the local hills. They were headed again for Cologne.

This was to be another strong effort with 200 bombers from all 14 Canadian Squadrons joined by an additional 270 bombers from the RAF.[15] Bob's brother Jack would be among them. The stream would arrive over the target at between 16,000 and 20,000 feet.[16] The Kalk-Nord railway marshalling yards was the primary target. Enroute, Bob flew due east over France and then headed northeast between Liege and Brussels to avoid any flak or searchlights. One last turn to starboard set them on a direct run into the target. Cologne was a city known for its deadly flak and, with a full moon, Ron worried that their plane would be sillouetted against the clouds, making them an easy target. Ron's eyes strained to exhaustion as he scanned the sky for both enemy fighters and Allied bombers that might veer too close to their airspace. Bill, the upper gunner, also scanned the sky above for movement. Al estimated they would arrive at the target in less than twenty minutes. Bob, determined to stay near the top of the bomber stream to avoid being hit by an errant bomb from above, approached the target at an elevation of 18,500 feet. The bomb load consisted of one 4,000-pound "cookie," six 1,000-pound, and six 500-pound bombs that were all released at 9:09 PM.[17] The target had been marked by sky markers and upon bomb release, a broad reddish glow could be seen through the clouds that were making observation difficult.[18] As soon as the mandatory photo was taken, Bob took control of the plane and headed home.

The photos confirmed that extensive damage had been inflicted on the railway yards, including the destruction of two ammunition trains, which were there at the time of bombing.[19] In his log book Ron noted it was a "good trip," which was reinforced by the fact that no planes were lost. Bob, with the navigation assistance of Al, brought WL-D home to a safe landing just after midnight. They had been airborne for almost seven hours and covered one thousand miles. SE-G, piloted by Jack Henry, had already landed even though it had started out a full half hour after WL-D.[20]

Bomber Group 6 was quite active in December. It flew 1,947 sorties, with a loss rate of 0.8 percent, which was much lower than the November rate of 1.3 percent.[21] These results were encouraging as the bomber penetrations had gone deeper into Germany and the heavily defended Ruhr industrial area. For Ron, December marked his twentieth birthday, his twenty-first operation, and a move to a new aircraft, the Canadian-made Lancaster KB-830. And as he discovered on New Year's Eve—in a letter from Kay dated December 17—he was also becoming a bit of a public figure.

> *Your Mom called me up just the other day, as she saw a picture of you and Bill in the* Herald, *one taken a while back after your seventh "Op," you and Bill are certainly hitting the news.*

Ron had now accumulated over 328 hours of flying time, which included 114 hours of combat experience.[22] As the New Year dawned, he remained hopeful that the war in Europe would come to a timely conclusion with only the Pacific theatre left to resolve. The challenge for Ron and the crew was to make sure that they were around to celebrate the victory.

12

A New Year

With the arrival of 1945 came a short lull in the war over Germany, at least for "A Flight," whose first combat mission of the year would not be until January 5. Some of the crews in "B Flight" were not so lucky and, on the evening of January 2, seven "B Flight" aircraft from 434 Squadron joined aircraft from other Canadian bases to attack the giant I.G. Farben chemical factory at Ludwigshafen, a port on the west bank of the Rhine near Mannheim.[1] The sprawling I.G. Farben plant covered over 1,200 acres and had been attacked on numerous instances over the previous two years with mixed success. This time, however, significant damage was inflicted on the plant, with no planes lost.[2]

Since Ron was not on active duty this day, he strolled over to the mess to find a quiet table. With "B Flight" occupied, it was nice and quiet as he sipped some coffee in an old metal mug and composed a note to his parents.

Dear Mum and Dad, All best wishes for a Happy New Year and I hope to see you again before next Christmas. I guess you know Bill and I spent Xmas in Hastings at Gran's. We really had a swell time but not nearly the same as being at home as you can understand. What with no snow and all the family missing it made quite a difference. All day on Xmas, I was wondering what you were all doing and could pretty well visualize it.

Well I'm back on the job again and have done a total of 21 ops.

I was thinking of you and dad especially on your wedding anniversary, did you have all the old gang in for a get together as per usual?

Ron added in reference to the Montreal *Herald* article,

So Bill and I hit the news; well it's about time I made the paper somehow. If we looked tired in the picture it's because we were, we actually had just come back from a raid and ten hours later we took off on another one back to the same German city. When we got back we were just about asleep on our feet. That's the only time we've ever had to do two in one day thank goodness.

Well I think I'll have to close now so give my love to all at home. Your loving son, Ronny

The crew, now refreshed and well rested, attended the next briefing on January 5. It had been five days since their last flight over Germany. Ron and the crew had only nine missions to go. They could sense that the end of their tour of duty was getting closer.

Their next target was now unveiled: Hannover, in northern Germany. During the war, Hannover had key factories which produced armoured military transport vehicles. The thought of going on operations after a five-day break was unsettling. Sometimes to go at it full tilt seemed a better option. If that wasn't enough, Squadron 434 had already lost five planes on earlier missions to Hannover.[3]

The crews had a two-hour void to fill before takeoff. This window allowed Bob to chat with his brother who once more would be on the same mission—his seventeenth.[4] Now that Jack had more than ten trips under his belt, Bob felt a little more comfortable about his brother's chances. (Jack would be flying with 431 Squadron's mascot, Warrant Officer 2nd Class Minnie Simcoe, who would be second pilot in SE-D.[5] Minnie, in reality, was a doll that had provided good luck to all previous 431 Squadron crews who had flown with her.)

On this trip, Flying Officer H. Rubin, who would later be awarded the Distinguished Flying Cross (DFC), would fill in for Frank who had a severe cold. But Ron still had some time on his hands so he decided to head over to the mess to see if he had any mail. He was quite surprised to receive both an aerogram and a letter from Kay dated December 28.

My Dearest Ronny, Gosh Ronny I have so very much to tell you I just don't know where to begin. In a few days we'll be celebrating the New Year, the nicest thing that "1945" could bring would be to see the end of the war and to see you home again.

How do you like flying Lancasters Ron? At least "Kay" saw fifteen ops, that's quite a few, fifteen more than me anyway. I think of you flying dear and always like to think that you'll know somehow that I'm with you in heart and every thought.

We had a lovely Christmas Ronny, everything was swell. Christmas is a grand time, don't you think so dear?

I received your Bracelet, gosh I think it's grand, I'm worth something now. Now if you could just manage to steer your Lancasters over this direction it would be swell.

I was down at your house Christmas Eve Afternoon, and had a lovely time. It would have done your heart good Ronny to see how cheery and Christmasy the house was decorated, it was just grand. Santa was sure wonderful to me. Thank you for your lovely Compact and beautiful Scarf, they were truly swell. Well Dear, I've just about ran out of news, take care of yourself Ronny, and God Bless, All my love, Kay. P.S. Happy New Year Darling

Having finished reading his letters, Ron rounded up the rest of the crew and headed out to grab transportation to the tarmac. All the crew were suffering from the letdown which followed a seven-day leave, knowing that they were now back to reality and were once more engaged in a desperate effort to bring closure to a war that seemed to stretch on forever. With Bob at the controls, WL-D taxied onto the runway and, once in the queue, with the flash of the green light and the four engines at full throttle, Bob released the brakes and they were away on the tail of WL-W. Bombers from 434 and 431 Squadron joined aircraft from eleven other Canadian squadrons. After takeoff, Bob started to fly in a circuit with the other bombers to gain altitude before setting out across the North Sea in a southeasterly direction toward Germany. A total of 190 planes had been vectored to the target from Bomber Group 6, while additional planes lifted off from RAF bomber bases to join the stream at altitudes of 18,000 to 20,000 feet.[6] WL-D was at the top of the bomber stream.[7] Fourteen Lancasters from 434 Squadron participated in this mission.[8] From the cockpit the bomber stream stretched out as far as the eye could see. This would be the second attack on Hannover that same day. The previous wave of 390 bombers had attacked the city just hours earlier with a loss of twenty-five planes.[9] After flying for an hour and twenty minutes, WL-D crossed the French coast flying almost due east and then into Germany, skirting just south of Bremen before making one final turn in a southeasterly direction right into Hannover.

As Ron and the crew made ready for the final approach to Hannover, they were tragically unaware that they were passing almost directly over the Bergen-Belsen concentration camp. It was one of hundreds of concentration camps established by the Nazis to imprison, enslave, and exterminate millions of innocent victims during the war—a travesty against mankind. This camp held over sixty thousand emaciated and sick prisoners when it was liberated by British and Canadian troops just three months later. Ten thousand were so ill they would die within a week of being liberated. Spread amongst the living were thousands of unburied corpses littered throughout the grounds. Soldiers who first entered these concentration camps walked right into a living nightmare. The total deaths at Bergen-Belsen alone was estimated at fifty thousand from 1943 through 1945.

Thousands of feet above, the unknowing crew could make out fires from the earlier attack on Hannover. As they got closer they could also see large explosions below with black oily smoke rising as high

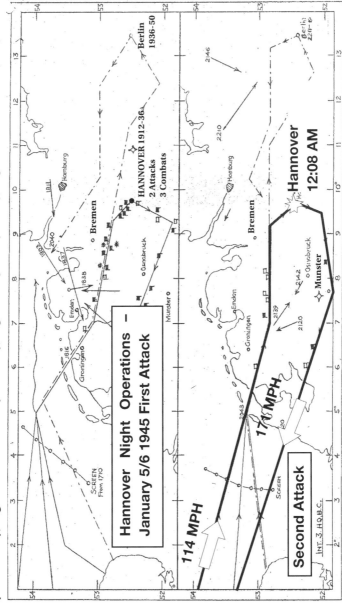

Crew: F/O R. Henry (1st Pilot), F/O A. Coleman (NAV), F/O H. Rubin (B/A), F/O H. Ward (WOP/AG), Sgt. A. Thomson (MU/AG), Sgt. R. Pyves (R/AG), Sgt. J. Casavant (F/E)

Hannover Night Operations – January 5/6 1945 First Attack

114 MPH

Second Attack

171 MPH

Hannover 12:08 AM

Outbound: 356 Miles, Inbound: 462 Miles, Total Distance Flown: 818 Miles

434 Squadron: WL-D (KB830), Bomb Load: 18 x 500 pounds

Source: *Night Raid Report No. 810*, Bomber Command, 1945. Reproduced with the permission of the Minister of Public Works and Government Services Canada, 2009.

as 6,000 feet.[10] A large stretch of buildings was engulfed in flames.[11]

The target area could now clearly be seen and spare bomb aimer H. Rubin released the load on the red target indicators.[12] It was a very good attack. On the return leg, fires from this massive raid could be seen for over one hundred miles on the horizon.[13] As WL-D recrossed the enemy coastline the entire crew breathed a sigh of relief although they still had another hour and twenty minutes of flight time before arrival back on *terra firma*.

The devastation delivered by the two attacks on Hannover came at a staggering cost. The target had been well defended this night, with numerous enemy aircraft observed in the area, including Ju-88s and Me-110s.[14] A combination of flak and enemy aircraft activity resulted in significant losses, with a total of thirty aircraft lost in the two waves, including eleven Canadian bombers.[15] Only one Canadian aircraft was lost in the second wave.[16] The 5.8 percent loss rate for Bomber Group 6 over the two waves was appalling, although miraculously no planes were lost from Croft.[17]

The crew had been in the air for almost six hours and had watched the destruction of several Allied bombers. They were physically exhausted and let out a sigh of relief as they touched down at Croft. Bob would have to wait another twenty minutes before Jack and Minnie arrived safely back at base.[18]

This was their worst mission to date in terms of overall losses. Over half the men in the stricken Canadian bombers managed to bail out, and although taken prisoner, they at least survived the demise of their aircraft.[19] This 50 percent survival rate was far higher than the normal 29 percent for fatally damaged Halifaxes.

The next day Ron and the crew were stood down for a few days, although on the evening of January 6, other crews from 434 Squadron were involved in an attack on a key railway junction in Hanau, fifteen miles east of Frankfurt.[20] Hanau was known as the hometown of the Brothers Grimm who, in happier times, had written a series of famous German fairy tales. But no matter now. A total of 189 bombers from thirteen Canadian Squadrons participated in this attack with one plane lost from 415 Squadron and one downed from 431 Iroquois Squadron (SE-P) with the loss of all crew.[21] Another effort was put forth the following evening which involved a small force of thirty Lancasters from Middleton St. George and Croft, including twelve planes from 434 Squadron. They joined 615 aircraft from RAF Bomber Command that attacked Munich. There were no Canadian losses although fifteen bombers were destroyed.[22] On the return trip, all 431 and 434 Squadron aircraft were diverted to other bases due to inclement weather at Croft.[23] With the persistent bad weather it would take several days before all diverted aircraft returned to base.[24]

Ron and the crew did not get off of the ground for eight days. Oddly, Ron did not write any letters home to either Kay or his parents over this period. But he did find one of Kay's letters when he went down to pick up his mail.

> *Dearest Ronny, Hello dear, have you got over the holidays yet? Everything is just about back to normal now; I like it better too, sort of.*
>
> *Gosh they say another snowstorm is heading this way. I never saw Montreal with so much snow; if this keeps up we'll be able to ski to work.*
>
> *Have you done any more "ops" Ronny, gosh 21, they certainly have kept you busy. I bet you'll be pleased when you complete your Tour, and I don't blame you. It's bad enough when I think of you dear flying, but I'm afraid I would never be as brave.*
>
> *Well dear as it's getting late I'll say goodnight to you for now Ronny, but only for a little while. Goodnight Dear, All my love, Kay*

The crew was scheduled to participate in an operation on the evening of January 12.[25] The main briefing scheduled for 2:00 PM had been pushed to 10:00 PM, raising the anxiety level of all crews on that night's duty roster. Shortly after the briefing though, the operation was scrubbed due to inclement weather.[26] All aircraft were left bombed up in anticipation of the next mission.

Two days later Ron and the crew were back on the active duty roster. This would be the first of four consecutive flights that did not include Hal.[27] For the third time, Pilot Officer H. Morris would fill in as the wireless operator and backup air gunner.[28] The crew attended the delayed briefing at 4:30 PM.[29] Now with twenty-two operations under their belts, it was Ron and his crewmates that the rookies listened attentively to when the flight leader unveiled the target. This time it was Merseberg, located deep inside Germany, just one hundred miles west of Berlin. The target: the largest synthetic oil refinery in all of Germany, protected by a belt of 450 flak guns, making Merseberg one very tough target.[30] Combined, these guns were capable of firing almost 7,000 shells per minute—which equaled 140,000 pounds of shells per minute all loaded with high explosives capable of reaching heights of 25,000 feet. It is no wonder that a sense of trepidation and fear could be felt throughout the room. Even the most experienced aircrews were more than a little concerned.[30] With the current surprise German offensive in the Ardennes, the supply of oil to the German army reached a critical phase if it was to have any success with its Panzer divisions, which depended on mobility for success. This then was an absolutely critical mission, and little wonder it would be led by Wing Commander Paul Blackburn.[31] Knowing that this would be one of their deepest forays into Germany to date, the four-hour wait before takeoff in Lancaster WL-D seemed like an eternity.

The goal was to have Lancasters from four Canadian squadrons (434, 431, 419, and 428) attack Merseberg, while the balance of Bomber Group 6 (in Halifaxes) targeted the rail yards at Grevenbroich.[32] Over three hundred bombers from the RAF were also scheduled to join in the Merseberg attack.[33] Squadron 431 were the wind-finding force, responsible for measuring the wind speeds on the way to the target and providing this information to the other bombers.[34] This allowed the navigators to calculate a more accurate flight plan while in the air.

When given the chance, Bob would meet with his brother before each mission to compare notes and share feelings on the imminent mission. This would be the nineteenth trip for Jack and the twenty-fourth trip for Bob.[35]

At 6:00 PM the crew headed out to their ship and proceeded to go through all the necessary checks before departure. This routine helped take the edge off their nervous energy and seemed to help

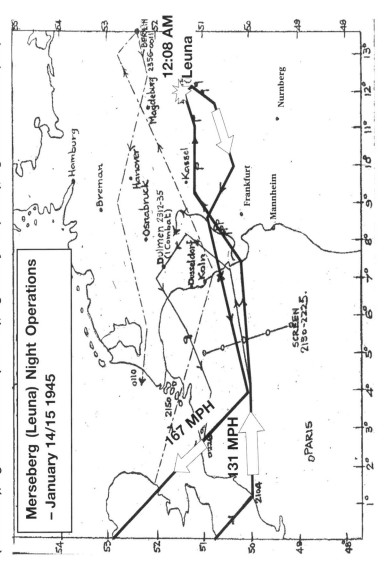

Crew: F/O R. Henry (1st Pilot), F/O A. Coleman (NAV), F/O F. Welsh (B/A), F/O H. Ward (WOP/AG), Sgt. A. Thomson (MU/AG), Sgt. R. Pyves (R/AG), Sgt. J. Casavant (F/E)

Merseberg (Leuna) Night Operations – January 14/15 1945

12:08 AM Leuna

167 MPH

131 MPH

Outbound: 727 Miles, Inbound: 733 Miles, Total Distance Flown: 1,460 Miles

434 Squadron: WL-D (KB830), Bomb Load: 1 x 4,000, 6 x 500, 5 x 250 pounds

Source: *Night Raid Report No. 816*, Bomber Command, 1945. Reproduced with the permission of the Minister of Public Works and Government Services Canada, 2009.

calm nerves. Bob and Joe worked in tandem to successfully get the four large Merlin engines started. Once done, Bob taxied onto the perimeter track and joined the queue of fifteen 434 Squadron Lancasters that waited for their green lights.[36] One of the first planes to leave Croft was WL-Q, piloted by Wing Commander Paul Blackburn.[37]

After takeoff Bob spent the first three-quarters of an hour circling in order to get to their planned altitude of 21,000 feet. They then headed almost due south for over 230 miles. At this point they turned a few degrees to port and crossed the French coast heading due east. With their final turning point just south of Kassel, it was pretty much a straight run into the Leuna oil refinery that had just been bombed three hours earlier. Coming in on this second wave had some advantages—most of the German fighters were on the ground refueling. However, the flak barrages were heavier on this attack. The four Canadian squadrons were soon over the target, having flown well over seven hundred miles from England in just under five hours. They then released over a half-million pounds of high explosives on the Leuna refinery at elevations of 18,000 to 21,000 feet.[38] For only the second time, Ron and the crew dropped a 4,000-pound bomb as part of their payload. It was just after midnight from 21,000 feet. Jack had just passed through the target area three minutes earlier.[39] Frank had at first been instructed by the Master Bomber to bomb on sky markers but, since the markers had burnt out, he aimed on red target indicators as well as green and red flares.[40] He observed one large orange explosion with a massive cloud of black smoke, most likely from their 4,000-pound "cookie."[41] (In his log book Ron wrote "heavy flak" and noted that it felt like they had just passed through a hail storm.) Bob then quickly set the plane on a return course. It turned out to be a long flight back: they didn't touch down at Croft until 4:15 AM, having flown over 1,400 miles.[42] This had been the crew's longest combat mission to date: they had been airborne for over nine hours. It was all the crew could do to get out of their flying gear, collapse into bed, and get some sleep once the adrenalin settled down.

Although Frank reported that the overall attack had been poor due

Crew: F/L R.Henry (1st Pilot), F/O. Coleman (NAV), F/O F. Welsh (B/A), P/O H. Morris (WOP/AG), F/S A. Thmson (MU/AG), F/S R. Pyves (R/AG), Sgt. J. Casavant (F/E)

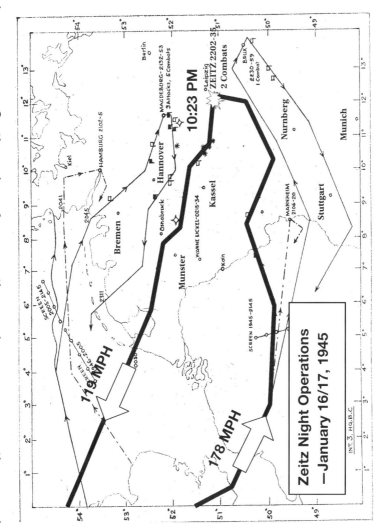

Zeitz Night Operations —January 16/17, 1945

10:23 PM

119 MPH

178 MPH

Outbound: 735 Miles, Inbound: 548 Miles, Total Distance Flown: 1,283 Miles 434 Squadron: WL-D (KB830), Bomb Load: 1 x 4,000, 10 x 500, 2 x 250 pounds

Source: *Night Raid Report No. 817*, Bomber command, 1945. Reproduced with the permission of the Minister of Public Works and Government Services Canada, 2009.

to the weather, in reality the entire refinery had been severely damaged. As expected, the oil refinery had been fiercely defended and the resultant losses were high: ten planes were destroyed including three planes from Bomber Group 6.[43] One bomber from 431 Squadron, flown by Flight Officer M.A. McLeod on his nineteenth trip, was lost when it collided with a Messerschmitt Me-109.[44]

Two days later the crew was again put on the active duty roster. Things were starting to heat up. In early afternoon, the entire base's active crew membership, including Jack Henry's, attended a briefing for that evening's mission. The new target: an oil plant in Zeitz, deep inside Germany about twenty-five miles south of Merseberg. The Allied strategy focused on strangling the flow of oil and fuel to the German military. Like many previous missions, the flight path to this target was indirect and in this instance involved six different key turning points before the final run into the target.

After they completed the normal pre-flight checks, Lancaster WL-D received clearance for takeoff. Ron then watched as the runway disappeared below him, leaving the safety of Croft behind. As in the previous trip, a small number of Lancasters from Croft and Middleton. St. George were vectored to Zeitz, while the balance of 127 Canadian bombers were sent to Magdeburg on the Elbe River as part of a larger RAF effort.[45] And once again Pilot Officer H. Morris filled in as the spare wireless operator.[46] After four and a half hours Bob approached the target at 18,500 feet.[47] The sky appeared well lit up with "bags of searchlights." On the run into the target, ground detail was quite clear as Frank released a mix of bombs, including one 4,000-pound, ten 500-pound, and two 250-pound explosives.[48] Fires, which had been started before the arrival of WL-D, helped light up the target area, although Frank used the target indicators as his aiming point.[49] As soon as the bomb load had been released and the photo taken, Bob banked WL-D in a sharp turn to port and then, like a sailing ship in the ocean, zigzagged four times over the next 180 miles until just south of Osnabruck where he set WL-D on an almost direct course to Croft some 370 miles ahead. Ron noted in his log book afterward that it had been a "good prang," though twenty-seven kites were missing from the two missions, including eight planes from Bomber Group 6.

It was another Herculean effort with WL-D airborne for almost nine hours. They landed safely at Croft in almost total darkness (there was almost no moonlight) and right on the heels of Jack. They had flown almost 1,300 miles on the round trip.

The attacking force on Zeitz consisted of 328 Lancasters, including 51 Lancaster bombers from Bomber Group 6.[50] They suffered the loss of 10 planes including 1 plane, WL-O (for "Oboe") from 434 Squadron, flown by Flight Lieutenant A. Kiehlbauch, an experienced pilot who had already flown on 24 combat missions.[51] The entire crew was lost.[52] Included in the 17 aircraft lost on the Magdeburg mission were 6 Canadian planes with over 50 percent of the aircrew taken prisoner.[53]

While Ron had been airborne over a Germany in flames, Kay was safely ensconced at home penning another letter to Ron.

> *Dear Ronny, I feel so darn swell, I just received a letter from you today. As I hadn't heard since before Christmas, I just couldn't wait somehow to hear from you and to know how Xmas went and all.*
>
> *One thing dear—even if your Christmas lacked a few of the good old Canadian traditions, it was grand to know that you were with relatives and friends, and I bet your Grandmother was delighted to have you there too.*
>
> *You say you only have 10 more ops to do, I shouldn't say "Only" because I know how thrilling and tense it must be flying so often over Enemy territory, and I think of you always Ron, and every time you go up you must feel that a little prayer of mine goes along with you.*
>
> *Tonight is a good night for listening to the radio, there's Fibber McGee & Molly and Bob Hope. I think he's tops.*
>
> *I don't want to get my hopes too high dear, but gosh Ron it would be truly wonderful if you did get home on leave. I'm hoping so much you do. That would be something to work and hope for!*
>
> *Dad and I are doing our best to get a smaller place to live, it's so crazy just us two and seven rooms, while we could be in a four room apartment easy.*

Well Dear, I'll say goodnight to you for now Ronny, but just for a very short while. All my love always Dear, Love, Kay

For the next four days there were no operations or training scheduled due to gale-force winds, heavy icing, and below-freezing conditions—even in the daytime. This presented a welcome break for the crews whose missions were becoming increasingly more dangerous. Ron took advantage of this lull to write to Kay.

Dearest Kay, It's hard to know how to start telling you how happy I am because <u>happy</u> I am. First of all yesterday I received one of your treasured letters and the personal greeting Record, darling, you don't know how wonderful it was to hear your voices again. I too will be very happy when I can talk to you again personally, but in the meantime if my morale had slipped at all, that record sure boosted it again in a hurry. It's really swell being able to hear your voices as much as I like.

Well dear what's new? Besides the Zombies deserting by the thousands. I don't understand fellows like that; they must be just plain yellow I guess. They're to be pitied more than anything. I'm darn sure if I had stayed home when our country was in a tough spot I'd never have a clear conscience again and would be thoroughly ashamed of myself. I suppose things like that don't worry them.

We haven't been flying much lately. I've still only got 25 ops done. Oh well, we'll get them done sometime I guess. I mean I know we will.

I've only been off camp once since our last leave that's once in about three weeks. So you see I've been a good boy. We stay in camp, get a good fire going in our room and listen to the juke box and play cards and write letters. You should see the way the boys all congregate in our room to get warm and hear some good music. They're making an awful racket in here just now and I can hardly hear myself think. That's one of the pleasures of having company eh! Dear. They're a swell bunch and you would probably think we were arguing all the time, the way we kid each other along.

Well dearest I'll say goodnight now with all my love and kisses for you darling always, Ronny

Having not flown for nine days, Bob decided to take the crew up for a short flight in WL-D to keep the team sharp. The aircraft first had to have the bombs removed to make it safe in the event that they encountered any mechanical difficulties over the local countryside. They then left Croft mid-afternoon and were back on the ground just before sunset. The following day, Ron wrote one last letter to Kay before he went back on operations.

Dearest Kay. I'm the one who is really happy today after receiving one of your wonderful letters.

As you can probably tell by my letters, sometimes I get the blues and feel as though I've got all the cares of the world bearing down on me, but you soon fix that in a hurry dear. I guess everybody gets in a blue mood once in a while eh! Kay? It's just human nature for a person to be alternately happy, worried etc.

I like your little cartoon of me dear with all the bottles around me. I'm not a bad boy really about drinking. About the only times I really bother about it over here is when I'm on leave or after we've done a few ops in a row and my nerves are a bit jumpy, and believe me they do get jumpy from the long tense hours on ops. When you're over enemy territory every sense is really alert and you're all keyed up. After eight or nine hours of that at a time, it begins to tell on you and makes you feel as though you can't stay awake any longer for anything, but of course you have to. No matter what the drawbacks, life on a squadron makes life really interesting.

It makes me have a sort of contented feeling inside of me to know that you're thinking of me on ops dear. Whenever I'm flying or on the ground I'm thinking of you always. I hope to be back and we'll be going out together again this summer, with luck and some good flying weather. I can do it. That's something I dream of quite often, getting off the train in Central Station and seeing you there. Gosh it'll be wonderful. I mustn't daydream though, there's too much grim reality between now and then.

I'll say goodnight, now darling with all my love for you always. Love, Ronny P.S. 25 ops done

On Saturday, January 28, they were back to the deadly business of air warfare with an early evening trip scheduled for the railway yards at Kornwestheim, just four miles north of Stuttgart. For the thirteenth time, both Jack and Bob would take part in the same mission. This attack would be a major effort with just over 500 bombers converging on the target in two waves, including 179 planes from Bomber Group 6.[54] On this trip, Sergeant G. Cloake stood in as wireless operator for Hal Ward.[55] All aircraft taking off from Croft did so through snow flurries that encircled the base. After reaching his cruising altitude of 20,000 feet, Bob pointed WL-D due south before crossing the English coastline and then starting his flight over France. They flew north of Paris and ninety minutes later were just north of Kornwestheim heading directly into the target. On the final approach, significant cloud cover obscured the marshalling yards, resulting in scattered bombing. WL-D was one of the first bombers to arrive at the target. Frank aimed at sky markers, releasing 10,000 pounds of high explosives.[56] Jack, in SE-D, bombed the target just seven minutes later.[57] Joe checked the bomb bay to make sure that all bombs had been released. It was a routine which he carried out on every mission. To his surprise, one 500-pound bomb remained hung up in the bomb bay, a scary first for the crew.[58] Joe first tried the bomb jettison button directly in front of him but to no success. He then frantically turned the bomb jettison control handle, also with no luck. Although this bomb was technically armed, fortunately it could not detonate without first falling several thousand feet through the air.

Once the photoflash bounced off the clouds below, Bob continued due south for four miles before turning the plane sharply to starboard, setting them on a path that ran parallel to their long, inbound journey. As the bomb could not be shaken loose, Bob decided to close the bomb-bay doors to reduce the air drag on the plane. He then skirted Paris to the north and proceeded to Spilsby, an operational RAF Bomber

Crew: F/L R. Henry (1st Pilot), F/O A. Coleman (NAV), P/O F. Welsh (B/A), Sgt. G. Cloake (WOP/AG), F/Sgt. A. Thomson (MU/AG), F/Sgt. R. Pyves (R/AG), Sgt. J. Casavant (F/E)

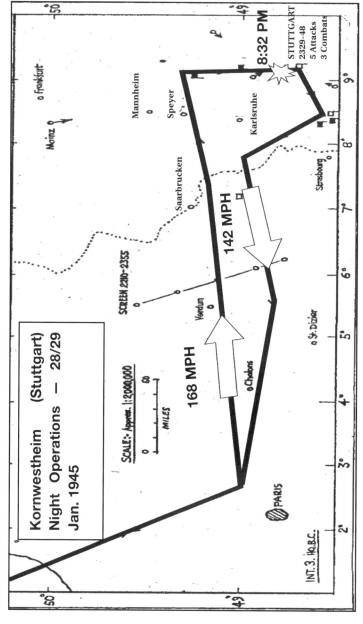

Kornwestheim (Stuttgart) Night Operations — 28/29 Jan. 1945

8:32 PM

STUTTGART
2329-48
5 Attacks
3 Combats

142 MPH

168 MPH

Outbound: 655 Miles, Inbound: 546 Miles, Total Distance Flown: 1,201 Miles
434 Squadron: WL-D (KB830), Bomb Load: 1x 4,000, 13 x 500 pounds

Source: *Night Raid Report No. 824*, Bomber Command, 1945. Reproduced with the permission of the Minister of Public Works and Government Services Canada, 2009.

Command Base near the east coast of England in Lincolnshire.[59] Here he executed a soft landing making sure that their unwanted cargo did not shake lose. It had been a long trip, and although the crew had only flown on four missions in January, they were now flying deeper into Germany which meant that their actual accumulated combat flying time of almost thirty-four hours represented a 25 percent increase over December.[60]

The crew debriefed and then scrambled to find some overnight accommodation in an air base overflowing with displaced flyers. This had been a long, stressful trip of over 1,200 miles, the last 600 of which included an unwanted 500-pound bomb hung up in bomb bay. It would stay there until removed by the ground crew the next day. Flak over the target area had been slight but enemy fighters had been active and accounted for at least two of the five Canadian planes lost on the mission.[61] Of the other three bombers lost, one had crashed on takeoff, with the others either downed by flak or enemy aircraft.[62] Thankfully, no planes were missing from Croft.[63] For the German populace who lived in Stuttgart and its outlying areas, over 67 percent of their housing had now been destroyed from the cumulative missions of Bomber Command.

The next day Kay wrote her first letter in almost two weeks while Ron and the crew were stuck in Spilsby due to the inclement weather.

Dearest Ronny, I received your letter of the 7th, and gosh Ronny, you just can't imagine how I love each and every letter.

Twenty-three "ops," they certainly must find your crew pretty capable. It would be grand Ronny if you did get a Commission, you certainly rate one, I think that you're doing a swell job and I feel very proud of you too. I was chatting with your Mom on the phone and we both agreed that you're not so bad.

We're still right in the middle of Old Man Winter here in Montreal, it was 15 below Friday.

At noon today, the gang of us from the office were having dinner downstairs in the Coffee Bar, and a woman told me she had been admiring my bracelet, she said it was very nice. She wanted to know if it had brought me any luck since I've been wearing it. Well between us, I think my lucky time was being up North and meeting each other as we did, so I feel sure that I'm pretty lucky.

You asked me about my plans and dreams for the future, I guess Ron, that that's a very big question dear and really calls for a smart answer, and a sincere and honest one too. We all individually have numerous dreams and plans, but actually when you place them altogether they add up to pretty much the same idea, we all want to be "<u>happy</u>" in our own way.

You know Ron, about asking a girl to get engaged, even though you're doing dangerous work, that I know wouldn't make the slightest bit of difference, and I know the girl wouldn't hesitate for a second on that account, what's more important is being certain about each other and their feelings. I think Dear that we're both wise enough and patient enough to wait and see one another, the right kind of love Ron is always worth waiting and fighting for, and that's the only kind too, I know you think the same way dear.

I hope Ron that you'll be lucky enough to be home soon, that sure could be swell.

Take care of yourself always, and remember that this letter is sent with all my love, Kay

While WL-D was stuck at Spilsby, 434 and 431 Squadrons won the Bristol Challenge Trophy for the highest rate of bombing accuracy among Bomber Group 6 stations.[64] The trophy had been received with pride by Wing Commander Blackburn from the Chief of Air Staff, Air Marshal Robert Leckie.[65]

It took until midday on February 1 for Bob to obtain clearance to depart the still-overcrowded Spilsby. The flight back took less than an hour. But when Ron returned to his hut, he discovered that his entire kit had been redistributed among those who shared his accommodations.[66] Apparently there was some misunderstanding as to whether WL-D had made it back from Kornwestheim. It was common practice for crews to sift through the kits of missing colleagues, leaving behind personal belongings that would be returned to next of kin. Ron therefore had to spend most of the afternoon reclaiming his lost articles.

Bomber Group 6 had just completed its worst month for losses since Ron and his crewmates had been put on active duty. A total of thirty planes were lost, which represented a loss rate of 2.5 percent.[67] This was triple the rate for December and October and twice the November loss rate. For a war that most people expected to wind down in 1945, January had gotten off to a bad start for the Canadian bomber squadrons. The one source of pride for the group once known as the "Chop" Squadron was that its loss rate was now significantly below the average rate of attrition for all Canadian bomber squadrons.

Three new crews were posted into 434 Squadron in January with the loss of one crew for the month.[68] When Ron first went into active combat duty in September 1944, there were twenty-five Halifax bombers available for operations. In January 1945, there were only nineteen bombers available, and these were all Lancasters.[69]

With twenty-five missions now in the bag and five left to go, Ron could now see light at the end of the tunnel and could almost taste the relief which would come with the safe completion of the last sortie. However, he and the crew of Lancaster WL-D were about to be thrown a curve ball.

13
Night Madness

B y early February the German military was being severely pressured on a number of fronts. The Russian Army under Marshal Georgi Zhukov was less than fifty miles from Berlin while Canadian and British infantry would complete their objective to drive the Germans out of the Netherlands. The American First and Third Armies had simultaneously crossed into Germany across a broad front, pushing through the first layer of the two Siegfred Lines of defence, which consisted of concrete pillboxes and tank traps set out in depth to slow down the advancing enemy. The Canadian government had decided early in 1945 to send overseas, elements of the Canadian Home Defence Army which were comprised mainly of draftees. The first of these troops had finally arrived in England to provide desperately needed reinforcements for Canadian troops already in the field.

Sending draftees overseas had been quite a controversial move. When conscription was introduced in 1940 under the National Resources Mobilization Act, Prime Minister William Lyon Mackenzie King had promised Canadians that conscripts would not be deployed overseas. This promise necessitated a referendum held in 1942 to release the government from its earlier commitment. The referendum had been divisive in that it was supported by 83 percent of English-speaking Canadians but only 27 percent of French-speaking Canadians. Although some seventeen thousand conscripts were designated for service overseas, in reality fewer than three thousand ended up in front-line service before the war in Europe ended.

Activity in the Canadian area of operations since early November 1944 had been focused on holding a defensive position in the Netherlands. This included the key bridgehead at Nijmegen while the Battle of the Bulge raged farther south. On December 16, 1944, a major surprise attack had been launched by the Germans through the Ardennes region of Belgium. The objective was to recapture the Port of Antwerp which had just become functional to the Allies in late November 1944. Although the Germans had some initial success, their limited supply of fuel and the tenacious resistance offered by the Americans ultimately resulted in the German advance grinding to a halt well short of their goal. The Americans, who bore the brunt of the German offensive, experienced significant casualties: over eighty-nine thousand soldiers were killed or wounded. With resolution of the Battle of the Bulge, the Canadians would now once more go on the offensive.

On February 8, Canadian and British troops attacked the German army between the Maas and Rhine Rivers. The Germans had to be removed from the area before the Allies could attempt to simultaneously breach the Rhine River at multiple locations in the coming months. During the next eighteen days of fighting, the First Canadian Army, consisting of both Canadian (20 percent) and British (80 percent) troops, sustained over eight thousand casualties.[1] However, they successfully achieved their objectives.

In February, Bomber Group 6 focused primarily on oil refineries and key railway junctions in Germany. Also included were efforts to support the advance of the Russian Army on the Eastern Front, including missions to Dresden, Chemnitz, and Magdeburg. On February 1, while Ron and the crew were still in Spilsby, 434 Squadron made eleven aircraft available for operations to Ludwigshafen, Germany.[2] As well, on the next day, fourteen aircraft from 434 Squadron bombed Wiesbaden.[3] One plane from Bomber Group 6 was lost in the Ludwigshafen attack with three additional planes missing in the Wiesbaden operation, which included one plane lost while landing back at base.[4] There were no planes lost from Croft.[5]

On February 3, Flying Officer H. Rubin, who had flown with Ron and the crew on January 5, was screened from operations. He had completed thirty-one trips.[6] Ron and the crew were informed that after their next mission they would be given a seven-day personal leave. This was sufficient incentive to get another mission checked off the list—and they didn't have long to wait. On February 4, they attended a midday briefing where Bonn was unveiled as the target. Ron wrote in his log book that the objective was to surprise the enemy and impact morale. Bonn was located just twelve miles south of Cologne so Ron and the crew were familiar with the area since they had visited Cologne as recently as December 30. Bonn would be a good trip. It wasn't located too deep inside Germany and its proximity to water—the Rhine—would help both Al and Frank better locate the target.

The crew performed pre-flight preparations and boarded Lancaster WL-D. It felt like walking inside a refrigerator it was that cold. It took almost an hour before the plane started to feel warmer, at least in the forward part of the bomber. Bob received clearance for takeoff at 5:27 PM.[7] As WL-D quickly climbed skyward, Ron was treated to a spectacular sunset with bright pink clouds backlit by the setting sun. Surely this was a good omen. For just the second time since starting their tour of duty, navigator Al Coleman did not make the trip due to illness, and Flying Officer A. Dunn stood in for him.[8] Pilot Officer J. Woodstock also replaced Hal Ward who remained unavailable.[9]

In total, 100 aircraft from Bomber Group 6 were joined by another 138 bombers from the RAF.[10] Bob's brother Jack was also on the mission, despite having already participated in raids on Ludwigshafen and Wiesbaden in the last three days. The flight path took the bombers to an elevation of 17,000 to 20,000 feet over the target, but a solid blanket of cloud covered the city, which resulted in scattered bombing with minimal impact. Frank bombed on sky markers. The entire bomb load consisted of thirteen canisters of incendiaries, which carpeted the target with 1,800 four-pound bombs.[11] The extensive cloud cover meant that in this case no enemy aircraft were seen and the flak was ineffective. Bob set his aircraft for home as soon as Frank announced "bombs away" and the photo flash from the plane's camera bounced back off the clouds. Jack was in SE-D, just eight minutes behind Bob's plane.[12] He was at 19,500 feet and while the usual photo was being taken, Jack was forced to make a steep turn to starboard to avoid hitting another bomber, which had just crossed his path.[13] It was a near call that shook up the crew and sent chills down Bob's spine when he heard about it back at base. On the return flight, many of the bomber crews could see an orange glow through the clouds as far as sixty miles from the target. Later during debriefing, Frank reported that the target appeared well ablaze over an extensive area.[14]

Bob made a smooth landing back at Croft just after midnight, thankful that their air base had not been socked in with clouds like at Bonn. They had flown for six hours and thirty-five minutes. Jack in SE-D landed safely just fourteen minutes later.[15] Two aircraft from 428 and 419 Squadrons were lost on the Bonn trip due to a mid-air collision.[16] With hundreds of planes flying in tight formations, mid-air collisions were not uncommon. It was a miracle that they did not occur more often.

The crew was officially on leave after the Bonn debriefing, but just before departing base they received a bombshell of their own. The RCAF had changed its system of ops just when they were nearly finished their tour. Instead of the original requirement of thirty, each crew member would now have to do anywhere from thirty-five to forty missions, depending on whether anybody else in their crew lagged behind. This change in policy seemed like a death sentence—and for many in the RCAF, it quite literally was. Having to do an additional five to ten trips could clearly mean the difference between finishing one's tour safely and tempting fate one time too often. Hal at this time had five fewer trips than anybody else, due primarily to recurring ear problems. If Hal did not do any spare trips, then the rest of the crew might have to do as many as forty. In addition, there was also a new point system. Four points were given for each trip to a major target in Germany, with just three points given for minor targets or closer targets such as those in France. So in addition to the extra number of missions, each crew member now needed to accumulate a minimum of 120 points to be screened from operations. Some of the crews reacted negatively—*especially* those who were near the end of their tour based on the old criteria. And some thought it a matter of faith: how could the crews now trust that when and if they completed the new requirements, Bomber Command wouldn't once again up the ante? Ron received only one piece of good news this day: his commission to Pilot Officer had been approved. His daily pay would almost double—from $3.40 to $6.25—which was grand as long as he was around to collect it.

Ron, accompagnied by Bill, visited his grandfather, Robert Hall Pyves, in North Shields. Returning from leave, and despite the tour of duty changes, Ron was delighted to receive a letter from Kay. He put his camp chair next to the coal burning stove to ward off the incessant winter chill, and quickly opened the letter.

Dearest Ronny, The mail seems to be better now, and I'm glad that you received the records and letters. You mentioned Ronny that you were sent overseas so soon after we met, that's certainly true alright. There were so many things we could have done and said together, it's funny in Wartime how these things happen, everything so mixed up, and it will be wonderful when the War is won and everyone all over the World has an equal chance to find their happiness.

One letter dear you mentioned you were waiting around to go out on "ops," I agree that there's a queer feeling about waiting around, I think perhaps it leaves too much time to think about it. Everyone now and then experiences that feeling now and then, and I guess it just makes you enjoy all the more the times when you haven't a thing to worry over.

Gosh dear 25 ops you've nearly completed your tour or whatever you call it, I think you fellows must be pretty proud. It certainly would be grand if you came home on leave, gee that would be an answer to all my hopes and I know your Mom and Dad would be so gosh darn happy too. The only thing as you say dear, it's not right to day-dream too much, but just the same it's worth every second of the time.

I'll be writing again soon dear, take care of yourself always. All my love, Kay

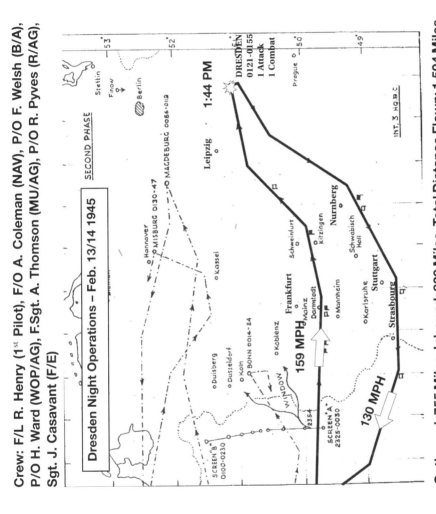

Crew: F/L R. Henry (1st Pilot), F/O A. Coleman (NAV), P/O F. Welsh (B/A),
P/O H. Ward (WOP/AG), F.Sgt. A. Thomson (MU/AG), P/O R. Pyves (R/AG),
Sgt. J. Casavant (F/E)

Dresden Night Operations – Feb. 13/14 1945

Outbound: 755 Miles, Inbound: 839 Miles, Total Distance Flown: 1,594 Miles
434 Squadron: WL-D (KB830), Bomb Load: 1 x 4,000, 7 x 1,000 pounds

Source: *Night Raid Report No. 837*, Bomber Command, 1945. Reproduced with the permission of the Minister of Public Works and Government Services Canada, 2009.

Now back at Croft, the reality of having to do as many as nine more trips, rather than just four, began to weigh heavy on Ron and the crew. Whenever Ron thought of the extra trips, his stomach started to ache thinking whether he really would make it back to Kay. While on leave, only one of five planned missions got off the ground on February 7, due to foul weather. Fifteen bombers from 434 Squadron, as part of a larger RAF and RCAF effort, set out to Goch, Germany, but turned back due to poor visibility over the target.[17]

Since joining Bluenose Squadron in September, Ron had already seen almost a third of the squadron aircraft and their crews lost in action.

On February 13, just before Valentine's Day, the crews of 431 and 434 gathered at the briefing hut to see what was in store for them that evening. The target was identified as Dresden, the seventh largest city in Germany and at this late stage in the war, a key communications and transport centre on the Eastern Front. With a normal population of 650,000 people, Dresden had recently been flooded with refugees fleeing the Russian advance which was just sixty miles away. This attack was communicated to the crews as a Russian Army co-operation to disrupt the movement of German reinforcements to the Russian front. Dresden had only been bombed twice previously, by the United States Air Force as a secondary target on October 7, 1944, and more recently on January 16, 1945.[18] As Germany responded to a new offensive by the Russians, which had commenced in early January, dozens of German divisions were scheduled to pass through Dresden on their way to the Eastern Front. Most of the anti-aircraft defences had been moved from the city to key strategic cities in the Ruhr Valley, as well as to army units desperate for increased firepower to stave off the Russians.

Dresden was now selected as a key strategic target by not only the RAF and RCAF, but also by the American Air Force. Over a period of twenty-six hours, Dresden would be hit by three waves of bombers, which would drop over seven million pounds of high explosives and incendiary bombs.

RAF Bomber Group No. 5 made up the first wave. They special-ized in low-level sector bombing to maximize the intensity and impact of high-explosive and incendiary bombs, which their 244 Lancasters dropped on the city starting just after 10:14 PM.[19] A total of 800 tons of bombs were released from an elevation of 10,000 to 13,000 feet, although the visibility was poor due to heavy cloud cover rising to as high as 9,000 feet.[20] The bombers took indirect routes, which meant that the citizens had almost no warning before the first target indicators, and then bombs started to fall around the aiming point, which was the sports stadium located next to the Altstadt, or old town.

Lothar Metzger, a child living in Dresden during the war, would later write about his experiences this night:

"There were nonstop explosions. Our cellar was filled with fire and smoke and was damaged, the lights went out and wounded people shouted dreadfully. In great fear we struggled to leave this cellar. My mother and my older sister carried the big basket in which the twins were laid. With one hand I grasped my younger sister and with the other I grasped the coat of my mother.

"We did not recognize our street any more. Fire, only fire wherever we looked. Our 4th floor did not exist anymore. The broken remains of our house were burning. On the streets there were burning vehicles and carts with refugees, people, horses, all of them screaming and shouting in fear of death. I saw hurt women, children, old people searching for a way through ruins and flames."[23]

Individual fires quickly merged together with results visible for one hundred miles as the bombers started on the return trip homeward. The smoke reached as high as 15,000 feet. Only one Lancaster was lost from this first phase of attack.[21] The seeds for what would become a firestorm of significant magnitude had been sown.

The second wave was scheduled to arrive in Dresden three hours after the start of the first. This follow-up wave was a tactic developed by Bomber Command to catch the German emergency services, including fire fighters, in the open where they would be battling the initial fires. Bomber Group Nos. 1, 3, and 8 from the RAF and Canadian Bomber Group No. 6 would participate.[22] A total of 529

Lancasters would bomb the primary target with an additional 1,800 tons of bombs.[23] The aiming point was now the city centre. The first bombs were released at 1:21 AM. The marking and bombing were highly concentrated due to less cloud cover.

WL-D would arrive in this second wave. The fully bombed-up Lancaster took off from Croft at 8:59 PM.[24] It was just the third bomber from 434 Squadron to lift off and join the small group of sixty-six Canadian Lancasters.[25] It was common practice for the slower planes to be placed near the front of the queue so they would not be left behind in the bomber stream as it headed to the target. The Canadian bombers merged with a much larger stream of 484 planes rising from RAF stations in the south.[26] With Dresden situated about one hundred miles south of Berlin, it took them almost five hours to reach the target. After they crossed the English coastline south of Dover, Bob made a sharp turn to port and headed due east for just over 380 miles before they reached their next turning point at 150 miles out from Dresden. Al found navigation to the target easy since he could see the Dresden fires from a hundred miles out. The unusual combination of dry weather, incendiary bombs, ancient buildings, and a high concentration of bombs created the perfect recipe for a firestorm of extraordinary proportions. Such extensive damage and loss of life had only occurred once before when a firestorm in Hamburg took the lives of fifty thousand two years earlier. This widespread, raging inferno in Dresden resulted in an extraordinary level of military and civilian casualties. Even from the bomber's viewpoint some 20,000 feet above, one could clearly see a maelstrom of fire below where the target should have been—this was truly a scene of night madness. Flak was almost non-existent as what little defences the city had were already overwhelmed by the first wave of bombers.

Although visibility over the target was fairly clear in terms of clouds, massive amounts of smoke forced Frank to use the target indicators as an aiming point.[27] The bomb load consisted of one 4,000-pound and seven 1,000-pound bombs, which were released at 1:42 AM at an elevation of 18,000 feet.[28] The crew observed large fires that lit up the whole city south of the river and at the time they felt it had been a very good attack.[29]

Bob then turned WL-D toward home knowing that they still had an exceptionally long journey back to Croft, especially with the strong headwinds that gusted to 85 miles per hour.[30] The return route took the crew on a flight path just south of Nurnberg, Stuttgart, and Strasbourg before they started to head in a northwesterly direction home. As they left Dresden, the fires could be seen for over 150 miles.

Twenty-four-year-old Margaret Freyer lived through the Dresden firestorm and would later recall:

"The firestorm is incredible, there are calls for help and screams from somewhere but all around is one single inferno.

"To my left I suddenly see a woman. I can see her to this day and shall never forget it. She carries a bundle in her arms. It is a baby. She runs, she falls, and the child flies in an arc into the fire. The woman remains lying on the ground, completely still. Why? What for? I don't know; I just stumble on.

"Suddenly, I saw people again, right in front of me. They scream and gesticulate with their hands, and then—to my utter horror and amazement—I see how one after the other they simply seem to let themselves drop to the ground. Today I know that these unfortunate people were the victims of lack of oxygen. They fainted and then burnt to cinders. I fell then, stumbling over a fallen woman and as I lie right next to her I see how her clothes are burning away.

"Insane fear grips me and from then on I repeat one simple sentence to myself continuously: 'I don't want to burn to death.' Once more I fall down and feel that I am not going to be able to get up again, but the fear of being burnt pulls me to my feet. I do not know how many people I fell over. I know one thing: that I must not burn.

"I try once more to get up on my feet, but I can only manage to crawl forward on all fours. I can still feel my body; I know I'm still alive. Suddenly, I'm standing up, but there's something wrong, everything seems so far away, and I can't hear or see properly any more. As I found out later, like the others, I was suffering from lack of oxygen. I must have stumbled forwards roughly ten paces when I all at once inhaled fresh air. There's a breeze! I take another breath, inhale deeply and my senses clear. In front of me is a broken tree. As I rush towards it, I know that I have been saved.

"I walk on a little and discover a car. I'm pleased and decide to spend the night in it. I spent all the daylight hours which followed in the town searching for my fiancé. I looked for him amongst the dead, because hardly any living beings were to be seen anywhere. What I saw was horrific, that I shall hardly be able to describe it. Dead, dead, dead everywhere. Some completely black like charcoal. Others completely untouched, lying as if they were asleep. Women in aprons, women with children sitting in the trams as if they had just nodded off. Many women, many young girls, many small children, soldiers who were only identifiable as such by the metal buckles on their belts, almost all of them naked. Some clinging to each other, in groups as if they were clawing at each other."[31]

W/O Nick Nicholson, from RAF 35 Pathfinder Squadron, also participated in the second wave of attack. He would later recall how as they turned for home, all he could see was a bright red glow that reached to the horizon. It was a sight he had never seen before. Nick continued to watch the bright flames as his plane slowly pulled away from the target area. Like many of the crews, he felt badly for the people on the ground but nevertheless felt that the crew had done a good job that night and he had no regrets about the mission.[32]

The brown and yellow patchwork of the farmers' fields around Croft seemed in stark contrast to the boiling cauldron they had left behind. Due to fuel shortages, a number of planes had to land at alternative bases.[33] Bob and the crew were lucky that they did not, as they had flown 1,595 miles in a plane that normally had a maximum range of 1,650 miles. They were literally flying on fumes by the time they arrived back over the airfield at Croft, touching down at 8:09 AM.[34] This eleven-plus-hour flight was the longest that the crew would experience during their tour of duty. Four Lancasters were downed with an additional five planes crash landing, but no planes from Bomber Group 6 were lost on this trip.[35] A third wave of attack was conducted the following day by the USAF 1st Bombardment Division with 431 B-17s scheduled to bomb Dresden.[36] Only 316 B-17s bombed the primary target, the marshalling yard in the Friedrichstadt district of Dresden, just after noon, dropping almost 750 tons of bombs while the balance of the force misidentified their targets, bombing Prague, Brux, and Pilsen.[37]

On the ground that morning, eighteen-year-old Goetz Bergander recalled the experience,

"The city was absolutely quiet. The sound of the fires had died out. The rising smoke created a dirty, gray pall which hung over the entire city. The wind had calmed, but a slight breeze was blowing westward, away from us. That's how, standing in the courtyard, I suddenly thought I could hear sirens again. And sure enough, there they were. I shouted, and by then we could already hear the distant whine of engines. We rushed down into the cellar. The roar of the engines grew louder and louder, and the daylight attack began. This was the American 8th Air Force, and their attack came right down on our heads.

"Normally, there were only 20 to 25 of us down in the cellar. But now, with many people off the street, including those who'd stopped over at our house, there were about 100 of us. Nevertheless, no one panicked—we were too numb and demoralized from the night before. We just sat there. The attack rolled closer, and then a bomb hit. It was like a bowling ball that bounced, or jumped perhaps, and at that moment the lights went out. The whole basement filled with dust. When the bomb carpet reached us, I crouched in a sitting position, my head between my legs. The air pressure was immense, but only for a moment. The rubber seals on the windows and steel doors probably helped to absorb some of the impact. Someone screamed, and then it was quiet. Then a voice shouted, 'It's all right, nothing's happened.' It was the shelter warden.

"Someone turned on a flashlight. We could see again, and that meant a lot. If it had remained dark, I don't know if the people wouldn't have jumped and screamed to get out. However, after this flashlight went on everyone relaxed, and in spite of the loud crash that made me think the whole house was caving in on top of us, a loud voice shouted 'Calm down. Calm down, nothing's happened.' Although the drone of the bombers faded away, we heard another load of bombs explode in the distance. The entire episode lasted about 15 minutes.

"We listened for it to become quiet again. The deathly silence that ensued was a stark contrast to the previous minutes. Our house was still standing, a true miracle. There were no more windows and the entire roof had been torn off and strewn about the street. In front of the house there was such an enormous crater that I thought, my God, it's not even 20 yards away, how did this house ever make it through as well as it did?"[38]

The three waves of attack destroyed over 78,000 dwellings and another 27,500 were made uninhabitable.[39] It is estimated that at least 25,000 residents and refugees in Dresden were killed. Many suffocated while in their bomb shelters as the air was literally sucked out to feed the raging fires outside.

The decision to bomb Dresden would not only haunt Bomber Command but many of the crews who were ordered to attack this target on Valentine's Day. Although Dresden had been a city of beauty and culture with many historic buildings and structures, it had also been a key centre of war manufacturing. It was home to over 110 factories employing at least 50,000 individuals in various war industries, including aircraft components, munitions, and the manufacture of anti-aircraft and field guns.[40] For Ron in particular, it would be a seminal event in his wartime experience—one which would haunt him to the end of his life.

Ron debriefed, ate, and although still wound up from the eleven-hour mission, felt overwhelmed from exhaustion and crashed for a few hours. He and the rest of the crew were on the order of battle for later that day.

The crew was called at 12:15 PM to eat before the main briefing scheduled for 2:30 PM.[41] Ron woke up in a dream-heavy fog. He slipped off the side of his bunk and the cold floor on his bare feet brought him back to reality: he suddenly remembered that he was scheduled to fly on another operation that day. At briefing, Chemnitz, a key manufacturing area in eastern Germany, was revealed as the day's target. Seventeen aircraft from 434 Squadron were scheduled to participate in the attack, joining an additional 102 planes from eleven other Canadian squadrons, which included their sister squadron 431.[42] Takeoff was scheduled to commence just before 5:00 PM. The crew headed out to WL-D and went through all the pre-flight checks. When Bob and Joe started up the engines they had difficulty with the outer starboard engine, which the ground crew was unable to fix.[43] They were then scratched from the operation. WL-H also experienced mechanical problems and was scratched.[44] To compensate, a spare crew from 434 Squadron was required to participate in the mission.[45] This spare crew, as in most operations, had been on standby in a fully loaded bomber (SE-C from 431 Squadron).[46] Sadly, they were rookies flying on their first combat mission and would be one of seven crews from Bomber Group 6 lost on this raid.[47] Tragically, the loss rate on this mission reached almost 6.2 percent.[48]

When the crew heard that the rookies from SE-C had been lost, they were devastated and couldn't help thinking about how unpredictable life could be. Ron, still shaken from his trip to Dresden, decided it was time to catch a few more hours of sleep.

That same day Kay sat writing at the kitchen table back home in Montreal, glad that she had gotten through the first half of the work week.

> *Dearest Ronny, Hello dear, I hope that you're receiving my letters fine and that everything is swell with you.*
>
> *It's Valentine Day today, and it's funny but I can't help thinking of someone very special, that I would like to be with on St. Valentine's Day, so the next best thing was to write him telling him how I felt. I do very much dear wish you were here, and I hope that soon that wish will be fulfilled.*
>
> *I hope you had a grand time on leave, and I bet it's not so welcome going back to your base.*
>
> *The weather here has been lovely lately, sun shining, and it gives you a lift to know that Spring will soon be here, sort of a "glad to be alive" feeling.*
>
> *You mentioned Ronny that all the gang like to drop into your room. It's swell when there's a gang like that. I love people, that's a simple statement but true, I do.*
>
> *I was down to see your Mom the other night, Edna was over, we had a lot of fun too, but then when three women get together for a chat you can always count on that. I like Edna very*

much, she has a good sense of humor and is a good sport, and confidentially I think her husband is pretty nice too, but I still prefer his younger brother, maybe because he's such an enthusiastic "skier"—could be!

I sure hope that soon this War will be won, and that people will be able to get used to being home again.

Remember Ronny that there's somebody that cares, and hopes that it won't be long before that someone waits in Central Station. Goodnight Dear, All my love Always, Kay

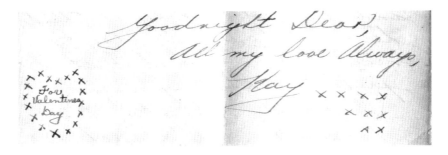

All operations were cancelled the next day due to inclement weather, offering a brief break for the crews of 434 Squadron, who had flown on back-to-back missions the previous two days.[49] For Ron, having the day off provided another opportunity to pen a quick note to Kay as he never knew when it might be his last chance to write.

Dearest Kay, I received your letter of January 29th. I guess that is a better idea of yours Kay to wait until we see each other again, so we can be sure of each other. After all it's a big decision to make and lasts for a lifetime. There is nobody I'd rather share my life with, darling than you. I'm sure of that. I guess if you saw me now dear you'd probably notice a bit of a change in me. I know I feel different anyway. I sort of feel as though I've grown up quite a lot since leaving home.

All my love sweetheart, Ronny

Foggy weather for the next four days kept the crews grounded but ground training continued unabated. All pilots and wireless operators were expected to attend a lecture on both H2S and Fishpond.[50] Fishpond was an extension of the H2S system used by the wireless operator to detect the approach of enemy aircraft. On February 19, after an inspection of all station personnel by the station commander, the crew was given a heads up that they would be on the active duty roster the next day. That afternoon, Ron attended a turret training session for all air gunners.[51]

Early next evening, on what could only be characterized as a typical cold and blustery English winter day, the crews gathered at the briefing hut. They lined up in school assembly style in front of their briefing tables, waiting for the latest information on the night's mission. The briefing had already been delayed twice that day, which did not help to settle already-stretched nerves, given this was, for most crews, their first operation in five days. The navigation officer revealed the target as Dortmund, with the marshalling yards the primary aiming point. Although a new target, Dortmund was not totally unfamiliar. It was located in the Ruhr, ten miles north of Hagen, which 434 Squadron bombed on December 2. Nevertheless, each new target raised mixed emotions because it offered the unknown, which could be unsettling. For Bob, who had been on leave, this would be the first time in over two weeks that he would be flying on the same mission as his brother.[52] Jack was beginning to close the fraternal experience gap—this would be his twenty-sixth mission and the thirtieth for Bob, what would have been his last mission if not for the recent changes.[53]

This trip involved another late departure with the crew bussing out to their ship just after 8:00 PM with the dampness easily penetrating their flight gear. After the pre-flight checks, Bob started up the engines one at a time. Tonight the engines hesitated and then sputtered into life, building to a high whine as Joe monitored the fuel mixture to make sure the engines were warmed up and ran smoothly before takeoff. With one final check through the intercom system, Bob rolled the plane along the perimeter track and then turned Lancaster WL-D onto the main runway. Bob kept the brakes on, building up the revs on the four engines until they screamed.

When the green light was given, Bob released the brakes and reported liftoff at 9:28 PM.[54] Jack's plane—SE-D—had already taken off thirteen minutes earlier.[55] The crew were now on their way to

Crew: F/L R. Henry (1st Pilot), F/O A. Coleman (NAV), P/O F. Welsh (B/A), P/O H. Ward (WOP/AG), F/Sgt.
A. Thomson (MU/AG), P/O R. Pyves (R/AG), Sgt. J. Casavant (F/E)

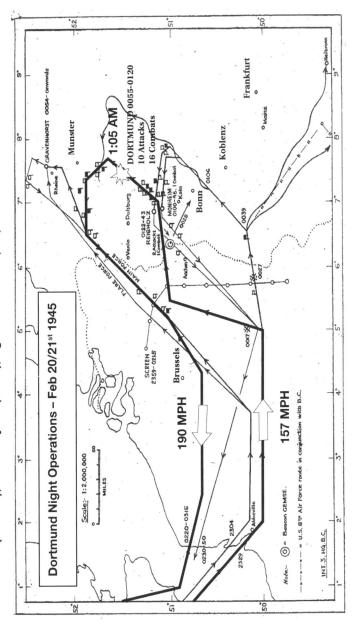

Dortmund Night Operations – Feb 20/21ˢᵗ 1945

Outbound: 570 Miles, Inbound: 522 miles, Total Distance Flown: 1,092 Miles
434 Squadron: WL–D (KB830), Bomb Load: 1 x 1,000 pounds, 16 Canisters Incendiaries

Source: *Night Raid Report No. 843*, Bomber Command, 1945. Reproduced with the permission of the Minister of Public Works and Government Services Canada, 2009.

Germany as one of only eighty-four planes from Bomber Group 6, all Lancasters from 419, 424, 428, 431, and 434 Squadrons.[56] An additional 444 planes from RAF Bomber Groups 1, 3, and 8 also formed part of the bomber stream that stretched out in front of Bob to what seemed like infinity.[57] Concurrently, 112 Canadian Halifax bombers along with an additional 16 aircraft from Bomber Group 8 were directed to an alternative target at Monheim, an oil refinery north of Cologne.[58]

The flight to and from Dortmund was expected to be four hours shorter than the recent trip to Dresden. This comforted the crew—a shorter trip should provide better odds of returning unharmed, even for a target in the well-defended Ruhr Valley.

Having climbed to an altitude of almost 17,000 feet, Bob set his aircraft on what had become a familiar southeasterly route across the English Channel at its narrowest point to France. Once across, he headed due east and then banked steeply to port, heading almost due north and flying parallel to a Mandrel Screen, which had been employed to block out the German early warning radar system.[59] Then penetrating the Mandrel Screen, Bob banked the plane to starboard and once again headed due east. Just north of Manheim, he made one final turn to port to position WL-D on a northeasterly direction to bring them right to the target. Bob flew at an elevation of 18,000 feet near the bottom of the bomber stream, increasing the possibility of being hit by an errant bomb from above. Although the target was covered with broken stratocumulus clouds, Frank managed to bomb on a concentration of red target indicators.[60] The bomb load was released to deadly effect.[60] Sixteen canisters of incendiaries and one 1,000-pound bomb accurately rained down on the railway yards below.[61] Frank and the crew observed two large explosions just after bomb release with large fires burning below. Frank felt it had been a very good attack.

Bob then continued on the same flight path just long enough to get the requisite photo and then banked the plane for home. Just south of Brussels, he set the plane on a course due west and made a dash for the coast with the four Merlin engines driving the plane forward at 190 miles per hour. They were assisted by a 40-mile-per-hour tail wind. Once across the English Channel, Bob set the plane on a northwesterly course arriving back at Croft at 4:35 AM.[62] Jack's plane had arrived twenty-one minutes earlier.[63] Even with the strong tailwinds WL-D had the dubious honour of being the slowest aircraft in 434 Squadron. The crew was now anxious to hit the sack after debriefing because another trip was expected the next day.

Three Canadian planes were lost out of the eighty-four bombers that attacked Dortmund.[64] An additional nine RAF bombers were lost on this mission.[65] Seven of the twenty-one crew members from the destroyed Canadian bombers were killed, with ten becoming prisoners of war. Four managed to bail out over friendly territory.[66] One additional bomber, WL-P from 434 Squadron, suffered the loss of the wireless operator who was killed by flak even though the plane made it back to Croft.[67] The overall loss rate on this trip for the entire attacking force was 2.2 percent, but was considerably higher amongst Bomber Group 6 at 3.6 percent.[68] Flak played its part but crews also reported heavy enemy aircraft activity over the target area. Within the other Canadian bomber stream, an additional two planes were lost.[69] A post-analysis of photos taken by the Lancaster bombers confirmed that significant damage had been inflicted on the marshalling yards.

By the time Ron finished his debriefing and crawled into bed, the sky had started to lighten, making it difficult to get to sleep. The rising sun was an unfamiliar sight given the bad weather over the last week. Finally, the utter physical exhaustion took over and Ron dropped into a deep sleep—only to be abruptly aroused by Frank shaking his shoulder. It took a few moments for him to become oriented, but then reality set in. Damn, it was time to get up and eat before shuffling over to the mid-afternoon briefing.

Somehow the level of chatter was more subdued than normal. Most of the aircrew were getting weary of the long hauls into Germany and just wanted to get the war over with. When the target was unveiled, one could hear the groans: another trip to Duisburg. For Ron and the crew, this was a target that 434 Squadron had already visited on three previous occasions with the loss of two planes. The primary target would be rail traffic in the local marshalling yards. This mission called for an early evening departure, with Bob releasing the pent-up fury of WL-D's four engines just after 7:00 PM.[70] Once again, the

Crew: F/L R. Henry (1st Pilot), F/O A. Coleman (NAV), F/O F. Welsh (B/A), P/O H. Ward (WOP/AG), F/S A. Thomson (MU/AG), P/O R. Pyves (R/AG), Sgt. J. Casavant (F/E)

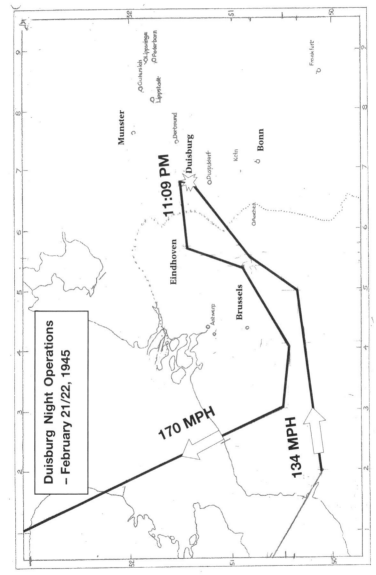

Duisburg Night Operations
– February 21/22, 1945

11:09 PM

170 MPH

134 MPH

Outbound: 534 Miles, Inbound: 482 Miles, Total Distance Flown: 1,015 Miles

434 Squadron: WL-D (KB830), Bomb Load: 1 x 4,000 pounds, 14 cluster bombs

Source: *Night Raid Report No. 844*, Bomber Command, 1945. Reproduced with the permission of the Minister of Public Works and Government Services Canada, 2009.

Canadian bombers rising from seven different air bases in Yorkshire were vectored toward two different targets. A smaller group of eighty-two Lancaster bombers, which included planes from Croft, headed for Duisburg. They were joined by 291 RAF bombers from Bomber Groups 1 and 8.[71] The other 102 Halifax bombers from Bomber Group 6, directed at Worms, merged into a smaller stream of 237 RAF bombers from Groups 4 and 8.[72]

After gaining altitude, Bob joined the bombers streaming almost due south. Over the next four hours Bob would make four course corrections before arriving over the target at an elevation of 19,000 feet. Although haze and cloud covered it, Frank could clearly see the target indicators. As he released the bomb load, which included a deadly mix of one 4,000-pound bomb and seven cluster bombs, the plane jumped upward and Bob had to fight the controls to keep the plane level until the automatic photo was taken.[73] Once through the target area, Bob headed north for ten miles to escape flak. A little over three hours after leaving the target area, Bob brought WL-D in for a soft landing, touching down at 1:59 AM.[74] No Lancaster bombers were lost in this attack, but the Halifax bombers which attacked Worms were not as lucky—six planes were lost, which represented a horrific loss rate of 6.1 percent.[75] At debriefing, Frank reported that the bombing appeared scattered over a large area due to poor visibility. However, fires could be seen glowing through the clouds for one hundred miles as the bombers left the target area.[76]

The base medical officer grounded Ron after the Duisburg mission for a few days. He had a bad cold and desperately took cough medicine and nose spray three times a day to clear it up because he didn't want to miss any trips with the rest of the crew.

As for Frank, he would fly as a spare bomb aimer on February 23 with Flight Lieutenant Hall from 431 Squadron. His mission was to Pforzheim, with the railway marshalling yards the primary target. This was the twenty-eighth mission for Frank and the only time he would fly in combat with a different crew. Fortunately he was flying with a seasoned aircrew on their seventeenth mission—and in WL-D, which he was quite familiar with. Frank's plane left Croft in late afternoon and merged with a small group of thirty-seven Lancasters from Croft and Middleton St. George as part of a much larger RAF bomb raid.[77] Frank's plane carried one 4,000-pound "cookie" as well as seven cluster bombs that were dropped on the target.[78] Strong fighter opposition appeared both over the target and on the first portion of the return leg. Frank arrived back at Croft late in the evening having been airborne for almost seven hours. He was quite relieved that his mission with an unfamiliar crew had been completed without incident.

After seeing Frank off, Ron headed to the mess to pick up his mail, which included a note that Kay had written just one week earlier.

> *Dearest Ronny, Hello dear, I hope that everything is alright with you. I haven't heard from you for awhile, but know that you've been on leave.*
>
> *Gosh Ronny, it looks as if spring is just around the corner. It's strange but you can always tell it's spring or just about by looking around you, the days seem so much sunnier and longer, and the wind just doesn't seem the same but most of all it's by people themselves, they seem happier somehow as if everything is going to be brighter and smoother, and they have something to look forward to.*
>
> *Last year at this time dear you were going away, and I just can't help feeling that this year you'll be home soon, that would be beyond my fondest dreams, but I can't stop hoping somehow.*
>
> *Goodnight for now dear, and take care of yourself always. Love, Kay"*

Ron wrote home on February 26 while still recovering from his cold.

> *"Dear Mom and Dad, I received one of your swell letters yesterday. It was the first one for quite a while; the mail seems to be quite poor lately.*
>
> *Things are about the same as usual here. Well we're right back on the job now after a pretty good leave. We've done two or three ops since we came back off leave, but they were fairly quiet trips. That gives me a total of 29 ops now. I still have a few more trips to go.*

I've just about got used to eating in the officer's mess now. At first I felt kind of strange, but I guess that's understandable, eh! The other day somebody called me sir and I almost looked around to see who he was talking to. Oh well! That's life.

Say Mum, how about sending me a copy of that picture of Bill and me. I think almost everybody except us has seen it.

I was out the other afternoon buying some of my new clothes. I really enjoyed it too. I can certainly use and will greatly appreciate any shirts and socks you can send me mum. Do you know all clothes are rationed and we only get a certain number of coupons?

Well mum and dad I'll say cheerio for now. Your ever loving son, Ronny

Ron returned to active duty on March 1 having missed one bombing mission to Mainz on February 27 in which one Canadian bomber from Leeming crashed on takeoff.[79] Ron's crewmates flew on this mission in Lancaster WL-D. Pilot Officer W. Hannaberg replaced Ron as rear gunner.[80] Fortunately, the defences over the target area were negligible and they returned unscathed.

Ron also missed an aborted mission. Exactly one hour after takeoff on a mission to Neuss, Hal received a recall to base due to poor weather expected over the target area.[81] Bob decided to jettison one 4,000-pound bomb in the North Sea before they returned to base. This move would make for a safer landing as they still had a significant amount of fuel in the tanks.[82] It also allowed them to bring back the balance of the bomb load. Frank later recalled that the "cookie" made an impressive explosion upon impact with the ocean.

Although the Allied armies had made good progress and were almost at the Ruhr, danger still lurked in the skies above Germany. Cities and industrial complexes were still heavily protected by flak and enemy aircraft.

By the end of February the Allies had pushed back desperate German defenders on both the Eastern and Western Fronts. Hitler was now in permanent residence in his bunker in Berlin with the Russian Army less than forty miles from his command headquarters. The last

German forces on the west side of the Rhine River had been recently displaced after an attempt by the Germans to recapture American-held Strasbourg. As more and more of Bomber Command's previous German targets fell into Allied hands, the need for more co-ordination between land and air forces was required to prevent inadvertent "friendly fire" casualties. March was thus shaping up to be a tough one for Bomber Command.

14
Screened

There was a hint of spring in the Yorkshire air on this first day of March. The sun crept over the horizon, quickly dissipating the fine mist that swirled around the entrance to the Officers' Mess. It seemed so strange for Ron not to be able to have breakfast with Bill and Joe anymore. However he could now enjoy the company of his fellow officers, Bob, Frank, Al, and Hal at mealtime. Luckily this kind of segregation did not create a barrier between crew members. When off base, there were many opportunities to eat and drink together in local pubs, which helped cement the warm friendship and camaraderie among the crew. Sharing common experiences, which included intense episodes of danger and relief, as well as embracing the basic goal of survival, were key ingredients that bound the crew together.

After breakfast, Ron sauntered over to the briefing hut where he met up with other aircrew to learn what their target would be for today's daylight raid. It was Mannheim, a mid-sized city at the junction of the Rhine and Neckar Rivers in the southern part of Germany. The aiming point would be the heavily industrialized portion of the city. They didn't have long to wait after the main briefing. They were quickly transported to Lancaster WL-D which now carried one 4,000-pound bomb and twelve canisters. After all pre-flight tests were completed, Bob taxied their kite to the lead position on the runway for takeoff—a first for the crew. WL-D then broke the bonds of gravity at 11:20 AM.[1]

Wing Commander Paul Blackburn, piloting WL-G, personally led this mission.[2] For the sixteenth time, Jack Henry was on the same mission as his brother.[3] He took off eight minutes later.[4]

Not having to battle through turbulence created by aircraft ahead of them was a welcome change for Bob. However, it was odd for Ron because this was his first daytime combat mission in over four months. Somehow night missions provided a greater sense of security when a combination of cloud and darkness shrouded the aircraft.

Now at almost 18,000 feet, the crew of WL-D could make out the bomber stream as it stretched beyond the horizon. Bob merged his aircraft with the other 159 Canadian bombers vectored on Mannheim.[5] Included were twelve other planes from 434 Squadron and another thirteen bombers from 431.[6] An additional 318 aircraft from Bomber Groups 1 and 8 also joined.[7] While on approach to the target, WL-D was hit by flak but luckily did not suffer any serious damage.[8] Al and Frank were also challenged by a cloud-covered target that made the aiming point very difficult to locate. Their training paid off when Frank bombed on blue smoke puffs as directed by the Master Bomber, releasing his lethal load at 3:19 PM.[9] Bob then banked the Lancaster into a sharp turn to head for home. This trip had required quite a deep penetration into Germany. The result was a near eight-hour round trip. Much to Bob's relief, Jack's plane landed just six minutes later.[10] Flying on the same mission never got easier, especially knowing that both of them could be lost to their parents at the same time. Overall, though, it had been a good trip. Three Lancaster bombers were lost, but none from Bomber Group 6, although the wireless operator in WL-R had been wounded by flak.[11] For Ron and the crew this was their thirtieth trip; it should have put them across the finish line.

With the Allied armies pushing hard on both the Western and Eastern Fronts, there was increasing urgency for the bombers based in England to provide tactical support to soften up the enemy. The intensity and frequency of the bomber attacks was building to a crescendo. In order to make up for the missed trip due to illness, Ron awakened just after 1:30 AM and went over to the briefing hut. It was a freezing night but with a bright full moon. For Ron, the idea of not flying with his regular crew left him uneasy; he had only flown combat

with that one crew—and he had made it back safely on thirty consecutive trips. All crewmen tended to be superstitious and would go
to extremes not to change routines. And they specifically did not want
to change crews. Nevetheless, at briefing Ron discovered he would
be flying with a relatively inexperienced crew that had only eleven
trips under their belts.[12] If he had his wish, Ron would have picked
Jack and his crew, who were now on their twenty-seventh mission
together.[13]

The target this time was Cologne, which Ron had visited on three
previous occasions.[14] Cologne had become a more critical target; the
American 1st Army was pressing its attack into the outskirts so it could
occupy the heavily industrialized Ruhr Valley. Flying as mid-upper
gunner for the first time, Ron departed from Croft in Lancaster WL-H
just as the sun started to warm up the chilly morning air.[15] The mid-
upper gunner position presented a unique experience for Ron since
he didn't feel the same isolation and loneliness there that he did at
the tail end of the plane.

On the way to the target, the rear turret became unserviceable, so
his position as mid-upper gunner became even more critical.[16] This
mission was a maximum effort with 703 aircraft scheduled to attack
Cologne.[17] Included were 182 planes from 13 Canadian squadrons.[18]
They experienced clear weather all the way to the target and no enemy aircraft were reported in the area, although a number of bombers
were damaged by light to moderate flak in the run in to the target. Flying Officer R. Prime approached the target at an elevation of 19,000
feet. The bomb aimer, Flight Sergeant A. McLeod, released the bomb
load at 10:12 AM, after visually identifying the target.[19] This would be
the last attack by Bomber Command on Cologne—and once again
the ancient Cologne Cathedral was spared from total destruction.
One bomber from 408 Squadron did not return from the mission,
with most of the crew bailing out and ending up prisoners of war.[20]
Nevertheless, Cologne would be captured by the American Army just
four days later. After debriefing, Ron met up with a number of his
regular crew, including Bob, who was waiting for his brother's safe
return. When Jack's plane did not return to Croft, Bob became very
concerned. Due to both inoperable hydraulics and an unserviceable

electrical system, Jack had been forced to make an emergency landing at Woodbridge, the same airfield where his brother had landed on November 1, 1944, when they had lost an engine.[21] After landing, Jack quickly sent off a message to Bob saying he had made it back safely.

For Ron, it was not only his first but also his only combat trip with an unfamiliar crew. With two missions under his belt in a little over thirty hours, Ron received a forty-eight-hour break from combat. But he still had to attend a parade ceremony where Air Commodore R.C. Simon of Bomber Group 6 presented the bombing efficiency trophy to Wing Commander Paul Blackburn, who accepted it on behalf of the entire squadron.[22]

Early in the morning of March 4, Croft was rudely awakened by cannon fire from several Messerschmit Me-109s which had followed a group of returning Halifax bombers that were almost out of fuel.[23] The runway lights had just been turned on. One distressed Halifax was shot down in the meleé but the crew managed to bail out.[24] One intruder then turned his attention to the base, letting loose with several bursts of cannon fire. Luckily no injuries were sustained.[25] This was a stark reminder that even at Croft, nobody could assume that they were safe from enemy attack. Indeed, the geography of the European theatre of war was fairly tight. Thankfully, this was the first and only time that Ron experienced an enemy attack at Croft.

On Sunday morning March 5, Ron once again flew in Lancaster WL-D with his regular crew on a short training exercise over the English countryside. They returned just before noon. Fortunately, they were not put on active combat duty and missed a tragic attack on Chemnitz where Bomber Group 6 suffered horrific losses due to severe icing problems during takeoff, enemy flak, and fighter plane activity. Unfortunately, Hal Ward, the wireless operator, was put on the battle order for the Chemnitz raid. He had flown on fewer missions than his regular crewmates and needed to catch up. If not, the entire crew would have to fly extra missions to compensate for Hal.

Hal, like all the crew, did not like to fly with others if avoidable. At the briefing, Hal was assigned to fly with Pilot Officer J. Kitchen in WL-L (for "Love").[26] They achieved liftoff at 4:35 PM.[27] Nine other aircraft from Bomber Group 6 were not so lucky, crashing shortly after takeoff due to severe icing.[28] The toll included three Halifaxes from 426 Squadron.[29] The outward-bound trip to Chemnitz remained uneventful until they arrived in the target area, with clouds reaching as high as 7,000 feet.[30] Between the clouds Hal could see German and Russian artillery firing at each other. One bomber behind WL-L was hit by an artillery shell, blowing its nose cone off. Quickly afterward at least one crew member jumped out from the front of that airplane. The rest of the crew were lost as the bomber plummeted to the ground in a swirl of black smoke and flames. As WL-L released its bomb load a Junkers Ju-88 twin-engine night fighter attacked a Halifax within sight and shot it down.[31] (The destroyed plane was most likely Halifax OW-J from 426 Squadron flown by F/Lt. J. Kirkpatrick with only one member of the crew surviving.)[32] The fatally damaged Halifax then struck the tail end of Hal's plane, damaging the rear turret so it would no longer rotate.[33] Before the rear gunner had even recovered from the shock, the Ju-88 turned its attention on WL-L. The enemy plane attacked from the rear starboard position with the rear gunner, F/Sgt. Riggs, first seeing the German fighter at a distance of 1,500 feet.[34] He yelled to the pilot to corkscrew to starboard.[35] As WL-L started into a steep dive, both the rear gunner and mid-upper gunner, Flight Sergeant Heisler, both opened fire at a range of 1,200 feet. Each gunner fired off four hundred rounds at the Ju-88, with the fighter returning in kind.[36] Although both gunners claimed to have hit the Ju-88 (which broke off its attack at nine hundred feet), serious damage had already been inflicted on Hal's plane. Miraculously, none of the crew had been hit.[37] The bomber sustained damage to the starboard elevators and undercarriage as well as the hydraulic systems, and although one of the gas tanks was holed, it didn't catch fire, as WL-L had been outfitted with self-sealing tanks.[38]

Pilot Officer J. Kitchen realized that his kite had been badly mauled. He would need to reach the closest emergency airfield on the return leg of the journey. The navigator provided directions to Carnaby on the coast of East Yorkshire. Carnaby was an emergency RAF airfield with an extra-large runway that could accommodate a bomber in distress.

When Hal's plane approached the area where they expected the base to be, there was nothing but blackness below.[39] With just enough fuel to make one attempt at landing, Hal in desperation fired off a flare down the flare chute, a covered opening located on the floor of the Lancaster just forward of the mid-gunner station.[40] To the entire crew's relief the emergency runway lights immediately blinked on in front of them, which allowed the pilot to make a superb landing.[41] Luckily for Hal, he had flown with an experienced aircrew who had already been on fourteen missions.[42] Later, the ground crew showed Hal an 88-millimetre shell they found in the nose cone.[43] Fortunately it was a dud. If it had exploded, the front of the bomber would have been torn apart, killing the pilot, flight engineer, and bomb aimer and, most likely, the rest of the crew. Hal could clearly remember this trip over sixty years later.

In total, nineteen planes were lost or severely damaged on this one effort, including SE-G from 431 Squadron flown by F/O S.K. Reid, lost over Germany with all crew killed.[44] It was their seventh trip.[45] Jack had left Croft just one minute before SE-G so was likely close to SE-G when it went down. An additional plane from 434 Squadron crashed on return but with no crew seriously hurt.[46] The loss of 19 out of 166 planes represented a horrific loss rate of 11.4 percent.[47] Even at this late stage in the war there was no guarantee that one would make it safely through a tour of duty. It remained dangerous times. And it was getting more dangerous every day as the German forces tenaciously defended what was left of their homeland.

On Tuesday March 7, Ron and the crew were put back on the active duty roster. They attended a 2:00 PM briefing and were surprised that the scheduled evening attack would be on a Junkers aircraft plant and marshalling yards in Dessau. In World War II, Dessau was a mid-sized town only sixty-five miles southwest of Berlin at the junction of the Elbe and Mulde Rivers. Ron knew this would be a long trip, but at least it would be in Lancaster WL-D—and with his own crewmates. An hour after the briefing the crew assembled and took a bus out to their aircraft and by 4:00 PM were ready for the trip. Bob started up the four engines and taxied to the dispersal point where he ended up at the head of the lineup waiting clearance from the

Crew: F/L R. Henry (1st Pilot), F/O A. Coleman (NAV), P/O F. Welsh (B/A), P/O H. Ward (WOP/AG), F/Sgt. A. Thomson (MU/AG), P/O R. Pyves (R/AG), Sgt. J. Casavant (F/E)

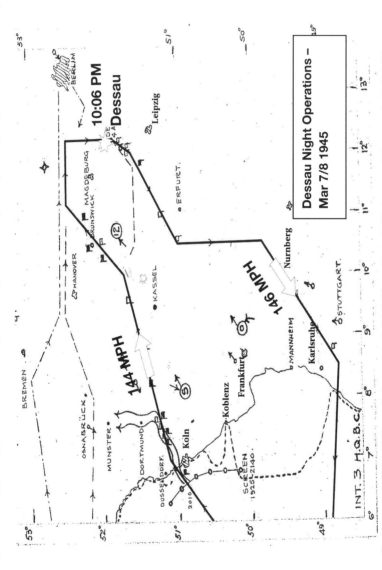

10:06 PM
Dessau

146 MPH

144 MPH

Dessau Night Operations –
Mar 7/8 1945

Outbound: 826 Miles, Inbound: 647 Miles, Total Distance Flown: 1,473 Miles

434 Squadron: WL-D (KB830), Bomb Load: 1 x 1,000, pounds, 14 Cluster Bombs

Source: *Night Raid Report No. 858*, Bomber Command, 1945. Reproduced with the permission of the Minister of Public Works and Government Services Canada, 2009.

control tower. Even with light rain, the visibility at takeoff remained fairly good, with the cloud base at 2,000 feet. With the release of its brakes WL-D careened down the runway and in less than a minute, became airborne and started to climb at a rate of almost 900 feet per minute. All the Lancasters from Bomber Group 6 that lifted off from Middleton St. George, Skipton-on-Swale, and Croft had a very long flight ahead of them. The 81 Lancasters from Bomber Group 6 were joined by an additional 450 aircraft from RAF bases in the south.[48] An additional 99 Halifax bombers from Bomber Group 6 were vectored to Hemmingstedt and were joined by an additional 157 aircraft from Bomber Groups 4 and 8.[49]

After gaining altitude, Bob merged into the bomber stream which headed almost due south. He remained on this course for just over 380 miles before he crossed the English coast and turned to port, heading easterly into France and then Germany. This leg of the journey stretched for 250 miles before their next turning point, midway between Düsseldorf and Köln, heavily defended cities to avoid. As Bob made a slight course correction to starboard at the turning point, all the crew kept a lookout for potential enemy aircraft. Less than an hour later, Al instructed Bob to turn forty-five degrees to port to set them on a northeasterly direction. Bob maintained this course for sixty-five miles, which placed them forty-three miles north of Dessau. At the next turning point Bob banked WL-D sharply to starboard, setting the plane on a course directly in line with Berlin. When they were within thirty miles of the city, one of the most feared and heavily defended areas in Germany, the bomber stream made a ninety degree turn to starboard to head due south, right into Dessau. This would be the closest Ron would ever fly to Berlin. In the Battle of Berlin—from November 1943 through March 1944—hundreds of planes from Bomber Command had been lost there, including ten bombers from 434 Squadron.[50]

The planes were greeted by both flak and enemy aircraft over the target area with several sightings of Ju-88s and a Focke-Wulf Fw 190 fighter. WL-D made the final approach to Dessau at an elevation of 15,000 feet.[51] With the target area partly obscured by cloud, Frank aimed at the red and green ground target indicators and released his bomb load of one 1,000-pound bomb and fourteen cluster bombs.[52] Although Frank thought the attack scattered, he could see many fires and explosions below. Right then, having already flown over eight hundred miles just to get to the target, flight engineer Joe Casavant informed Bob of a possible fuel shortage. Bob requested alternative landing bases from Al. Based on Al's input, Bob made a decision to head for Thorney Isle on the south coast of England just east of Portsmouth. This RAF Coastal Command air base would provide a safe refuge for fourteen planes from 434 Squadron by morning.[53]

As soon as Bob took over the aircraft after the photoflash, he banked the plane slightly to starboard and headed southwest for just over thirty minutes. As he set WL-D on a course due south he could still see fires from Dessau on the horizon. After flying on this course for twenty-five minutes, the navigator gave him directions to turn forty-five degrees to starboard and head in a southwesterly direction that would take them just north of Stuttgart. Then Bob turned WL-D forty-five degrees to starboard, placing them on a course due west toward England. They were now dangerously low on gas.

The crew had already travelled over one thousand miles, with more than five hundred miles of additional flying needed to reach the safety of Thorney Isle. Joe kept an ever-watchful eye on the fuel gauges and each engine's performance to try to minimize fuel consumption. At their current speed of 146 miles per hour the four Merlin engines were consuming 1.2 gallons for each mile flown. Feeling quite relieved they finally touched down, having been airborne for just over ten hours. For the second time in the last four missions, WL-D once again ranked the slowest aircraft to make the return trip.[54] This concerned Ron and the rest of the crew.

Out of the eighty-two Lancaster bombers from Bomber Group 6 that had participated in the attack, three planes had been lost but none from Croft.[55] This represented a considerable loss rate of 3.7 percent. Next day, Bob flew the plane and crew 220 miles back to Croft on a trip of almost one and a half hours.[56]

The following day fifteen aircraft from 434 Squadron were scheduled for an operation.[57] Ron had risen early, expecting to be on duty, but the mission was cancelled.[58] So he headed over to the Officers'

Mess to pick up his mail. He was ecstatic to receive a letter from Kay, postmarked March 2, in which she wrote,

> *Dearest Ronny, Do you know dear you're guilty of something pretty serious, making me so wonderfully happy when I receive your letter, I hadn't heard from you for awhile and just couldn't help wishing for news from you, and after reading that letter I was on top of the world.*
>
> *I'm glad Ron that you received your commission, you worked every bit for it and you must feel very proud, I know dear that I am very proud of you, one thing about you Ron is that you are determined and know what you want of life and you will be as wonderful a Pilot Officer as you were a Flight Sergeant.*
>
> *I'm sorry dear that they've changed the system of "ops"; I'll have to admit that I was inwardly hoping that you would be coming home soon; but let's hope it won't be too long before we keep the date we made nearly a year ago.*
>
> *You can feel spring in the air in Montreal now, it's so much nicer out it's a pleasure.*
>
> *Well dear, I'll say goodnight to you for now, but just for a little while. Take care of yourself and hurry home. All my love always, Kay*

On March 11, both 431 and 434 Squadrons were involved in a successful attack on Essen involving 186 bombers from Bomber Group 6, in which almost two million pounds of high explosives were dropped.[59] The total bomber force consisted of 1,079 with three Lancasters lost, including one plane from 431 Squadron flown by Wing Commander R. Davenport, an experienced pilot, and WL-Y, flown by F/Lt. R. Fern, who had completed twelve previous missions.[60] Tragically, just one of the crew from WL-Y managed to escape the downed aircraft.[61] He was soon a POW.

Things were moving at a pace, with Ron and the crew selected to participate in an early daylight attack on Dortmund the next day. It was a key transportation hub with a canal that linked the city to the North Sea. It was also a steel town, with many coal mines in the vicinity. Ron prepared himself for his thirty-third operation, but the pressure of combat duty had now manifested itself in a nervous trembling of his hands, which he controlled with some difficulty. As he neared the end of his tour, he found it more difficult to remain focused and was less and less keen to fly on upcoming missions.

Ron sat nervously in his cramped turret waiting for start-up of the four Merlin engines, waiting for that familiar smell of oil and exhaust fumes. Ron could feel the familiar shudder of their ship as the wheels lifted up off the blackened tarmac and soon he was up amidst the bomber stream.

In addition to the 192 Canadian bombers, a huge fleet of 916 bombers from RAF was also simultaneously targeted to Dortmund.[62] The bomber stream experienced moderate flak and few enemy aircraft were sighted over the target. With clouds topping out at 8,000 feet, even in daylight an accurate visual of the target could not be achieved. So Frank released their 12,000 pounds of explosives on blue smoke puffs.[63] He felt the bombing had been very concentrated, with large quantities of brown smoke mushrooming above the clouds to a height of over 8,000 feet.[64] Over 4,800 tons of high explosives were dropped, causing severe damage below.[65] Bob landed WL-D at Croft at 7:15 PM.[66] Two bombers from the RAF were lost.[67]

On March 14, fifteen aircraft from 434 Squadron participated in an attack on Zweibrucken in which there were no losses.[68] The following day, while Ron and his crewmates were stood down, fifteen bombers from 434 participated in a raid on Hagen in which 7 of 142 Canadian planes were lost, including WL-J, flown by Flight Officer J. Stewart, and SE-K, flown by F/L R.R. Haw.[69] WL-J had been flown by a rookie crew with just four missions under their belt while the crew in SE-K was, sadly, on their thirty-fifth trip, which would have completed their tour of duty.[70] This loss rate of 4.9 percent was quite staggering.

On St Patrick's Day, the crew was involved in an air test with Lancaster WL-D. This involved two hours of flight over rural England. The patchwork green passing below reminded Ron of Kay and the luck of the Irish, which hopefully would rub off and bring him safely home.

On March 18, Ron found some quiet time and, enjoying the first warmth of the sun, sat outside to pen a quick note to Kay.

Dearest Kay, How are you dear?

I got those five records mum sent me. The songs she sent are really swell, especially 'An Hour Never Passes.' It has lovely words, lovely because they are so true dear, you are beside me darling everywhere I go and <u>always</u> in my thoughts.

We're quite the old operational crew around the station now with 33 ops done and 2 more to do. When you get that many in you can get away with things you wouldn't even think of trying before. I never bother getting up before noon now, unless there are ops on. What a life eh! After our next two ops we're what they call screened, meaning you're finished operational flying. That's when the whole crew goes out and has a big celebration and sort of paints the nearest towns red.

Well darling I'll say goodnight now with all my love and kisses for you always, Ronny

On March 20, Ron and the crew were scheduled to participate on their second to last mission the next morning. It would also be the thirty-second mission for Jack and his crew.[71] The target was identified as the oil refinery complex at Heide in northern Germany near the Danish border. With the exception of the attack on the submarine pens at Bergen over five months ago, this would be the most northern target that the crew would attack. For this trip Ron and the crew were assigned Lancaster WL-A (for "Able"), the first time in the last fifteen missions that they would not fly in WL-D.[72] It was with some trepidation then that the crew lifted off from Croft.

Bob and the crew set out on a course almost due north and climbed to 16,000 feet. They worried that after thirty-three missions their luck might just run out now. Once they reached the English coast, Bob turned his ship to starboard and headed due east across the North Sea. After travelling 216 miles, the bomber stream took a southeasterly course skirting the German coastline just north of Wilmshaven and Hamburg. Bob maintained this line for less than thirty minutes before turning to port where they approached the target at 18,000 feet. With fuel becoming even more critical to the German Panzer divisions and air force, several enemy fighter planes vigorously protected the oil refinery. With thin clouds rising as high as 6,000 feet, Frank released his bomb load using the red and green target indicators.[73]

Crew: F/L R. Henry (1ˢᵗ Pilot), F/O A. Coleman (NAV), P/O F. Welsh (B/A), P/O H. Ward (WOP/AG), Sgt. A. Thomson (MU/AG), P/O R. Pyves (R/AG), Sgt. J. Casavant (F/E)

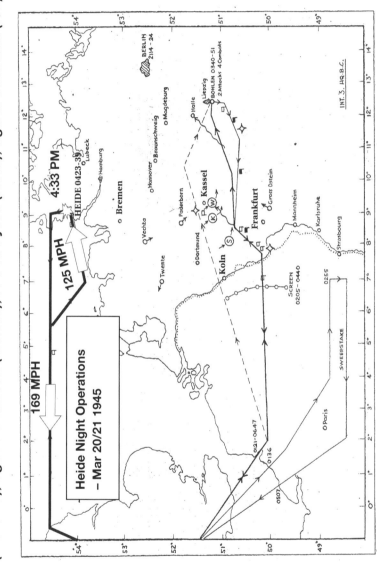

4:33 PM

125 MPH

169 MPH

Heide Night Operations
– Mar 20/21 1945

Outbound: 381 Miles, Inbound: 380 Miles, Total Distance Flown: 761 Miles

434 Squadron: WL-A (KB825), Bomb Load: 1 x 4,000, 16 x 500 pounds

Source: *Night Raid Report No. 871*, Bomber Command, 1945. Reproduced with the permission of the Minister of Public Works and Government Services Canada, 2009.

He could see many oil fires following the blast of their 4,000-pound cookie, with black smoke rising as high as 1,000 feet.[74] For Frank the attack was very concentrated, with fires from the target area seen for at least fifty miles.

After bomb release, Bob quickly banked the plane to port to avoid the flak, which rose as high as 12,000 feet. The strike by 110 Lancaster bombers from Bomber Group 6, with an additional 56 planes from Bomber Groups 1 and 8, inflicted significant damage on the primary target.[75] Ron noted "Good Attack" in his log book. Bob landed back at Croft at 7:14 AM, having flown just over 760 miles.[76] One bomber was lost on this mission. All said, this would be the crew's last nighttime bombing raid and the last mission that included both Bob and Jack.

***

On March 22, the crew anxiously attended the 8:00 AM main briefing for what would finally be their last combat mission. The target: the railway yards at Hildesheim. This ancient city was founded in the ninth century and was eighteen miles southeast of Hannover, a city the crew visited in early January. This day, all Ron's regular crew were slated to fly in their favourite ship, WL-D, which would provide a fitting ending. The crew was more nervous than usual, given that they expected to be screened at the end of this mission. It was then that Lancaster WL-F, right in front of them, got caught in a crosswind during takeoff. It swung wildly just before it became airborne and as the plane ran off the runway, its undercarriage collapsed and one of the engines caught fire; it could not be extinguished.[77] All the WL-F crew escaped safely and the pilots of the seven planes that had not yet lifted off scrambled to put some distance between their kites and the burning aircraft.[78] Bob yelled at the crew through the intercom to prepare to abandon ship once he moved WL-D a safe distance from the crippled aircraft, which had been so close only seconds earlier. The crew then jumped through the escape hatches and started to run for their lives, not knowing when the fire on WL-F might set off the bomb load. It was carrying one 4,000-pound bomb and 1,500 four-pound incendiary bombs.[79] They were familiar with WL-F as they had used this plane for an H2S cross-country exercise on December 11. Just minutes later, WL-F and its full bomb load blew up leaving a huge crater by the side of the runway.[80] A photo taken by the station photographer shows a scene that looks like a nuclear bomb had just gone off; and sitting forlornly in the foreground of the mushroom-shaped cloud in the photo was Lancaster WL-D.

Ron and the rest of the crew were extremely disappointed that they had not been able to takeoff on what should have been their last trip, but were thankful they were able to get clear of the explosion and no crew had been injured. That said, two of the eighty Canadian Lancasters which participated in the Hildesheim raid were lost, including SE-Y, flown by F/L J.P. Duggan from 431 Squadron.[81] He was on his thirty-second mission.[82]

The crew now had to wait another forty-eight hours before their last mission became available. Ron found it difficult to eat and keep his food down during the wait. Like their first combat mission so many months ago, the crew hoped for a soft target, especially given what had just happened on the runway at Croft.

The next target was officially unveiled at an 11:00 AM briefing on March 24. They knew right away that it would not be a milk run. The target, a benzol plant in Bottrop, deep in the Ruhr just ten miles southwest of Duisburg, would be a modest effort with seventy-five Lancaster bombers from Bomber Group 6.[83] This daylight raid included ten aircraft from 434 Squadron and an additional 110 aircraft from Bomber Groups 1 and 8.[84] At least this last trip would be in WL-D, which miraculously had escaped damage on the runway just two days earlier. The crew was transported out to their ship where pre-flight checks were very diligently completed and the crew, for one last time, tested the intercom system with a quiet rendition of "Mairsy Doates." For the third time in March Bob's plane would be the first to take off. They lifted off at 12:48 PM and climbed to join the bomber stream, but this day the sky somehow seemed clearer and brighter than normal.[85] After three hours of flight at an elevation of 16,800 feet, Frank took command of the plane for the last time and gave Bob the final instructions to make sure that this last bomb load would be smack on target. Their final payload consisted of twelve 1,000-pound bombs, one 500-pound bomb, and as a final token, one brick with a note to Hitler attached to it.[86] When Bob asked Frank what he wrote, he replied, "He wished Hitler well in his new life."[87] With a shout of "Bombs & Brick Away" from Frank, Bob yelled "Let's get the hell out of here before Hitler reads our note. Beers are on me when we get back to base." He then turned WL-D for home. Oily black smoke could be seen rising as high as 2,000 feet over the target area.[88]

The elated crew struggled to maintain their focus on the return leg. Just prior to landing, Bob dove toward the control tower, veering off just before impact. A number of the ground crew could be seen diving for the dirt as WL-D headed directly toward them. Several onboard, including Ron, were startled by Bob's shenanigans, which were totally out of character. But Bob had been planning this manoeuvre for some time. Buzzing the control tower was forbidden except when crews completed their tour of duty. All said they finally touched down at Croft at 6:53 PM.[89] No planes were lost on their last mission. Once safely on the ground, the crew circled WL-D, giving the old dog a few pats before they boarded their transport over to the debriefing hut.

The entire crew felt the tremendous weight lifting from their shoulders as the realization set in that, at least for now, their war was over. This good news became even better when they remembered that there was still time to get to the local pub before closing as they wouldn't be flying again for some time, if ever. Earlier, Hal had received a bottle of Canadian rye mailed to him in a loaf of bread from his wife, which he shared with the crew to toast their successful tour of duty.[90] That same day, the crew were officially screened from duty and awarded a ten-day personal leave. As for WL-D, it would go on to be flown for an additional nine combat missions by different crews, with its final mission to Wangerooge, Germany, on April 25, 1945.[91]

The 434 Squadron Operational Records noted that Flight Lieutenant Bob Henry had completed thirty-six trips, accumulating 137 points; followed by Pilot Officer Ron Pyves with thirty-five trips and 133 points; Flight Sergeant Bill Thomson with thirty-five trips and 133 points; Sergeant Joe Casavant with thirty-five trips and 133 points; Flying Officer Frank Welsh with thirty-four trips and 130 points; Flying Officer Alan Coleman with thirty-four trips and 130 points; and Pilot Officer Hal Ward with thirty-three trips and 125 points. Since the start of Ron's flying career, he had logged just over 441 hours of flying time, which included 212 combat hours over Germany, France, and Norway.[92]

While flying with 434 Squadron at Croft since September 13, 1944, Ron had experienced the loss of twelve out of twenty-five planes in his squadron, including fifty-three crew killed and twenty-three crew who were taken prisoners of war.[93] For 431 and 434 Squadrons combined, the loss of twenty-five out of forty planes and 117 crew killed represented a loss rate of 62 percent of the base's effective aircraft over the last six months.[94] Although the losses at Croft were very high, they were not as catastrophic as those suffered in the two squadrons based at Middleton St. George, the most northerly of the Bomber Group 6 airfields. This air base suffered a loss of 36 planes and 180 crew killed over the same time period.[95]

While the crew were on leave, 434 Squadron lost another crew while on a bombing mission to Hamburg, when WL-W, flown by Flight Officer G. Haliburton on his seventh combat mission, disappeared without a trace.[96] This would to be the last crew lost by 434 Squadron while on combat operations.[97] Hal had just flown with them ten days earlier. Bob's brother Jack was luckier; this attack on Hamburg was his last mission before he too was finally screened.

On March 26, Ron cabled Kay:

"Have finished tour of ops Love Ronald Pyves".

It seemed Ron's war was finally over.

***

On April 14, Bill, the mid-upper gunner, received his well-deserved promotion to Warrant Officer Second Class and was posted out five days later to a repatriation depot.[98] Bill stayed on in England to marry his English girlfriend, Edna Weeks. Hal was assigned to the adjutant's office at Croft and returned to Canada in August 1945. Frank, the bomb aimer, was transferred to Heavy Conversion Unit No. 1659 at Topcliffe as an instructor and didn't return to Canada until late 1945.

On April 19, Joe received his promotion to Flight Sergeant and returned to Canada in late June 1945. On May 10, Al, the navigator, was posted out from Croft to Heavy Conversion Unit No. 1666 in North Yorkshire as an instructor. He was seriously injured in a training flight in November 1945 when his fog-shrouded Lancaster crashed into a hill in the Yorkshire Dales. He didn't return to Canada until 1946. On April 19, Bob, the pilot, was moved to a repatriation depot in Warrington, England, enroute to Canada for a thirty-day personal leave. He had volunteered to fly a second tour. Ron also volunteered for "Tiger Force," an initiative to utilize experienced Canadian bomber crews in the Pacific Theatre. He too would be repatriated back to Canada before joining the Force.

***

While Ron looked forward to going home, he also had time to fully reflect on his tour of duty. Over Ron's 212 combat hours and 35 missions, the crew dropped over 260,000 pounds of high explosives and almost 9,000 incendiary bombs on the enemy. He could still see the endless stream of bombers and the bright burning fires below.

Ron's own survival seemed incredible considering the enemy fighter attacks, his guns jamming, the hung-up bomb, the coning by enemy searchlights, the loss of hydraulics, the endless flak, the wayward bomb that vaporized another plane, the vicissitudes of weather, and the ever-present dangers of mechanical failure and human error.

Yet through it all, he'd fallen in love with a woman whom he had dated only three times before. And it was her letters that provided his anchor of sanity in a world gone mad. She had become his true love and now, he was going home.

(1)

F/S P. HENRY

COMBAT REPORT PRO-FORMAN

1. Date : 27.11.44   Target: NEUSS   Group :   No.6   Squadron: No. 434
2. Aircraft type & mark : Halifax III   A/C Letter & Serial No. "D" M2435
3. Special Equipment carried : FISHPOND
   Say whether serviceable,u/s, or not used at time of combat ? U/S
4. Time: 19.33 Height: 15,000 ft. Heading: 231'T Position : ~~540WT (GERM~~ 50.43N - 0615E
5. Homeward and on Track.
6. Weather: Full Moon - Cloud below.
7. Searchlight activity, flares, flak, etc., prior to or during combat ? None
8. What was first warning ? Visual
9. Which equipment warned) N.A. Immediate action taken? Corkscrew Port.
10. If the first warning was not on Special equipment, did it warn later ? N.A.
11. First visual : range 300 yds. position: ASTERN/LEVEL against DARK SKY.
12. Which member of crew obtained first visual ? Rear Gunner
13. Type of E.A. ? 109   No. 1   What lights on E/A ? None
14. Direction of attack or Approach ? Dead Astern *below*
15. Direction of breakaway of E.A. ? Port Quarter down   Range ?   200 yds.
16. What combat manoeuvre was taken ? Corkscrew Port.
17. Did fighter fire ? No
18. Who opened fire first ? R/AG

19.

	REAR GUNNER	M.U. GUNNER
Name	R209215 SGT Thomson,A.	SGT Pyves,R.
Rounds fired	250 rounds	-
Opening range	250 yards	-
Closing range	200 yards	-
Stoppages	No. 2 Positions - 4 Guns	-
Training A.G.S.	No. 9 B&G School	No. 9 B&G School
O.T.U. & H.C.U.'s	22 O.T.U. & 1659 CU	22 O.T.U. & 1659 CU

20. Were you able to clear stoppages ? Yes
21. Which crew position was searching away from the attack ? M/U Gunner
    Other A/C seen ? None
22. Loss of height during the attack ? Bomber descending
23. Mechanical defects or damage previously sustained affecting combat ? None
24. Damage to Bomber ? None
25. Casualties to Crew ? None
26. Damage to fighter ? None
27. No claims.

F/L A.D. Lewis
Squadron Gunnery Leader
No. 434 Squadron (R.C.A.F.).

Combat report filed by Ron Pyves and Bill Thomson at debriefing due to attack by enemy aircraft on November 27, 1944 in mission to Neuss, Germany. Note that positions of rear air gunner and mid-upper gunner have been inadvertently reversed.

© National Defence. Reproduced with the permission of the Minister of Public Works and Government Services Canada 2009.
Source: National Defence collection/RG24-E-7, Operations Record Book, 434 Squadron, Microfilm reel C-12310

COMBAT REPORT PRO-FORMA

(Fill in for all "Attacks" and "Combats".)

F/L R. HENRY

1. Date: 2.12.44   Target: Hagen   Group: 6   Squadron: 434
2. Aircraft type & mark: Halifax III   A/C letter & Serial No. "D" MZ435
3. Special Equipment carried: Visual Monica, Fishpond
   Operator: Trained
4. Time: 20.58   Height: 17.00   Heading: 0.90   Position(Lat.& Long)5135N
                                                                    0700E
5. Outward, Homeward. Off track.
6. Weather: Vis Good, 10/10 cloud below. Moon on starboard ·
7. Searchlights: Nil   No flares.   Moderate-Heavy flak.
8. What was first warning? - Visual
9. Which equipment warned? VISUAL Immediate action taken? Corkscrew Port
10. If the first warning was not on special equipment, did it warn later? N.·
11. First Visual; range: 400 yds;   position ASTERN. Below against Dark sky·
12. Which member of crew obtained first visual? Rear Gunner.
13. Type of E.A. Single.What lights on E/A: None
14. Direction of Attack or Approach: Dead astern below
15. Direction of breakaway of E.A.: Below   Range: 300 yds.
16. What combat manoeuvre was taken? Cork screw port.
17. Did fighter Fire? : No.
18. Who opened fire first? : Rear Gunner.
19.
        Rear Gunner
    Name   Pyves,R.L. Sgt.   R.219049
    Rounds fired: 200
    Opening range: 400 yds
    Closing range: 300 yds.
    Stoppages: None
    Training A.G.S.   No. 9 B.& G., Mont Joli
    O.T.U. & H.C.U. :   22 O.T.U.   1659 C.U.

20. Were you able to clear stoppages?   N/A
21. Which crew position was searching away from the attack, or in the
    dark part of the sky? Mid Upper   Other A/C seen: No.
22. Los of height during the attack: Nil
23. Mechanical defects or damage previously sustained affecting combat: Nil.
24. Damage to bomber: Nil.
25. Casualties to crew: Nil.
26. Damage to fighter: None seen.
27. Fighter claimed Destroyed/Probably destroyed/Damaged: Nil

                    (A.D.LEWIS) F/Lt.

                    Gunnery Leader,
                    No.434 Squadron (R.C.A.F.).

Combat report filed by Ron Pyves at debriefing due to attack by enemy aircraft on
December 2, 1944 in mission to Hagen, Germany.

© National Defence. Reproduced with the permission of the Minister of Public Works and Government
Services Canada (2009)
Source: National Defence collection/RG24-E-7, Operations Record Book, 434 Squadron, Microfilm
reel C-12310

Jack and Bob Henry at Croft between combat missions. Jack was a pilot with 431 Squadron while his younger brother Bob was a pilot with 434 Squadron. Source: Library and Archives Canada/National Defence collection/Accession 2008-0377- PL - 43116.

Devastation in Dresden after the attacks on February 13/14, 1945. Copyright Deutshe Fotothek. Photographer Blick vom Rathausturm

On March 22, 1945, in what should have been Ron and his crewmates' last mission, the bomber directly in front of their plane slid off the tarmac, which resulted in a broken undercarriage and a resultant fire and explosion. Prior to the explosion Ron and the crew evacuated their plane, WL-D, which can be seen in the foreground. Source: Library and Archives Canada/National Defence collection/Accession 2008-0377-PL -44939.

Photo taken at Taylor Studios in Darlington, Yorkshire, shortly after the crew finished their tour of duty in March 1945. In front row from left to right is Bob Henry, Al Coleman, and Frank Welsh. In back row from left to right is Hal Ward, Joe Casavant, Bill Thomson, and Ron Pyves.

December 17th, 1944.

Dearest Ronny,

Hello dear, I hope this letter reaches you in time to send you my love at Christmas Ronny, but if I'm too late I hope you had a Merry one. Are you receiving my letters O.K., I hope so, yours are coming through fine dear, & how I love every one of them too.

Well Ronny, this past week or so we've had enough snow for the whole darn world to have a White Xmas, you'd really be amazed at your Montreal. Phil & a few of the gang from work are going up to Morin Heights skiing, weekend following New Years, I've only been up there once, but if I remember right I think you liked it up there didn't you? I hope the hills aren't too steep.

Your Mom called me up just the other day as she saw a picture of you & Bill in the Herald, one taken a while back after your seventh "Op," you & Bill are certainly hitting the news. Gosh Ron there's plenty of excitement in the air these days, everyone looking forward to celebrations and all, but with all the rushing & confusion dear, I just can't help thinking how it would be if you were here Ron, that would be wonderful. I hope that it won't be long before we get our wishes fulfilled.

Jim is still working hard in Sherbrooke, he really likes it there a lot. Confidentially we never thought that he'd like it so much, he's coming in next Saturday for Christmas, gosh I'm always so glad so see him too.

The other evening Phil & I went to see "Kismet" with Ronald Colman & Marlene Dietrich, it was pretty good, but really far fetched alright. Have you seen any good movies lately? There's a swell song becoming very popular over here, "Suddenly my Heart Sings" it's a lovely song too, have you heard it yet?

Well dear, I'll say goodnight to you for now with all my love. Take care of yourself always, all my love,

May

Merry Christmas Dear.

Jan; 27 1945.

Dearest Kay,
I'm the one who is really happy today after receiving one of your wonderful letters. Honestly dear there's nothing that can make me more cheerful than hearing from you. As you can probably tell by my letters, sometimes I get the blues and feel as though I've got all the cares of the world bearing down on me, but you soon fix that in a hurry dear. I guess every body gets in a blue mood once in a while eh Kay. It is just human nature for a person to be alternately happy, worried etc.

I like your little cartoons of me dear with all the bottles around me. I'm not a bad boy really about drinking. About the only time I really bother about it over here is when I'm on leave or after we're done a few ops in a row and my nerves are a bit jumpy, and believe me they do get jumpy from the long tense hours on ops. When you're over enemy territory every sense is really alert and you're all keyed up. After eight or nine hours of that at a time, it begins to tell on you and makes you feel as though you can't stay awake any longer for any time, but of course you have to. Each op is just the same thing over again with perhaps a little more or a little less excitement than the previous one. No matter what the drawbacks life on a squadron is really the tops. It makes life really interesting.

Darling I've been trying to get a Valentine card for you all around here, they just don't seem to be making them over here now. I want you to know dear there's nobody else anywhere I'd even want to send one to. So sweetheart will you be my Valentine? You can bet I'll make up for it next year. It makes me have a sort of contented feeling inside of me to know that you're thinking of me on ops dear. Whenever I'm flying on or on the ground I'm thinking of you always. Every night I look up at your picture smiling down at me and say goodnight sweetheart. I often wonder why it had

to be dear that I didn't meet you sooner than I did. I only wish I had, it seemed such a short while after I met you that I was stuck over here. I enjoyed every hour every minute of your company dear. I hope to be back and we'll be going out together on our this summer, with luck and some good flying weather I can do it. That's something I dream of quite often, getting off the train in Central Station and seeing you there. Gosh it'll be wonderful. I mustn't day dream though there's too much grim reality between now and then.

I'll say goodnight now darling with all my love for you always.

Love and Kisses
Ronny

x x x x
x x x x

P.S. 25 ops done

15
Reunion

After Ron and his crewmates were screened, events in Europe started to move quickly. Benito Mussolini was captured near Milan and executed on April 28, precipitating the surrender of the Italian military two days later and the surrender of German forces in Italy on May 2. With the Russians fighting in Berlin, and just a few city blocks away from Hitler's bunker, Hitler married Eva Braun and then committed suicide on April 30 to avoid being personally humiliated by his would-be capturers. Then, on May 7, Germany finally signed an unconditional surrender.

On May 8, known as "Victory in Europe Day," Kay returned home early from work, as most businesses in downtown Montreal had shut down to celebrate. She took in the euphoria of the milling crowds on St. Catherine Street then decided to share this moment with her father. At home in the parlour, she sat with her dad listening to the radio broadcast on the CBC. It was Prime Minister Mackenzie King who was addressing the Canadian people from a United Nations conference in San Francisco.

"In the name of our country, I ask the people of Canada at this hour to join with me in expressing our gratitude as a nation for the deliverance from the evil forces of Nazi Germany. We unite in humble and reverent thanksgiving to God for his mercy thus vouched safe to the peoples of our own and other lands.

"Let us rejoice in the victory for which we have waited so long and which has been won at so great a price. Our rejoicing however would fail to give expression to our true feelings if our first thoughts were not of those who had given their lives that victory this day might be ours and not our enemies. We would not be true to ourselves were our thoughts not also of those who are sorrowing today for the loved ones taken from them in the terrible holocaust of war."[1]

Just one month earlier Kay was informed that her brother-in-law Lieutenant William Albert Bennett had been killed in Normandy. Mackenzie's remarks were thus profoundly felt. And as King continued, her thoughts turned to Ron.

"We shall now eagerly await the triumphant return of those who have fought the fight of freedom at sea, on land, and in the air and who have survived the vicissitudes of war."[2]

Further into his address to the nation, Kay was struck by and felt hopeful of King's words.

"Finally we must fight to a victorious close the war against war itself. The hard struggle for peace will go on long after the guns cease firing. Until we win that struggle, we cannot truly say that we have won the war."[3]

Thousands of miles across the ocean, Ron and Bob sat in a pub in Warrington near Liverpool. They were celebrating with dozens of locals and military. Suddenly everyone in the bar stopped and strained to hear the radio. It was Prime Minister Churchill announcing the unconditional surrender of Germany after six long years of conflict. In congratulating the Allies he was quick to remind his listeners that,

"We may allow ourselves a brief period of rejoicing; but let us not forget for a moment the toil and efforts that lie ahead. Japan with all her treachery and greed, remains unsubdued."[4]

It was for this very reason that Ron and Bob had both volunteered to serve a second tour of duty with the RCAF's "Tiger Force." But before this, both Bob and Ron were waiting to return to Canada for a thirty-day leave.

***

Over the war, seventy-two German cities bore the brunt of Bomber Command's wrath, resulting in the destruction of seventy-eight square miles of built-up area, which represented almost half the downtown core of each city. It would take decades before all rubble had been cleared and churches, cultural centres, hospitals, schools, dwellings, and other key infrastructure were rebuilt. Some of the cities 434 Squadron bombed incurred damage in excess of 50 percent, including Bochum (83%), Cologne (61%), Dessau (61%), Dortmund (61%), Dresden (59%), Hagen (67%), Hamburg (75%), Hannover (60%), and Mannheim (64%).[5] A United States Strategic Bombing Survey conducted in 1945 estimated that 20 percent of all dwelling units in Germany were either completely destroyed or heavily damaged, resulting in the displacement of over 7 million German civilians.[6] The need to feed, cloth, and shelter these displaced civilians placed a significant burden on the German economy, during and after the war. In addition, over 300,000 civilians were killed and another 780,000 required hospitalization due to the Allied bombing campaign.[7]

The war in Europe took a terrible toll in terms of lives lost, property damaged, and lives disrupted and changed forever. Although accurate figures of military and civilian deaths at the end of World War II were impossible to ascertain, it is estimated that the Axis suffered approximately 12 million war dead while the "victorious" Allies had a death toll in excess of 44 million. Shockingly, the total number of non-combatants or civilians killed by disease, famine, bombing, and genocide was estimated at 35 million, or over 60 percent of the total fatalities.

In Canada 1.1 million people served in the military forces with over 47,000 killed and an additional 53,145 wounded. Over 249,000 Canadians served in the RCAF with 15,478 killed or missing, representing a 6.2 percent casualty rate versus 3.1 percent for the Canadian army. For the Allies, active combat crew in Bomber Command, excluding the American Air Force but including Canadian Bomber Group 6, numbered 125,000. Casualties within this group reached over 55,000 killed and an additional 18,000 wounded for a staggering aircrew casualty rate of over 58 percent. Air Marshal Arthur "Bomber" Harris's aircrew flew under the most adverse combat conditions and had made the ultimate sacrifices, especially in the early war years when Fortress Europe was impregnable to Allied land forces.

Just seven days after VE-Day, Ron set sail from England for New York City on the *Ile de France*, a luxury liner requisitioned as a troop carrier for the duration of WW II. In peace time, the *Ile de France* would carry almost 1,800 passengers at a time, but as a troop carrier it could convey over 4,000. With a top speed of twenty-four knots, the ship zigzagged its way across the ocean to make it a more difficult target for any lingering enemy submarines. It was here that Ron's thoughts once again turned to Kay, whom he had not seen for over a year. He now felt uncertain about meeting up with Kay given that their relationship had really developed through letters. He felt that in many ways he was now a changed person. Although Ron still had an abundant sense of humour, somehow he felt more mature and serious and hoped that Kay would still have feelings for this different man.

Ron arrived in New York on the morning of May 22.[8] When he stepped off the ship he wanted to kiss the ground, he was that excited to be back home, even if not yet in Montreal. Ron called his parents to make arrangements to meet at Central Station in Montreal and suggested they invite Kay as well. He now couldn't wait to get back. It seemed like a lifetime ago since he had last seen his parents and Kay.

Ron's train pulled out of Grand Central Station in New York City in mid-morning. It chugged along at a leisurely pace. Ron stared out the window at the many apartment buildings and tenements slipping by. It looked so different from war-ravaged Europe. His thoughts then turned to the many letters that he and Kay had exchanged over the last year and what he would say to her when they met again for the first time in almost fourteen months. How could he tell her he had volunteered for a second tour of duty in the Pacific? Before they both knew it, he would be back into the thick of fighting, facing down Zeros in the rear turret over Japanese territory.

Soon the train pulled into the countryside, which looked so peaceful. Nine hours later, he crossed the border into the beautiful countryside and farms of the Eastern Townships. Everything looked so green and fresh. After what seemed an eternity (but in reality just over twelve hours), his train pulled into Montreal. Ron picked up his kit bag, which contained all Kay's letters safely stashed inside a metal tin box, and then lingered in his car, nervously anticipating the reunion. Only after most of the other passengers had disembarked did Ron finally step off the train and search the station platform. With the keen eyesight of a tail gunner, Ron could see his mom and dad at the end of the platform looking for him, and how could he miss that young lady who had flown with him in spirit on all those missions. He dropped his kit bag and, in his haste to run down the platform, almost tripped over it. He shouted a loud hello and before he knew it, was embraced in one giant hug by both his parents and Kay. Everybody was shedding tears of joy. No one knew where to start the conversation; each had so much to say but in a way it had all been said in the over two hundred letters exchanged over the last year.

After a bite at a local delicatessen, Kay and Ron went back to his parents' home on Adam Street and talked into the late evening. Ron escorted Kay home by taxi with the promise that after tomorrow they would see each other every day. Kay had booked off an early summer vacation over the next two weeks and Ron did not have to report back to duty until late June. They spent time together at the beach in Terrebonne Heights, revisited the night spots in Montreal, including the Tic Toc and Picadilly Club where they had spent their last evening together before Ron went overseas, and got to know each other again.

On June 26, Kay met up with Ron at his parents' house and accompanied him down to the station for the train to St. John's, Quebec, located some twenty-four miles southeast of Montreal. Kay embraced Ron, not wanting to let him go. It was a difficult parting given that they had just been together for the last month and didn't know when Ron would get his orders to proceed to the Pacific. They might not see each other for a long time—if ever. It didn't seem fair that once again they might be separated across thousands of miles of ocean. Somehow going off to the Pacific seemed even more remote, more unknown.

It was not long before Ron wrote Kay his first letter from the new station. It was June 27, the next day.

Dear Kay, I'm here and it's not too bad by first judgement anyway. Of course you can't go by that.

It seems we do nothing and get a 48 hour (pass) every weekend. So if I get paid I'll see you Friday night about 7:30-8:00— so expect me eh! Dear.

There is quite a bit of flying going on here so that makes me feel a bit better, it's all navy training here—you know Fleet Air Arm.

I've got your picture sitting in front of me while I'm writing and I can see the order written on it, so don't worry starry eyes, I'll always love you now or fifty years from now, it makes no difference

Goodnight darling, All my love always, Ronny

By now the romance was heating up but the threat of having to go on a second tour of duty hung like a spectre in the background. Kay wrote,

Dearest Ronny, Gosh dear, this is the first time I've written to you since you've been home, but I'm afraid I just can't tell you how very much I miss you, there just doesn't seem to be any words that really express my feelings. I keep hoping that the phone will ring and it will be you back in Montreal, it just never stops being exciting to hear your voice. Good night dear and always remember that I do so love you. All my love, Kay

By the middle of July, Ron just couldn't wait to get back to Kay permanently and get on with living.

My darling Kay, I've just been sitting around thinking about last night. Gosh it was swell just to be near you again dear to talk to you and look at you, that's one thing I could never tire of dear no matter how much time we spend together. The time went by so very fast yesterday. From the time you came down the beach to meet me until we said goodnight seemed like a few minutes, but a wonderful few minutes.

Just knowing that we love each other more than anything else is all that matters don't you think so dear. Until Friday

*Starry eyes remember I love you darling, so much it hurts. All
my love Darling. Always, Ronny*

Not long after this, an event occurred that changed the world forever and at the same time expedited the end of World War II. In order to minimize the number of expected casualities from an Allied invasion of Japan, a decision had been taken to drop the first of two nuclear bombs on the morning of August 6, 1945. The *Enola Gay* dropped "Little Boy" on Hiroshima, killing over 70,000 outright with almost another 80,000 seriously injured. Three days later *Bockscar* dropped "Fat Man" on Nagasaki, which brought the total killed in the two attacks to 120,000 people, mainly civilians.

Even before the second attack it was clear to Canadian military authorities that Tiger Force had been made redundant. On August 8, Ron was taken off strength from the base at St. John's and officially discharged from the RCAF ten days later.[9] He was ecstatic. Ron was then transferred to a special section of the air force reserve in the event of a national emergency. Ironically, just three days later he received official notice that he had been promoted to Temporary Flying Officer effective May 11, 1945.

On leaving the air force Ron's medical records showed that the only physical ailment he experienced at the time included periodic blurred vision and sore eyes, due to the strain of night flying. Also, if Ron sat down for a long time his knees would begin to ache. This was diagnosed as being caused by cold-weather flying and long flights where he sat in one position with little space to move. Aside from the occasional shaking of his hands on his last month of operations, at this time there were no other visible signs of other medical problems.

With the surrender of Japan, Ron would not have to face another long separation from Kay. And he had certainly already seen enough killing and destruction to last a lifetime. Japan's surrender was good news and Ron soon returned to his parents' home and became a permanent fixture at Kay's father's house. They were both thankful that they could enjoy each other's company up close and take advantage of the personal freedom to do what they wanted—when they wanted—with no intervention by the military. Now that the war was finished, they quickly made a decision to become formally engaged.

On March 23, 1946, just a little over two years after Ron and Kay first met at St. Sauveur, they were married at Trinity United Church in Montreal North. It was an intimate wedding reception with twenty-two friends and family, followed by a honeymoon at the New Sherbrooke Hotel in the Eastern Townships.

Ron and Kay's marriage and future life together would include many personal challenges and accomplishments, but would always be cemented in love for each other. It was a love that had been forged in a unique time and place when the world was engulfed in a struggle for good over evil, democracy over autocracy, and freedom over slavery.

16
Post Traumatic Stress Disorder

For as long as humans have experienced or witnessed actual or potential life-threatening events, people have naturally responded with intense fear or horror. These frightening situations may include combat, sexual or physical assault, natural disasters, and serious accidents such as a car crash. The ensuing symptoms from such trauma are often identified in military terminology and include such labels as "shell shock" used in WW I, and "battle fatigue" or "lack of moral fibre" utilized during WW II.

After World War I some nine thousand Canadian veterans were receiving pensions for "shell shock and neurosis"—they were the lucky ones. In World War I hundreds of British soldiers suffering from "shell shock" were charged with desertion, cowardice, or refusal to obey orders and executed in front of their peers. Twenty-three Canadians also suffered such a fate. (Only Australia would not allow its soldiers to be shot for desertion.) It was only in 2001 that the Government of Canada offered an apology and formally announced its regret for these killings. The British government followed suit five years later, granting posthumous conditional pardons to all their "Shot at Dawn" soldiers.

The term Post Traumatic Stress Disorder (PTSD) was first coined by the American Psychiatric Association in its *Diagnostic and Statistical Manual of Mental Disorders, Fourth Edition* in the early 1980s.

This followed U.S. involvement in the Vietnam War where over 30 percent of returning Vietnam veterans at some point in their lives relived distressing wartime experiences.[1] As of 2008 there were over 229,000 American veterans of the Vietnam War receiving PTSD compensation from the Veterans Benefits Administration in addition to another 55,000 who had been involved in the Iraq/Afghanistan conflict.

Symptoms of PTSD can include avoidance of stimuli associated with the original trauma such as loud or sudden noises like fireworks or engine backfiring, the recurrent and intrusive recollection of the original event, including associated images or thoughts, recurring dreams of the event, and anxiety.[2] PTSD may manifest itself shortly after an individual is exposed to a traumatic event but in many instances, it may take years before symptoms become evident. There have been numerous cases where older veterans will first exhibit symptoms of acute PTSD fifty years or more after their military service ended. Although many people experience symptoms associated with PTSD after a traumatic incident, it is only when these symptoms persist over time and become chronic that PTSD is usually diagnosed.

Psychodynamic theories suggest that when an individual experiences trauma, defence mechanisms protect the ego from that experience, which is too difficult to process cognitively or emotionally. PTSD symptoms reflect the conflict within the psyche that is either trying to avoid re-experiencing the trauma, or trying to dull or eradicate that painful experience. The individual may thus unconsciously repress memories and experience dissociation—losing a sense of themselves for brief or longer periods. Consciously or unconsciously, the individual often becomes hypervigilant to factors which may precipitate a recollection or reliving of the trauma.

Although PTSD in its various forms has been around for a very long time, historically for combat personnel there has been a real stigma attached to it. This stigma has prevented many soldiers from admitting that they in fact have this health issue. They fear that their peers might consider them "weak" in character. PTSD sufferers within the military are also concerned that the reporting of their illnesses will jeopardize career opportunities and advancement. It is therefore difficult for a soldier to accept that he or she has been psychologically wounded and needs help. In fact, many Canadian forces personnel with PTSD leave or are released from service without being diagnosed or treated for their ailment. In addition, military health professionals over the years have been reticent to recognize PTSD as a real disease, which requires proper attention and treatment. To further complicate the matter, many American World War II veterans who were experiencing PTSD symptoms were hesitant to seek medical help because one of the remedies for it was an ice-pick frontal lobotomy—conducted under local anesthesia. This procedure turned out to be ineffective.

Until recently, neither the Canadian, British, or American Forces have kept proper statistics to quantify PTSD, nor have they provided timely and effective treatment. Only in late 2002 did the Canadian Forces commission a study, *The Canadian Forces 2002 Canadian Community Health Survey Supplement*, to quantify the incidence of various mental illnesses, including PTSD, within both current Regular and Reserve Forces. This study found PTSD to be the fourth most prevalent mental illness behind depression, alcohol dependence, and social phobia. Among members of the Regular Forces who have been deployed three or more times, the lifetime incidence level of PTSD in 2002 was 10.3 percent, or roughly 35 percent higher than in the civilian population.[3] More recent data suggests that between 15 and 20 percent of Canadian Forces members deployed return suffering from PTSD.[4] The study also found that less than 25 percent of Regular Canadian Forces personnel suffering from one or more mental illnesses felt that their needs had been met by mental health services.[5] A more recent Canadian Forces PERSTEMPO (Personnel Tempo) study conducted in 2007 found that members who spend more time away from home, whether in combat or non-combat roles, have a greater propensity to suffer from PTSD.[6] In increasing the time away from home from 120 to 240 days the rate of PTSD doubled.[7]

Treatments for PTSD include the use of support groups, medications, and cognitive-behavioural therapy, which may include helping the patient to relive parts of the traumatic experience.[8] The sooner PTSD is diagnosed, the better chance of success in treating the patient. It is believed that one of the most important factors for recovery for those still "on strength" within the military is the amount of positive support that the individual receives from his or her peers and unit.[9] In both WW I and WW II it was a common practice to keep PTSD patients close to the front while providing rest and nourishment, so they wouldn't completely break contact with their units. Although this short-term treatment was highly effective in the timely return of soldiers back to the front, it often only delayed the recurrence of PTSD.

Many PTSD sufferers turn to drugs, including alcohol, to self-medicate, especially when they do not want to admit that they are in fact suffering from PTSD. Tragically, alcoholism can easily reduce an individual's life expectancy by fifteen or more years. There is also a strong association between PTSD and elevated levels of attempted suicides (and suicides) although historically the Canadian Forces has not kept track of suicides among reservists and retired members.[10]

In 2010, the U.S. Department of Veterans Affairs made a landmark decision to allow all U.S. veterans regardless of length of service and whether they experienced combat to retroactively seek compensation for PTSD.[11] In the last few years, the Canadian Forces has begun to make the detection and proper treatment of PTSD a high priority, including outreach training for all personnel, although many of the recommendations made by the Canadian Forces Ombudsman in 2002 have not yet been fully implemented ten years later.

One of the objectives of Bomber Command in World War II was to disrupt and weaken the "morale" of the German people, who provided (along with forced labour) the manpower to produce weapons of war. With the bombing of major English cities, the German Luftwaffe similarly hoped to weaken the morale or psyche of the British. In both instances, except possibly near the very end of the war, the resolve of the respective civilian populations to fight on was only strengthened by the bombing campaigns. Jungian analyst Andrew Benedetto observes that the inherent danger of such a fight had a reverse effect—instead of aircrews destroying the psyche of their opponents, in many instances their own psyches were damaged in the long term.

PTSD does not differentiate between race, religion, sex, or rank. The most well-known and respected Canadian soldier to suffer the classic symptoms of PTSD is retired General Romeo Dallaire who was made a Senator in 2005.[12] In 1993, Dallaire was appointed Force Commander of the United Nations Assistance Mission for Rwanda.[13] Rwanda was in the process of being torn apart by a civil war fought between two rival factions, the Hutus and the Tutsis.[14] With inadequate forces and only a peacekeeping mandate, Dallaire was unable to prevent the subsequent genocide of eight hundred thousand civilians who were brutally murdered over a one-hundred-day period. Ten Belgium peacekeepers were also killed under his command.[15] This horrific experience caused Dallaire to suffer many PTSD symptoms including depression, anxiety, drinking, and an attempt at suicide four years later.[16] Dallaire was fortunate—he sought help and was able to receive therapy and medication, which helped him manage his PTSD. And as a Senator, he now plays an active role in the welfare of Canada's veterans as chairman of the Senate Subcommittee on Veterans Affairs.[17]

The first step in addressing PTSD is awareness and acceptance that there is a problem, and that this problem is a medical issue that must not be treated by self-medication. Drugs, alcohol, and suicide attempts are not sensible options. Professional treatment is required. It is critical that sufferers of PTSD and health providers recognize that a wound to the psyche is just as real as a wound to the body and equally deserving of attention, care, and appropriate treatment. For many veterans, this first step—realizing the need for help and asking for treatment—is the most difficult one to take.

17
A New Beginning

Housing shortages were still prevalent in 1946 right across the country as thousands of veterans returning home were unable to find adequate places to live. In Vancouver, over seven hundred frustrated veterans took over the Vancouver Hotel, which was being used as a warehouse. They refused to leave. The veterans ultimately occupied the hotel until well into the next year before they were provided with alternative rental housing. Ron and Kay solved the Montreal housing crisis after their honeymoon by moving into two small rooms which they rented while they shared part of the space with another family. They had to pay "pin money," equivalent to several months' rent, to obtain even these accommodations.

Just days after they finally found their new home, the two went shopping to pick up some items for their new residence. On the return trip, they jumped on a jam-packed streetcar with their many parcels and found it almost impossible to move. Kay recalled that they somehow became separated in the sea of passengers and, when the streetcar stopped abruptly, all the passengers were thrown against each other. Kay had been thrown forward, and was shoved in the side by a man of heavy-set proportions. Before she could check her temper she had blurted, "For heaven's sake, why don't you watch what you're doing?" The man replied disgustedly that "If she didn't like to ride the streetcar she could always take a taxi." Just then, Ron miraculously appeared at her side and demanded to know what the man was saying to his wife. The man, although surprised that Ron had suddenly showed up, made a quick recovery and muttered under his breath, "Look mister, I'm not interested in your wife." In the confusion Ron exclaimed with great inanity, "And neither am I." Ron and Kay would always get a chuckle when recounting the story.[1] This was the kind of good-natured ease that punctuated early post-war life for Ron and Kay, something that would become more complicated as Ron's health began to deteriorate.

Ron decided not to return to his pre-war employment at Vickers but instead started to train as a draftsman. He joined Canadair in August 1945, where he worked in the Engineering Department. He remained at Canadair until the spring of 1946 before moving on to Combustion Engineering, where he continued to hone his draftsman skills. Kay also made a career decision in August 1946, resigning from her stenographer and secretarial position at Heward Holden where she had worked for almost three years. This was in anticipation of their first child, Leslie Susan, who was born in early 1947. With the addition of a newborn, they searched for larger accommodations and, in early 1948, were successful in finding their very own apartment in east end Montreal.

In late 1948, at the age of twenty-three, Kay delivered a healthy baby boy, Richard Ronald. Sadly, Kay's dad died of a heart attack in March, so he did not get the opportunity to see his new grandson. Kay experienced a big loss with the sudden death of her father and so too did Ron, who in late 1948 once again decided to change jobs; he went to work at Canada Cement, where he remained until the start of 1950, when he then joined Dominion Textile where he produced piping and instrumentation drawings.

In 1950, Kay decided to take a correspondence course from the Palmer Institute of Authorship, located in Hollywood, California, as she had wanted to become a published author. She successfully completed the program in late 1955 and found her writing over the years offered a tonic to family demands. Early in 1951, Ron again changed jobs, moving to the engineering department at Canadian National Railways. In March of that year he was taken off strength of the primary Air Force Reserve, and with a growing family decided to register his own drafting business under the name of "Allied Technical Services" so he could take on extra work as it became available.

In 1952, Ron was twenty-eight years old and decided again to switch jobs. He joined C.D. Howe, a prominent consulting engineering firm in Montreal, started by the man who was then Louis St. Laurent's Minister of Trade and Commerce. The arrival of Ron and Kay's third child, Julia Roberta, born in 1952, necessitated another move to a larger housing unit on Lafontaine Street in the east end. It encompassed the entire top floor of a triplex and had a very large back porch on which the three kids could play.

One evening, Ron rang the doorbell and shouted up the stairs to Kay that he had a wonderful surprise. It turned out to be the family's first TV, a small black and white set with a twelve-inch screen. The entire family would gather around on Saturday nights to watch Maurice Richard and the Montreal Canadiens. In 1954, the last of Ron and Kay's four children, Colleen Deborah, was born.

Kay was thirty when she decided to work part-time to help out with the growing costs of family life. And over the next several years, Kay would work as a legal secretary for a number of firms. Ron, missing the camaraderie of his wartime days, decided to rejoin the RCAF, enlisting in the primary Air Force Reserve in 1954. He continued to participate in summer training on a number of occasions until he was once again struck off strength in 1957. He was thirty-three. At the time of re-enlistment, Ron weighed 150 pounds or about twenty pounds more than when he had first signed up almost eleven years earlier. At 5' 91/2", he was still pretty slim.

In 1955, Ron's parents sold their country property on Lake Nantel in the Laurentians where he had spent his summers. It was another big loss for Ron, and another life change.

In the summer of 1955, Ron moved to the Consumers Glass Company, having spent three years at C.D. Howe. It was the seventh job change for Ron in the last ten years. There, he worked on drawings associated with the huge Consumers Glass factory in Ville St. Pierre. He also had the responsibility of supervising two draftsmen and any contractors in the plant.

Given the long commute to Ville St. Pierre (a journey of over one and a half hours), Ron moved the family to an apartment complex on Walkley Avenue in the west end. The family resided on the ground floor and over the years made friends with many of the hard-working neighbours. In late 1959, Kay started to work on temporary assignments for Ogilvy, Cope, Porteus and Montgomery and over the next ten years worked for many of the law firm's senior partners.

When they moved to Walkley Avenue, it was a solid working-class neighbourhood, and fairly respectable. Over time however, the neighbourhood became a little rougher. On one occasion, the local police force, armed with machine guns, raided their building looking for a murderer. Another time the roof of their three-storey apartment caught fire while under repair. By the time the fire department put it out, Ron and Kay's apartment was covered in six inches of water, ruining almost all the family's clothes and furniture.

During this time Ron would sometimes take his son on fishing excursions to catch sturgeon as they migrated up the St. Lawrence River in spring. They would fish off the pier in Lachine near First Avenue or rent a rowboat and anchor it just off of the St. Lawrence Seaway buoys. With the approach of a lake freighter, Ron and Rick would adroitly turn the small boat into the waves to prevent being swamped. It was a nice way to spend a hot summer day on the weekend and it brought out the relaxed humour in Ron. And it was not uncommon to catch a four-foot-long sturgeon, which would necessitate a side trip to the local tavern to display the prize. Needless to say that on these side trips Ron never had to pay for his favourite beverage—a nice cold glass of beer.

In fall of 1959, Ron changed employers and moved to Rousseau Controls, a small engineering firm where he oversaw the purchasing department. A year later, he moved to Integrated Consultants, where he supervised draftsmen who produced detailed piping and layout drawings for an air reduction plant. As well, after a number of "exciting" experiences in the Walkley apartment complex, they decided to move to a quieter part of the city and in 1962, rented the top floor of a duplex on the border of Montreal West.

In the early 1960s, Ron became interested in hypnotism. He col-

lected over a dozen books on the subject and took a number of courses and by 1961 was an active member in The Canadian Institute of
Hypnotism in Montreal. Ron became quite proficient and on one
occasion successfully hypnotized his nephew who had *previously*
been averse to going to the dentist. On another occasion at a party,
he entertained the guests by hypnotizing a gentleman and had him
successfully regress back to his early childhood to recall forgotten experiences. To Ron's embarrassment, the gentleman did not wake up
readily and ended up sleeping for several hours, much to his wife's
displeasure. Ron never again used hypnotism at a public event.

In the fall of 1961, Ron, now thirty-five years old, joined Henry
J. Kaiser, an engineering firm where he worked on drawings for an
iron ore beneficiating plant in Labrador. This assignment lasted six
months. He then joined Brown & Root, a large U.S.-based engineering firm involved in the expansion of a petrochemical plant in Montreal and an oil refinery in Sarnia, Ontario. He was involved in these
projects for a year. In spring 1963, he moved on to work for DuPont of
Canada, where he assisted in an extensive expansion of the DuPont
plant in Brockville, Ontario, which produced nylon-based products.
Upon the completion of this project he moved back to Brown & Root,
which was building a new heavy water plant in Glace Bay, Nova Scotia. Shortly after his return from the war, Ron had done a short stint in
Chalk River working on one of the first operable nuclear reactors in
Canada, hence his experience in the nuclear field.

In 1966, Ron moved to Overload Services, producing the piping
layout for a bauxite plant expansion in Jamaica. Additional assignments in 1967 and 1968 included work on expansion of a Shell Oil
refinery followed by another assignment to DuPont Canada through
early 1970. By the age of forty-two, Ron had worked for fifteen different companies.

For the Pyves family, 1967 and 1968 turned out to be watershed
years in many ways. Ron bought everybody in the family a season's
pass for Expo 67, where Canada's centennial year was celebrated
along with the international theme of "Man and His World." It was
exciting times where everbody's *future* was spelled with a capital "F."
In early 1968, Ron and Kay also decided to buy a small cottage on a

two-acre country lot in Terrebonne Heights, just north of Montreal, and Kay became a full-time employee at Ogilvy Renaud, a prestigious law firm in Montreal founded in 1879, where she worked on a part-time basis for many years. Kay was in the intellectual property department, initially as a secretary and, over the years, worked her way up to a paralegal.

All said, marrying Kay and creating a close family unit appeared like a fairy tale to Ron, especially when compared to his experiences in World War II where he was never sure, from trip to trip, if he would ever survive his tour of duty. Sadly though, beneath the outside appearance of a happy, normal family life, an undercurrent of unrest, depression, and anxiety started to manifest itself in 1968 that stemmed directly from his wartime experiences. Ron's personal war was just taking flight, again.

18
A Personal War

By the middle of 1968, Ron, who for over twenty years had successfully earned his living and supported his family, became emotionally ill and suffered serious mental depression. Although not as evident in the early years after the war, he had nevertheless visited his family doctor from time to time to obtain tranquillizers, which in hindsight was most likely an early warning sign of what had now become a serious disability. In July, he sought emergency aid at the Reddy Memorial Hospital Outdoor Clinic in Montreal, and upon the recommendation of the attending staff, signed in at the Day Clinic for Psychiatry. He attended sessions each day for five weeks, returning home at night. He was therefore unable to work. After five weeks, and while still under medication, Ron attempted to find a new job. Although he found some temporary employment, he couldn't hold down these assignments due to illness. In one instance, he found a job opportunity as a design draftsman at a plant in Sarnia where he travelled by train. But he had a panic attack before he even showed up and immediately returned to Montreal. At this time, he decided to seek further psychiatric treatment.

Ron's mother, Laura Hilder, also died in 1968. It was his mother who always wrote to him during the war and, along with Kay, provided him with a link to the saner world in Montreal. It was this correspondence that helped him maintain his sanity in a world gone mad.

The loss added additional strain just at a time when the depression was getting worse. Compounding things, the daily news and endless war images coming out of Vietnam also set off war recollections and worsened Ron's condition.

Though there were happy times—in October 1968 for instance, Ron and Kay celebrated the marriage of their eldest daughter—the depression was in fact getting worse. So in February 1969, Ron decided to seek further help. As a World War II veteran, Ron was entitled to admission as a full-time patient to the Psychiatric Wing of the Queen Mary Veterans' Hospital. He stayed there for seven weeks, a good indication that Ron had a very severe case of depression that needed serious treatment. After the first week he obtained permission from his doctors to return home for weekends. During the week, he attended group therapy sessions and individual consultations with his psychiatrist. In addition, he attended Alcoholics Anonymous meetings, as he had taken to heavy drinking as a way to address his depression. Although Ron had always enjoyed an occasional beer, it was not until 1968 that an increase in alcohol consumption became evident. He was discharged from the hospital in April, and returned to his trade as a draftsman in 1970.

That year Ron and Kay celebrated the marriage of their second-eldest daughter, Julia; later in the year, Julia had a daughter, Michelle Leigh, Ron and Kay's first grandchild. But again such happy times only punctuated the depression and after a six-month bout of unemployment, Ron decided to take a less stressful job in the mail room at Robert Hampson & Son Ltd., a Montreal insurance company, where he remained for three years. Although the salary was less than half of what he made as a senior draftsman, it provided him with significantly less pressure—and it was honest work. This sabbatical from a more stressful job allowed him to get his health back on track. However, Ron continued to drink excessively as he was not able to shake off the depression. There were more happy times in 1971, with Ron and Kay's only son, Richard, marrying Judith Anderson. But the wedding and arrival in early 1972 of their second grandchild, Cindy Ann, provided only a brief oasis in Ron's ongoing depression.

In the spring of 1972, Ron lost his father to a heart attack. This loss had not been unexpected as his father had undergone a series of operations earlier in the year as part of a valiant fight with lung cancer. He had always looked up to his dad and related well to him, considering also that both had experienced combat in their youths.

In 1973, Ron accepted a job as an estimator and senior draftsman for Kingston Mechanical in Ville LaSalle. Despite Ron's drinking problems and recurring bouts with depression, he was a master at coming up with creative business solutions and, as necessary, personal solutions as well. On one occasion a huge snow storm hit Montreal, shutting down all public transportation. Ron did not drive and needed to find alternative transportation home from work. So he phoned the local B.B.Q. chicken joint and, upon confirmation that it was still making home deliveries, promptly ordered two whole chickens with assorted sides. When the delivery man left the restaurant Ron intercepted the driver and offered to pay for his gas if he was going in the same direction. Needless to say, he got his lift home, arriving safely with a treat for the whole family at a cost significantly lower than that of a taxi—if he could have found one. When the delivery man discovered the truth, he couldn't help but smile at Ron's ruse. Ron often used humour—especially with strangers—to mask his underlying problems with stress and depression.

Then in November 1978, Ron was laid off due to a shortage of work. He enjoyed his job at Kingston Mechanical and left on very good terms. But in many ways this job at Kingston Mechanical marked a watershed in his professional career. Ron, now fifty-four years old, could not find another full-time position. It marked the start of a serious decline in his health.

By late 1979, Ron was in constant touch with his doctors at the Queen Elizabeth Hospital. He continued drinking and was diagnosed with cirrhosis of the liver. The condition was life-threatening and doctors told him he would die unless he completely stopped drinking. Unlike many people who drink too much, Ron was never abusive to any family member and, although his condition could sometimes be embarrassing, he never presented a danger to anybody but himself. It was very frustrating for both Kay and the kids to watch while someone they loved and cared for was slowly killing himself.

With the cirrhosis scare, Ron became determined to stop drinking and attended over one hundred Alcoholics Anonymous meetings in 1980 and 1981, with Kay often sitting by his side. Without alcohol, his depression was more prevalent and he found it more difficult to cope with life. There were positives, of course. Ron and Kay now had six grandchildren to spend time with on holidays, vacations, and the occasional weekend when Ron was well enough. And in 1980, Ron and Kay attended their first RCAF reunion in Toronto, where they spent a great weekend renewing connections with Ron's fellow crewmates and their partners, including Bob and Erma Henry, Frank and Rita Welsh, Hal and Violet Ward, and Bill and Edna Thomson. Joe Casavant had been unable to attend and, unfortunately, Al Coleman had passed away in 1977. Despite Ron's concerns over the bombing of Dresden, the crew happily reminisced about their times together and the dangers at Croft as if it were just yesterday.

Then on New Year's Day 1983, Ron, who was on prescription medication for his condition, became seriously depressed and took an overdose of prescription tranquillizers. Luckily the dosage was weak and the next day Ron was admitted to the Psychiatric Department at the Queen Elizabeth Hospital as an in-patient. He remained there for the next two weeks. After release, he remained on medication. Kay recalled how, even with his ups and downs, he was always loved by her and the children. She knew that Ron was an honest, intelligent, and caring man who had a propensity for depression. He continued under the care of his doctor, who tried to treat both his mental and physical conditions, but he was never able to make a complete recovery and would never work again.

In March 1984, Ron experienced a serious, life-threatening haemorrhage in his throat due to back pressure created from his cirrhosis. He had to receive many blood transfusions to survive. He was released from hospital almost two weeks later but his health continued to deteriorate and he remained under constant watch by both his family and doctors.

He was sixty years old by the fall of 1984 when depression once more reared its ugly head. He planned to commit suicide at the scene where he spent one of his last best days in Canada before going overseas in 1944. Ron's parents had owned a lakeside cottage at Lake Nantel in the Laurentians north of Montreal. It was here, just before he left for war, that he had spent a leisurely day in his canoe on the lake, a memory he always treasured. It had been a place of tranquility and perhaps the last identifiable location where he experienced the "innocence of youth" that would be stripped away by war.

Ron hired a taxi driven by Frank, a neighbour. They were accompanied by Ron's close friend Glen who had no idea of his plan. They then headed up to Lake Nantel. Despite the cirrhosis, Ron and Glen drank heavily on the trip. Once there, they wandered around the old property. It had been shut up by the new owners for the season but Ron wanted to take a moored boat out on the lake. Frank tried to change their minds, telling them it was unwise. Frank refused to accompany them and instead waited onshore. It was quite some time before they finally returned. With the will to live overpowering his desire to commit suicide, Ron decided then not to end his life and returned home. It was here that he told Kay what his intentions had been. She was visibly shaken and right away called the Ste. Anne's Military Hospital for advice. They recommended that Ron and Kay camp on the steps of the Queen Elizabeth Hospital if necessary until they could get the medical help Ron desperately needed.

Kay went with him to meet a psychiatrist at the hospital. After Ron confirmed he had intended to commit suicide, the doctor referred him to the Jewish General Hospital where they could keep him safe until further suitable help could be provided. Ron felt terrible and expressed deep-felt guilt. He told Kay and the doctor that he wanted to get better, once and for all, and felt ready to take whatever action was required to make a full recovery. After three days at Jewish General, the Head of Psychiatry referred Ron to a new program at Montreal General with the promise of an early admittance. The doctor delivered and Ron was accepted into the program as an in-patient. He remained at the hospital for four weeks and after discharge, continued to follow up with additional treatments as an out-patient. The doctors interviewed Kay about his bouts of depression and concluded that they stemmed from deep within him and were not the result of family environment, which had always been strong, caring, and supportive.

Kay always knew when a new bout of depression was brewing because in each instance Ron would bring up the bombing of Dresden. In the heat of battle, Ron's bombing missions had separation of space between plane and target below. They were destroying things rather than people. It all seemed quite sanitary. You could be over a target one minute then hours later back at your base, safe from the ravages of war. It was only over time that the bombings really began to work their way through Ron's consciousness, which was often stirred by occasional arguments in the media about the role of Bomber Command and in particular, the necessity to bomb Dresden so near war's end. Ron had second thoughts, particularly about the role he played in the bombing of Dresden, and suffered recurring guilt over the years. Kay observed that he was not able to let go of the memory of the women and children who died as a result of this mission. But despite all this, he still felt proud of his contribution in World War II. He loved the Air Force and his fellow crewmates, keeping in touch with them all.

After his life-threatening experience in 1984, Ron continued under constant medical care due to the deteriorating condition of his liver. In late November 1986, he had a recurrence of his throat haemorrhaging and was rushed to the Queen Elizabeth Hospital where he remained for six weeks as an in-patient. At this time a team of seven doctors treated him for a number of ailments, which included pneumonia, liver damage, as well as an infection in his heart. But Ron miraculously pulled through with the help of his medical team. He lost seventeen pounds and when released was very frail. Try as hard as he could, he was unable to regain his health and vitality. At the time, he had to take over seventeen different pills each day. However this last hospital stay was his final wake up call: he would give it his best shot to take care of himself and totally abstain from alcohol.

Ron slowly regained the weight and diligently followed all the doctors' medical instructions. Sadly, it was too little too late. In July 1987, just six months after the birth of their latest grandchild, Rowan Phendler, Ron and Kay went up to Terrebonne Heights to spend some vacation time. Once at the cottage, Ron became seriously ill and had to be taken by ambulance back to the Queen Elizabeth Hospital in

Montreal. It was a trip of over thirty miles, which to Kay seemed like an eternity. Ron became very weak and suffered from excruciating headaches and nausea. Before being admitted, the attending doctor had Ron sent over to the Wilder Penfield Neurological Hospital for a brain scan where he was diagnosed with a cerebral haemorrhage. He underwent brain surgery, survived the initial operation, but post-operative bleeding set in and he slipped into a coma. On August 12, 1987, at age sixty-two, Ron lost his personal war. He was buried in the Field of Honour at the Lakeview Cemetery in Pointe Claire, Quebec, on August 14, where both his parents also rested.

Sadly, Ron Pyves's wartime experience as a very impressionable youth had contributed to his early demise. It would take Kay on an eight-year journey, starting in 1996, to confirm the connection between Ron's military service and Post Traumatic Stress Disorder, and his resultant depression and alcoholism. It would be a journey for Kay that, in many ways, would be as trying and demanding as Ron's first tour of duty.

19
Passing the Torch

Even before Canadians went overseas to serve in World War II, actions were set in motion by the Canadian government to ensure that individuals in the military would be recognized for service to their country and compensated for loss if disabled or wounded. Actions were also put in place to compensate dependents of those killed while in service. Some of the legislation which passed during wartime included the extension of the benefits provided through the Pension Act to individuals who served during World War II, the War Services Grants Act to assist in the re-establishment of a household by covering the purchase of household items, the Veterans Land Act to assist in the purchase of land for farming, and the Veterans Rehabilitation Act to assist in the establishment of small businesses and unemployment benefits. In 1944, the Department of Veterans Affairs was created to oversee all the various veterans' programs and to coordinate the activities of the government agencies involved in their administration. And in 1946, a Veterans Charter was established which embraced a host of previously approved legislation designed to assist returning veterans or their surviving dependents.

When Ron first become ill in 1968, he explored the possibility of whether he was entitled to any form of disability pension or compensation from the Department of Veterans Affairs, based on his war experiences. He discovered that Kay's income as a paralegal brought their family income above the threshold that would otherwise entitle them to any form of pension. If he had been a widower or divorced, or if Kay had earned less, then Ron would have been entitled to some degree of compensation. Although Ron knew that he was depressed at the time, he would not have been familiar with the symptoms of what would later be known as PTSD.

When Ron was so tragically lost by his family at age sixty-two, Kay decided to continue working, not only as a means of filling some of the void, but also to ensure that she would at least have a small pension after she retired. There were few financial reserves because Ron never received any financial assistance in the last ten years of his life when he was too ill to hold down a full-time job. Although at first Kay found it difficult to focus, with time it became a little easier; she continued to work until the retirement age of sixty-five. In 1991, Kay and Ron's youngest daughter, Colleen, delivered her second baby boy, Eric Ronald Phendler, named in honour of his grandfather. Kay now had ten grandchildren who helped fill the emptiness left by Ron's departure.

After retirement, Kay joined a local social club where members would watch old-time movies and critique them afterward. She also joined the Verdun Friendly Bowling League and quickly became a proficient bowler. These activities, along with weekly swimming sessions at the local YMCA, helped her from dwelling too much on Ron.

But one day in 1996, Kay, now seventy-one years old, picked up one of Ron's old notebooks that had fallen on the bedroom floor. As she picked it up, a pamphlet fell out and landed at her feet. It contained information on pensions for veterans. Then she noticed that Ron had scribbled a few notes on the cover of the brochure indicating that he had been planning to revisit the issue of a veteran's pension. She took this as a sign that Ron was passing her the torch.

Kay felt that she should first explore whether she had any entitlements to a pension as the spouse of a veteran who in her opinion had died prematurely as a direct result of his wartime experience. She felt strongly that if she were awarded a pension, it would be in recognition of all his suffering and that Ron himself would be posthumously helping Kay in her retirement years.

At the time Kay's annual income from all sources after working for over thirty-five years (including the last eighteen years as the primary wage earner) was $24,000, or approximately $19,700 after taxes on which to live. In November 1996, she wrote a seventeen-page letter to the Department of Veterans Affairs' regional office in Montreal. In it she outlined in detail Ron's personal history and medical emergencies and requested clarification on whether there could be any redress to a widow who knew that her husband's illness, including depression, excessive drinking, and death, was a result of his service to the nation. The Department of Veterans Affairs recommended that Kay follow up with her local Legion office to obtain assistance in exploring the possibility of applying for a widow's disability pension.

Just a few years earlier in 1995, the Canadian government introduced new legislation to streamline the application and appeals process for veterans' disability pensions. Prior to 1995, four separate organizations were involved in the pension process, including Veterans Affairs Canada, the Canadian Pension Commision, the Bureau of Pensions Advocates, and the Veterans Appeal Board. In other words, the application processing times had been lengthy. In late 1995, pension reforms delegated authority to Veterans Affairs to make first decisions on disability pension benefit claims. The Veterans Review and Appeal Board were responsible for first and second appeals by claimants.

Kay contacted her local Legion in Notre Dame de Grace (which she belonged to) for direction on how to proceed with her widow's pension claim. The Legion recommended she get in contact with Robbie Robertson, an experienced Provincial Service Officer from the Legion who helped veterans and their widows put together their disability pension applications.

Robbie would prove invaluable. Kay met with him for almost three hours in November. He advised her that she should proceed with a claim based on Post Traumatic Stress Disorder. Only in the last few years had PTSD come to be recognized as a valid reason for awarding veterans a disability pension. Robbie also felt it would be helpful for each of their children to submit a statement of personal recollections and experiences about living and growing up with their father and how the situation at home may have affected their personal lives. To establish a formal start date for the widow's disability pension, Robbie then filed an "intent to claim a pension" with Veterans Affairs Canada on behalf of Kay.

By the end of November, each of the four children had submitted a statement, which was attached to the claim. Although having to relive memories was a difficult and sometimes painful process, it was an exercise that they did willingly. For instance, Kay and Ron's youngest child, Colleen, recalled in her affidavit that:

"My earliest recollections of being aware that my life was maybe not as secure and safe as I had previously thought it was, occurred as early as 1966 when I was twelve. I remember that day well when I came home from school to find my father sitting in the backyard when he normally would have been at work. He told me that his job had come to an end. Even then, I sensed that it was more than a job that had come to an end. To me that was the end of an era and the beginning of a difficult one. Most likely there were problems before this but my realization of them became known that day. From that time on, with very few exceptions, family life seemed to change and my sense of security was very challenged."

Robbie then requested a copy of Ron's entire service file from Veterans Affairs to collaborate his actual military experience and combat duty. In addition, his medical history and files were pulled to gather additional input for the pension claim process. Indeed, Robbie had to do an extensive amount of work to put the final application together.

In August 1997, Robbie recommended that Kay also engage a forensic psychiatrist to conduct a post-mortem analysis of Ron's medical condition and cause of death, which would involve at least four depositions from Ron and Kay's children as well as a deposition from Kay. In November 1997, Kay engaged Dr. Jacques Voyer to conduct the required forensic analysis. The forensic work took a fair amount of time to complete. But in the end it concluded:

It appears to me that this veteran truly suffered from post traumatic stress disorder (DMV-IV) caused by his experiences as a rear gunner during W.W.II. The elements that led me to this diagnosis are:

- *The subject clearly experienced events where other individuals died and where he himself could have died.*

- *There is much evidence, in the file, showing that he constantly re-lived the above-mentioned traumatic events.*
    - *He was clearly a victim of recurrent and invasive memories of the event, as shown in his children's statements.*
    - *I also note "flashbacks" as if the traumatic event had just happened, as well as evidence of intense feelings of psychological distress when exposed to external elements. When the children were young, Mr. Pyves used to set off firecrackers for them but when asked by his daughter to take her to some fireworks he categorically refused saying that it was like flying through flak and watching planes fall.*
    - *I also note a persistent avoidance of stimuli associated with trauma experienced during WWII as 7 or 10 years after he was married he avoided watching movies or programs about the war.*
    - *I also note symptons representative of increased neuro-veg-atative activity as Mr. Pyves had sleep difficulties becoming a "light sleeper." This disturbance appeared 7 to 8 years after he returned from the war and only increased therafter.*

Lastly, his suffering was clinically significant as shown by the numerous hospitalizations in psychiatry and his suicide attempts. In addition there was a marked change in professional functioning; Mr. Pyves' records show difficulties working from 1969. In addition from 1978 until his death he no longer worked.[1]

In early April 1999, almost two and a half years after Kay had first approached the Royal Canadian Legion for assistance, her widow's disability pension application was completed and submitted to Veterans Affairs Canada for a decision. Although this had seemed like an inordinate amount of time to file the claim, it was important to recognize that when the individual was no longer living, there are unique challenges. Now that the application had been formally submitted, it became a waiting game to determine whether the application would be successful.

All the while life went on for Kay. She remained active with her social club, bowling, and swimming. She also went on weekend and summer trips to visit her children and grandchildren. They continued to be a close-knit family who appreciated get-togethers, having fun, and enjoying life, even if the road got bumpy sometimes.

Finally, Kay received a response from Veterans Affairs Canada in February 2000, eleven months after her application had been submitted. During that year, Veterans Affairs approved 66.8 percent of all first applications for a disability pension.[2] Kay's claim for a widow's disability pension was not one of them. She was visibly disappointed, not only because of all the effort put into the process, but more importantly, because in her heart she knew that on behalf of Ron, she had a strong case for compensation.

Kay continued to read the Department's response and encountered obvious errors of fact in the formal response. Her disappointment soon turned into anger. Ron had been referred to as a pilot and a bomber, although the military records submitted clearly noted he had been a tail gunner.[3] In addition, there was an insinuation that he had been manic-depressive (bipolar) and had been prescribed lithium, which was entirely untrue.[4] On one occasion, Ron had been prescribed Librium, which was a tranquilizer used to combat depression. This misinterpretation represented just one more example of the lack of professionalism and respect that had been applied to the initial application. Although some of these errors may not have been material in the decision taken, they did reflect the lack of attention to detail that had gone into the response. It made her wonder just how many other veterans' applications had also been handled in a similar fashion. Apparently she was not the only one asking that question. In 2000, Veterans Affairs initiated a study to determine the quality and consistency of decisions with respect to applications made for disability pensions. The study concluded that there were significant opportunites to improve the overall process, including clarity of communications with respect to the decisions taken by the Veterans Review and Appeal Board.[5]

For Kay, the decision was shocking, especially given the forensic psychiatrist's conclusion that "*Ron had suffered from Post Traumatic Stress Disorder leading to alcoholism and his untimely death.*"[6] Kay's children were also angered and disappointed, not only because of the inaccuracies, but because the whole application process had taken over three years. This had not been an easy experience for their mother.

Kay was a fighter and immediately contacted Robbie at the Royal Canadian Legion, indicating that she intended to appeal the decision. To that end, she applied her paralegal and writing skills and pulled together a thirteen-page draft rebuttal to the written decision. The writing was therapeutic, allowing her to redirect some of her initial anger in a positive effort, a well-written response for Robbie to review.

After meeting with Robbie in March to discuss how to proceed with the First Appeal, she sent him a final copy of the rebuttal in which she mentioned that Ron had suffered daytime nightmares, flashbacks, depression, and anxiety which spiraled until he could no longer work after the age of fifty-four. This time the application preparation process moved somewhat quicker. In April 2001, fifteen months after she had received the initial decision from Veterans Affairs, Kay's disability pension application, with the rebuttal, was submitted to the Review Panel of the Veterans Review and Appeal Board in Charlottetown, P.E.I.[7]

Kay received the Review Panel's deliberations in early August 2001. This time the board made a favourable decision and assessed Ron's disability at 20 percent due to Post Traumatic Stress Disorder, suggesting that the balance of his disability was due to other factors such as alcoholism and depression not related to PTSD. This would mean that Kay would receive 20 percent of the maximum payable amount for a spousal disability pension, or $241 per month tax free. The decision included retroactivity in terms of financial compensation going back three years to May 1998, even though Robbie had sent a notice of intent to apply for a pension entitlement in November 1996, some eighteen months earlier.[8] It is interesting that this 20 percent assessment had been made by the medical examiner for the Review Panel and was not consistent with the forensic psychiatrist's analysis. Dr. Voyer had concluded, "*As for the percentage of disability, I would assess it as more than 50% from 1969 and at more than 70% from 1978 considering the very marked suffering, numerous hospitalizations, with the use of medication, the constant monitoring which he required and the virtually total unemployment until his death."*[9] In the "Facts and Argument" section of the Review Panel's response, there was a comment that Ron's alcoholism had been pre-enlistment, a denial of the fact that his alcoholism had been a consequence of his PTSD.[10] This conclusion was not founded on any evidence: Ron had flown on thirty-five combat missions, and been promoted three times while serving in the RCAF for over two years with no signs of excessive drinking or alcoholism in his records, which were exemplary.

Some evidence that Kay could have submitted in the application process were the very letters that Ron had written to her while overseas. These letters would have reinforced the fact that Ron developed a nervous condition toward the end of his tour when he had the shakes, as well as confirmed that his consumption of alcohol had been limited during his tour of duty. At the time it had been over fifty years since these letters had been written so it is not surprising that Kay might have forgotten the details they contained. Nevertheless, she felt relieved the board had at least recognized that some degree of PTSD had resulted from his wartime experiences. But she also felt that the findings still did not truly reflect the extent to which Ron had been impacted by his tour of duty and, in particular, his role in the bombing of Dresden.

In August 2001, Kay met with Robbie and they agreed to proceed with a final assessment appeal to the Veterans Review and Appeal Board. Kay was determined not to let go of what she felt was a valid claim for compensation on behalf of Ron. In November 2001, the assessment appeal for Ron's PTSD and the entitlement appeal for alcoholism and subsequent death had been forwarded to the Appeal Board.[11] This time the appeal would be presented by Ms. Katharine Roney, service officer for the Dominion Command of the Royal Canadian Legion. Like Robbie, Katharine would turn out to be another very compassionate and efficient service officer who would steer Kay's application through the appeal process. However, the Veterans Review and Appeal Board decided in April 2002 not to increase the assessment of Ron's PTSD from 20 percent.[12]

In its decision letter, Ron was referred to as Ronald Reeves. Kay was devastated. Unless new and relevant evidence not previously considered came to light, Kay's only other possible recourse was the Federal Court of Canada. But this option was clearly beyond Kay's financial means. So in October 2003, Katharine Roney sent a "Request for Reconsideration" to the Veterans Review and Appeal Board. This request was based on an "error in fact": Dr. Voyer's letter dated March 1999 had clearly indicated that Ron's problem was *"Post Traumatic Stress caused by his experiences as a rear gunner during World War II."* And this assessment had not been considered as part of the medical evidence submitted with the original claim. Katharine also requested the opportunity to present the "Reconsideration Request" verbally.

In November 2003, Kay was informed that the Board had to first determine whether there were legal grounds on which a "Reconsideration Request" could be heard. Fortunately, a "Determination" hearing was approved in late January. Then, in February 2004, Kay received a letter informing her that the Board had increased Ron's assessment based on PTSD from 20 percent to 50 percent, which entitled Kay to a full survivor's pension.[13] Kay was now seventy-eight years old and had been working on the pension claim for almost eight years.

Although not confirmed in writing, Kay was told that the Panel changed its decision after revisiting the forensic psychiatrist's assessment submitted back in April 1999, some five years earlier. This was very good news; it reaffirmed Kay's belief that PTSD was the cause of Ron's medical condition. And it also provided Kay with a supplement to her small pension from work, which had a material effect on her quality of life because it almost doubled her after-tax income.

It was unfortunate, however, that the overall pension process took almost eight years to resolve and that a pension was not available until long after Ron's death in 1987. This meant that during his last years, Ron had been unable to receive any benefits for the many sacrifices he made serving his country. In Kay's mind a final, positive settlement on the widow's disability pension was at least some vindication for all the suffering that Ron had gone through over the last twenty years of his life.

Kay's tour of duty to bring some resolution to Ron's personal war had become an eight-year journey. But she had been more than determined to make it for a man who had been an honourable and loving partner and caring father. A man who had on that fateful day set out so innocently from his parent's cottage on Lake Nantel at age nineteen, and journeyed through a world of night madness.

***

The year 2004 marked Ron's 80th birthday and even though Ron had been gone for some seventeen years, Kay sat down and wrote him one last letter,

> *Dear Ron, Happy 80th birthday <u>here, and</u> in the <u>heavens</u>.*
>
> *I miss your earthly presence, but your love <u>remains</u> in my heart to warm my spirit.*
>
> *Ron I feel you have gained quite an entourage of loved ones around you <u>eternally</u> in your <u>heavenly</u> home—and here on earth too.*
>
> *You are <u>encircled</u> by all who love you, and that brings me comfort and peace.*
>
> *We have a loving family and they <u>never</u> fail to cheer and warm <u>my</u> heart.*
>
> *We all miss you dearly especially "yours truly"—but we feel you are <u>at peace</u> <u>at last</u>.*
>
> *Pass my deep loving wishes and prayers to all my loved ones, and dear friends, up there.*
>
> *Until we meet again...*
>
> Love always, Kay.

***

Having lived alone for many years, Kay developed a real passion for striking up conversations with friends and strangers alike. Never at a loss for words, Kay continued to be articulate, open-minded, and, to her grandchildren, a grandmother who kept up with the times.

In August 2007, Kay joined three of her children—Julie, Colleen, and Rick, along with Rick's wife, Judy, and two of her grandchildren, Rowan and Eric, in Ocean Park, Maine. Everyone stayed in a large Victorian-style house. It was a memorable vacation with trips to the beach, boogie boarding, and late-night Scrabble games. Sadly, this would turn out to be the last time that most of her children would be with her. On December 15, after an unexpected heart affliction, Kay, at age eighty-two, peacefully departed this life. She was surrounded by many of the people who had grown to love and respect this truly caring mother, nanny, wife, and advocate.

Kay first met Ron while skiing up north in St. Sauveur in March 1943, and her love for him would be cemented during their prolific correspondence during the war years. It never abated through both good and not so good times. And it most certainly continues to this day.

L38 S/O 17 25 GLT

28

MISS K EASON 3538 DORRION
ST MONTREAL QUEBEC =

HAVE FINISHED TOUR OF OPS LOVE =

RONALD PYVES ※

Ron and Kay at their wedding reception on March 23, 1946, at the Queens Hotel in Montreal

Ron working on a blueprint as a draftsman

Ron and Kay at their wedding reception. Directly behind Ron are his parents, Laura and Edward Pyves, and Kay's father, Bert Eason, in the front row on the far right.

Ron and Kay Pyves with their son, Richard Ronald, and daughter, Leslie Susan, in 1949

Ron and Kay Pyves's two youngest daughters, Colleen (on far left) and Julia (on far right), at Christmas in 1959

Ron and Kay Pyves (on the right) at a formal dinner with his older brother, Edward, and his wife, Edna Pyves (nee Campbell), in 1956

Bill Thomson (M/UG) with author, Rick Pyves,
May 2001

Frank Welsh (B/A) with Kay Pyves, December
2006

The Crew

Joseph (Joe) Xavier Riel Casavant
Flight Engineer

Joe Casavant was from the small farming community of Tisdale, Saskatchewan. Joe's parents were Emile Casavant, originally from St. Damase, Quebec, and Emelda Grenier from Thorne, North Dakota. He had eleven siblings, including eight sisters and three brothers. Most of his early years were spent assisting his father and siblings with the family farm and attending the local public country school known as Arpsville. By the time war broke out in 1939, Joe, who had finished school after grade nine, was anxious to play an active role in the growing global conflict. In 1942, he decided to join the RCAF and like most volunteers, initially aspired to be a pilot but eventually trained to be a flight engineer. Joe was 5'4", had clear blue eyes, light brown hair, and was quite athletic. He was also a hard worker. After completing his training, he met up with Ron Pyves and the rest of the members of his crew at No. 22 Heavy Conversion Unit at Wellesbourne, England, and would eventually complete thirty-five missions including thirty-three trips with Ron.

Joe was screened from operations on March 24, 1945, after the crew's final trip together to Bottrop. On April 18, 1945, he was promoted to Flight Sergeant. Joe was initially posted out to No. 64 RCAF base on June 4, 1945, and was then repatriated to Canada in late June.

After arriving back in Canada, Joe volunteered to serve in the Korean conflict but was never called up for service so he returned to

farming in Tisdale. Joe met Margaret Whitely, who, although originally born in Ontario, had moved with her family to Simpson, Saskatchewan, in the 1920s. They married on August 5, 1946. In 1951,
their first son, Daniel, was born, followed by two daughters, Deborah
in 1953, and Mary in 1955. Unfortunately both daughters were lost at
a young age to childhood diseases. Joe and Margaret's fourth and last
child, Gerard David, was born in 1958 in Winnipeg.

In 1955, Joe, like his fellow crewmates Bob Henry and Al Coleman,
decided to rejoin the RCAF on a full-time basis where he worked in
the aircraft maintenance area. Joe moved around to various military
installations, including Trenton, Lake Simcoe, and Barrie, Ontario,
before moving in 1957 to work at the RCAF maintenance facility in
Winnipeg. Here he worked on jet engines. Joe continued to work for
the RCAF until 1969 when he retired and took a position as Maintenance Manager at Simpsons-Sears, a position he held for almost
ten years.

In 1979, Joe decided to move to Pouce Coupe, a small town in British Columbia located just south of Dawson Creek, where the Alaskan
Highway starts. This began the migration of the family to British Columbia. While in Pouce Coupe, Joe worked in the engineering and
maintenance department at the local hospital. After living in Pouce
Coupe for a while, Joe moved Margaret to Richmond, B.C., while he
remained behind due to health issues. Following open-heart bypass
surgery he joined Margaret in Richmond where he spent time recovering from his operation. Unable to stay idle, Joe took on maintenance
work with the Oblate Priests, at their Mother House in Vancouver.

On February 7, 1990, Joe was struck by a fatal heart attack while at
work. Joe is buried at Valley View Memorial Gardens in Surrey, B.C.

***

The year 1990 was a tough one for the crew of 434 Squadron, who
had flown together forty-five years earlier. Both Joe Casavant and Bob
Henry were lost that year.

Alan (Al) Price Coleman
Navigator

Alan Price Coleman was a child of the prairies, born on September 26, 1924, in Magrath, a small Alberta farming community just thirty miles north of the U.S. border. His parents were Clarence Leo Coleman, a farmer, and his wife, Elizabeth Emma Mercer. Alan came from a military family as both his grandfathers, Leo Coleman and Ammon Mercer, served in the Canadian Expeditionary Force in WW I.

Life on a farm during the Great Depression was tough and from an early age Alan and his brother, Shelly, and two sisters, Patricia and Ruth, had to work hard to help their mother and father manage the farm. After he graduated from Magrath High School, Alan couldn't wait to get involved in the war and in July 1941 he attempted to enlist in the RCAF while in Calgary. To his great disappointment he was not accepted because he was underage. In 1942, Alan worked at the Monarch Door manufacturing facility in Tacoma, Washington, but on his eighteenth birthday, quit his job and returned to Calgary to enlist again. This time the RCAF accepted his application.

Like most RCAF volunteers, Alan aspired to serve as a pilot. When he enlisted, he had a fair complexion, brown hair, and piercing blue eyes, and with his slight build looked quite tall at 5'10". Alan also had a scar line just above his left eye as a souvenir of a basketball game in high school.

He first attended No. 2 Initial Training School in Regina and then moved on to No. 2 Elementary Flight Training School in Fort William. Here, like many other recruits, Alan was deemed not to have the necessary air sense and co-ordination to be a pilot even though his aircraft recognition and signal skills were very good. In May he was selected for navigation and sent to No. 5 Air Observer School in Winnipeg. After finishing his initial training course to become a navigator, Alan transferred to No. 3 Advanced Gunnery Training School in January 1944 in Trois-Rivières, Quebec. Alan embarked from Halifax for England in March 1944.

Alan met up with the rest of his RCAF crewmates at No. 22 Operational Training Unit in Wellesbourne in late May 1944. He served as the navigator for his crew in 434 Bluenose Squadron for thirty-two of his total thirty-four trips. Alan had also been fortunate to meet up with a local girl, Olga Victoria Coleman (unrelated), who he married on September 11, 1945, at St. Cuthbert Parish Church in Darlington, just six months after he completed his tour. Olga was only nineteen years old.

After Alan finished his tour of duty, he remained as a navigation instructor in England. While on a practice run, his Lancaster ran into severe fog and crashed into Beamsley Beacon in the Yorkshire Dales between Skipton and Ilkey. The resultant blaze was so intense that when the rescuers arrived they could not get within several hundred feet of the burning plane. Of the eight Canadian crew members, four were killed. One of the surviving crew members, Sergeant Joseph Balenger, managed to pull Alan and two of the other crew free from the plane wreckage. Alan suffered second degree burns to his face as well as multiple head and body lacerations. Three of the survivors, including Alan, were taken to Highroyds Emergency Medical Hospital in Menston. Alan remained in critical condition for four days and spent a number of months in hospital before he fully recovered. For someone who had survived thirty-four combat missions, this training flight had been an unexpectedly close call.

Upon his return to Canada in 1946, Alan attended the University of Alberta where he obtained a Bachelor of Commerce degree in 1950. His war-bride wife Olga gave birth to their first child in 1949, a daughter named Patricia Ann, followed two years later by a son, William Alan. Alan re-enlisted in the Air Force and spent a short period stationed in Edmonton before he moved on to a new assignment in London, Ontario, in May. By July of the same year, they moved to Moncton where Alan worked until May 1953. For the next three years, Alan and his family lived in Langar, England, where Alan served with No. 30 Air Material Base. He transferred back to Canada in July 1956 and worked at Air Force Headquarters in the Comptrollers Office in Ottawa. In October 1958, he was promoted to Flight Lieutenant and in 1960 he and his family moved to Trenton, where Alan continued to work in the Comptrollers Office for the next five years. He then moved to a similar role at RCAF Falconbridge northeast of Sudbury. In August 1969, he transferred to Ottawa and, in 1972, elected to retire from the RCAF, having by this time attained the rank of Captain.

Alan's brother, Leo Shelly, also an RCAF WW II vet, had also rejoined the RCAF in 1951 and unfortunately was killed in Sardinia while serving with 444 Squadron in Europe as part of NATO in 1957. Leo at the time was a pilot instructor flying Sabre jets.

Alan was only five years into an active retirement in Victoria, B.C., when he passed away prematurely on April 10, 1977 due to a heart attack. His final resting place is at the Royal Oak Burial Park in Saanich, B.C. Alan had served a total of twenty-three years in the Air Force and became the first of his crew to pass away. He was fifty-two.

Jack Carlton Henry
Pilot

Jack Carlton Henry, born on June 5, 1918, in Kingston, Ontario, was the second son of Thomas Reid Henry and Lottie Grace Williams. Jack spent his first several years in Kingston but then moved in 1920 with his family to Yorkton, Saskatchewan, and later Saskatoon, where his father owned a book and shoe store. In 1921, his younger brother Robert James Henry was born. Both would go on to have very similar careers in the RCAF during World War II.

When Jack enlisted in the RCAF on September 9, 1941, having worked at the Bank of Nova Scotia for four years, his manager provided a reference which stated that he was "a young man of good ability, steady habits and exemplary character." At the time of enlistment Jack was described as being 5'11", weighing 150 pounds, and being of medium build with brown hair and hazel eyes.

Jack first attended No. 2 Manning Depot in Brandon, Manitoba, from mid-September through early January 1942, learning some of the theories of flying. While there, he was interviewed by his commanding officer who felt "Jack was intelligent, well organized, and pleasant and should be recommended for a commission when qualified as a pilot." Jack was then transferred to No. 12 Service Flying Training School and then moved to No. 7 Initial Flying School in Saskatoon. Having done well, he was sent to No. 16 Elementary Flying Training School in Edmonton where he flew his first solo flight on a

Tiger Moth biplane. Jack graduated in June 1942 and was promoted to Pilot Officer in October.

With his proven abilities as a pilot, Jack was sent to No. 3 Flying Instructor School in Arnprior, Ontario, until the end of December. It was at this time that the career paths of Jack and his younger brother Bob would start to cross. For the first seven months of 1943, they were flight instructors at No. 6 Elementary Flying Training School in Prince Albert, Saskatchewan. During this period they flew together in training. In August 1943, Bob was shipped overseas. Jack would follow two months later.

After moving from Liverpool to No. 3 Personnel Reception Centre in Bournemouth, Jack finally moved in late February to No. 14 Advanced Flying Unit in Banff, Scotland, where he trained on two-engine bombers. Finally, Jack moved to No. 22 Operational Training Unit in Wellesbourne, Warwickshire, learning how to pilot two-engine heavy bombers, including the Wellington. It was while at Wellesbourne that Jack was promoted to Flying Officer and would meet up with the rest of his crew. Jack's regular crew members included Navigator F/O G.T. Williams (J37119), Bomb Aimer F/O J.W. Leblanc (J27403), Wireless Operator P/O H.G. Butler (J89434), Mid-Upper Gunner F/Sgt. K.L. Gregory (R254362), Rear Gunner F/Sgt. S. Gordon (R183357), and Flight Engineer Sgt. J.C. Baker (1605443). After completing the program at Wellesbourne Jack spent a short period at RCAF No. 61 Base before moving on to No. 1659 Heavy Conversion Unit located at Topcliffe, where he refined his flying skills on the four-engine Halifax.

On September 26, 1944, Jack joined 431 Iroquois Squadron. Jack's brother, Bob, was already flying out of the same air base. Over the following six months Jack and Bob would fly in separate bombers on twenty of the same missions. Jack would fly on his last mission to Hamburg on March 31, 1945, and was taken off strength from 431 Squadron in May 1945, having accumulated a total of 522 hours of flying, including 242 operational hours over Germany and France. Like his brother, Jack was awarded the Distinguished Flying Cross for "completing numerous operations against the enemy in the course of which he has invariably displayed the utmost fortitude, courage and devotion to duty." Incredibly, Jack and Bob flew on a combined seventy-two combat missions.

Jack returned to Canada in early August and would remain in the RCAF Reserve until November 1949. Jack then returned to his former Bank of Nova Scotia employer where he worked as a clerk until 1949. He then moved to New Westminster, B.C., where he continued to work for the bank.

By 1954, Jack had met and married his wife, Annabelle. Jack's career eventually took him to St. Boniface, Winnipeg, where in 1968 he worked as an accountant for the local Co-op Credit Union Society. In 1970, Jack became Manager of the Astra Credit Union Society where he remained until his sudden death on October 2, 1970, due to heart complications.

Robert James (Bob) Henry
Pilot

R obert James Henry was born in Yorkton, Saskatchewan, in 1921 and later moved with his family to Saskatoon. Bob attended the local public and high school, and after graduating decided to enlist in the RCAF in 1941 with the objective of becoming a pilot.

Like his brother Jack, he successfully completed the necessary courses at training schools in various parts of the country, flying in Tiger Moths, Avro Amsons, Fairchild single-engine Cornells, two-engine Cessna Cranes, and other now classic aircraft.

In 1942, his instructors rated him "an accurate pilot who coordinated his patter (instructions) with his flying very well." In August 1943, Bob was posted overseas, having accumulated over 850 hours of flying experience in Canada. His first assignment was at No. 14 Advanced Flying Unit in Banff, Scotland, involving the multi-engine Oxford. After completing this course, Bob was rated as a "high average" pilot and posted to No. 22 Operational Training Unit in Wellesbourne. Here he learned how to pilot twin-engine heavy bombers, starting with the Wellington. He completed his training at Wellesbourne in late July 1944. He then moved on to four-engine Halifax bombers at No. 1659 Heavy Conversion Unit at Topcliffe where, with a total flight time of 990 hours, was ranked an "above average" pilot, which was welcome news to Ron and the rest of the crew.

Bob completed his thirty-sixth mission and was screened along with the rest of the crew on March 24, 1945. He had accumulated an impressive 1,500 hours of flying time and was awarded a Distinguished Flying Cross. Bob volunteered for an additional tour of duty with Tiger Force and returned to Canada with Ron in 1945.

With the need to fight in the Pacific no longer required, Bob decided to continue with his career in the RCAF. In early January 1948, he joined No. 406 Tactical Bomber (Auxiliary) Squadron in Saskatoon, and initially flew the single-engine Harvard. By November he began to spend time on the two-engine Beech aircraft. While posted in Saskatoon, he met and married Erma Bernice Tweddle in 1947.

In 1949, Bob moved to the American-built Mitchell B-25 twin-engine bomber, which had been used so effectively in the war. He also flew two-engine Dakotas, with the commercial version known as the DC-3. In the summer of 1952, Bob and Erma's first child, Donna Lynn Henry, was born, to be followed two years later by their first son, William Robert Henry. Their second son, John Allen, was born in 1961.

Bob continued to fly mainly in the B-25 on training missions. By late 1956 he had accumulated almost three thousand hours of flying time since first going aloft in a Tiger Moth two-seater as a student in 1942. In December 1956, Bob, now thirty-five years old, started jet training and had his first solo flight in a CT-33 Silver Star jet trainer in early 1957. This single-engine jet, built by Canadair in Montreal, had a maximum speed of 570 miles per hour and a wing span of only thirty-eight feet. It was a far cry from the four-engine, thirty-four ton fully loaded Lancaster that Bob had to handle in WW II.

Four months later, Bob made his first solo flight in an Avro CF-100 jet fighter, which would become the mainstay of the RCAF in the 1960s. In August 1957, he transferred out to 414 All Weather Fighter Squadron based in North Bay, Ontario, flying CF-100s. In October 1960, he moved to Metz, France, where he was responsible for in-flight safety. Ironically, this is where he had his first serious flying incident since the war, when as second pilot in a CT-33, he had to bail out. Due to injury, Bob was flown by chopper to a U.S. Army Medical Command in Germany. Bob had suffered a broken elbow and a compression fracture in his back. He remained in hospital some two months, recovering from injuries, and did not recommence flying until 1961 when he flew once more in a CT-33.

Bob continued to fly CT-33s on a regular basis until September 1963 when he moved on to the Douglas-built C-47 two-engine plane used for transportation of military supplies. In 1964, he transferred to 129 Squadron based in Trenton, Ontario, and flew C-47s to various locations around the world. Former crewmate Al Coleman was also stationed at the Trenton air base, which allowed them to renew their friendship.

In 1964, Bob had his first solo flight in a CT-11 Tutor jet, then used by the RCAF for training. It is the type of aircraft still flown by the Canadian Snowbirds. He continued to add to his eclectic list of aircraft flown, and late in 1964 piloted the single-engine Otter built by De Havilland Canada.

At the time of his retirement in 1970, Bob had amassed an impressive 7,485 hours in the air, equivalent to being airborne for 312 days.

After his retirement from the Air Force, Bob followed in the footsteps of his father and, from 1976 through 1984, worked in Leslie's Shoe Store on Front Street in Belleville. Bob died on July 18, 1990, at age 69. He is buried at the Woodlawn Cemetery in Saskatoon. He was the fourth crew member lost to his comrades, family, and friends.

During the war, Bob had been one of the older crew members. He had played the role of an older brother to his crewmates, who, with the exception of Hal Ward and Joe Casavant, were several years younger at a time when even three or four years of additional experience and maturity could make a huge difference. Although it took the effort and expertise of every crew member to bring their ship back safely from each mission, the pilot had final control of the plane in all circumstances and the additional responsibility of moulding the young crew into an efficient team. As well, Bob had to make split-second decisions to avoid attacking enemy aircraft and whether or not to press on to the target under adverse conditions. All said, Bob was well respected by his crew for both his professionalism under fire and his great sense of humour.

Alfred William (Bill) Thomson
Mid-Upper Gunner

Alfred William (Bill) Thomson was born in Toronto on September 4, 1923. His parents were Alfred Truby Thomson and Marguerite Alberta Hopkins. Bill's father had been a member of the 81ˢᵗ Battalion as part of the Canadian Expeditionary Force in the First World War. Bill joined the RCAF in 1943 and like most volunteers aspired to be a bomber pilot. In fact, he already had a licence to fly single-engine planes. Unfortunately Bill was unable to complete the pilot training program for multi-engine planes so his training ultimately led him to become a mid-upper gunner. As one of the younger members of the crew, Bill felt a close affinity to Ron, the youngest, and also a gunner. In fact, Ron and Bill flew on thirty-three trips together during their tour of duty. Whenever the crew went on personal leave, Bill always joined up with Ron when he visited relatives. They were almost inseparable and remained close friends after the war.

While in England, Bill married Edna Weeks, who lived in Darlington, near Croft. When Bill completed his tour in March 1945, he remained in England until his first son, Bruce William, arrived, returning home to Canada in late 1945. Edna shipped out to Canada the following year, travelling with her son on the *Queen Mary*, a Cunard White Star Liner. When they arrived in Canada, housing was tight so the family had to spend their first two years with Bill's parents. But once settled in Toronto, Bill and Edna's family expanded with the arrival of their second son, Gary, and a daughter, Janice.

In 1947, Bill found a job at Simpsons and two years later changed employers to work as a clerk at Massey Harris. In 1949, Bill and Edna moved to their first home at Number 4 on Fourth Avenue on Ward's Island, just off the Toronto waterfront. It was a great venue to raise a young family. The following year Bill became a manager at *The Telegram* and a year later worked as a salesman at Yorktown Motors, moving on to another sales position at Danforth Motors in 1952.

In 1954, Bill made a significant career move which would take him in an entirely new direction. He accepted a position as an insurance adjuster for the Service Fire Insurance Company of New York. Then in 1957, he accepted a supervisory position there and moved to Scarborough. In 1960, Bill entered into a partnership with a business associate, establishing Crestview Auto Body. A few years later he decided to work as a driving instructor/tester for the province, working out of the Keele Street office in Toronto. Bill remained at this job for many years and ultimately moved into a supervisory role within the Motor Vehicle Bureau. In 1962, the family moved to another location in Scarborough where they lived for a number of years. By 1978, with the children moved out, Bill and Edna moved to an apartment building. Always on the go, Bill and Edna moved in 1985 to the Village of Queensville, in Ontario, and a few years later to a house in Bobcaygeon to enjoy the country lifestyle. They now had six grandchildren.

In 2001, after fifty years of marriage, Bill lost his wife and soulmate, Edna. Two year later, in September 2003, Bill was also lost to his friends and family. He now rests in Verulam Cemetery near Bobcaygeon, Ontario.

Harold (Hal) LeRoy Ward
Wireless Operator

Harold (Hal) L. Ward, the son of Clifford Ward and Verna Harris, was born in July 1921 in Dorchester, Middlesex County, in southern Ontario. He came from a line of Wards who had been in North America since the late 1700s. Although his father and grandfather, Thomas Jefferson Ward, had both been born in Canada, the reality was that the Ward family tended to bounce back and forth between Ontario, Michigan, and New York State.

Hal's father did various odd jobs to provide for his family and had been fortunate to obtain work at the Buick Plant in Flint, Michigan. Just five years after Hal's birth, his father died prematurely, leaving Verna to raise her young son. Hal attended the local schools in Dorchester and upon graduation decided to volunteer for the RCAF. He enlisted in February 1940, and like so many of the volunteers, aspired to be a pilot.

Due to a lack of training facilities, it wasn't until August 1942 that Hal received orders to report to No. 1 Manning Depot in Toronto to start his pilot training. Eventually Hal, like most of his future crewmates, became part of the 30 percent of students who did not qualify as bomber pilots, so he switched gears and attended the RCAF No. 4 Wireless School in Guelph, Ontario.

By March 1943, he had qualified to be a wireless operator. As wireless operators were also trained as backup air gunners, Hal attended the air gunnery school in Fingal, Ontario—the same station where Ron Pyves trained. He graduated from air gunnery school in early May and married his long-time flame, Violet Jean Wright. He then moved to No. 4 Air Observer School in London, Ontario, just five miles from home, and served as a wireless operator at this location until February 1944, on almost two hundred flights, where he flew in Anson bombers.

By May 1944, Hal had accumulated over eight hundred hours of flying time as both an air gunner and wireless operator, with the majority of his air time dedicated to the latter. After graduation from an advanced wireless operator school, Hal embarked for Liverpool. He then moved on to Bournemouth after processing and further training, then to Wellesbourne to meet the balance of his crewmates. Departure from Canada had been difficult for Hal, as his first child, Sharon Agnes, would be born shortly after Hal arrived in England.

After thirty-three missions—including twenty-five trips with his regular crewmates—Hal was screened after the final trip to Bottrop. He then worked for a time in the adjutant's office in Croft before returning to Canada.

After discharge from the RCAF in August 1945, Hal returned to London, Ontario, and like many other returning military personnel, found the hunt for a new job quite challenging. He had always wanted to work for the railway as an engineer and, fortuitously, came across an advertisement by the Canadian Pacific Railway (C.P.R.) that was looking for dispatchers. This would at least provide entry into a railway job. The Chief Dispatcher told him that his wireless experience made him a strong candidate, but he would need to go back to school to learn railway telegraphy. This form of telegraphy was based on a continental code different from the Morse code, which Hal had learned while in the air force. He attended and graduated from the Kasson School of Telegraphy in Toronto and started work for the C.P.R. as a stand-in for vacationing or sick dispatchers. During this time, Hal worked at Guelph Junction, as well as at Streetsville and the Windsor railway junctions, where he would issue train orders and pick up key messages with a wooden hoop as trains passed through the junction.

In 1948, Hal and Violet's second daughter, Cicily, was born. For five years they lived at a railway station in East Zorra Township, a rural community in Oxford County, Ontario, before they moved into their first residence in London, Ontario. In 1958, they moved into their dream home on McLarenwood Terrace in London, where they lived together for over fifty years.

In May 2010, having been happily married for over sixty-five years, Hal was lost to his family and is now buried in the Dorchester Union Cemetery in Dorchester, Ontario. He was in his ninetieth year. Hal at the time was the oldest surviving member of the group of young airmen who had met by chance in Wellesbourne, England, sixty-six years earlier.

Frank John Welsh
Bomb Aimer

Frank John Welsh was born in Birmingham, England, in the fall of 1923. Frank's parents were David Welsh and Kathleen Lockhart. In 1929, at the onset of the Depression, Frank's father lost his position at Sun Oil and with bleak job prospects in England, elected to strike out with the family to Canada. They were following in the footsteps of some close friends who had preceded them to London, Ontario.

Here Frank attended St. Martin's Elementary School with his younger siblings, Irene and Lawrence, followed by attendance at De La Salle High where he graduated in 1941 at age seventeen. One day in the spring of 1942, Frank decided to join the Air Force. Frank recalled that he had been playing pool at Ray's Billiards with two close friends. Here they talked about the possibility of getting drafted into the army when the Air Force was their service of choice. To address this issue they agreed to volunteer so they could choose where to serve. With no time like the present, all three put down their cues and hiked downtown to the RCAF recruiting office. At the time, Frank's two friends both failed their initial medical and returned home. But Frank ended up in the RCAF.

Frank wanted to be a pilot but did not make it through pilot school. Instead he trained as a bomb aimer and in 1943 was shipped overseas. After the required processing and training, he was posted out to No. 22 Operational Training Unit at Wellesbourne, where he met up with the rest of his new crew with whom he would fly thirty-three missions (and one with another crew) before being screened.

Frank then returned to Topcliffe as a bombing instructor. When the war in Europe ended, he too volunteered to fight in Tiger Force. But the atomic bomb precluded the need so Frank returned to Canada in late 1945 where he married Rita Madeline Tevlin in 1949. He then pursued an accounting degree through Queen's University and became a chartered accountant. In 1950, Rita gave birth to their first child, John David. The two would eventually have four more sons (Peter Francis, Paul Gerard, Stephen Michael, and Michael Joseph) and two daughters (Maureen Elizabeth and Suzanne Margaret).

Frank first articled in London, Ontario, and in 1954, set out on his own, forming a practice that he ran successfully for many years.

In 1970, Frank sold his practice and then joined another in Tilsonburg, Ontario, as a comptroller. And in 1973, Frank finally obtained his pilot's licence. He not only flew within Canada but also down in Florida, piloting various Cessna and Piper aircraft. He would accumulate over five hundred hours of flying experience. Unlike wartime, Frank loved the solitude and control that he had flying his own plane.

High interest rates in the late seventies caused Frank's employer, a real estate developer, to shut down and Frank found himself unemployed in his fifties. So in 1974, he re-established a successful public accounting practice to support his family. By 1999, Frank and Rita had fourteen grandchildren.

In early 2000, Frank lost Rita after fifty years of marriage. They had raised seven children who had all grown up and raised families of their own.

Frank eventually sold his business but continued to work for the firm until his eightieth birthday, at which time he decided to slide gracefully into full retirement. He remained active for many years playing golf and providing the occasional babysitting service for his many grandchildren. On June 26, 2010, Frank passed away in his eighty-seventh year. He is buried in St. Peter's Cemetery in London, Ontario.

Abbreviations

A.G.T.S. – Air Gunnery Training School
A.F.U. – Advanced Flying Unit
A.O.S. – Air Observer School
B/A – Bomb Aimer
B & G. S. – Bombing and Gunnery School
B.C.A.T.P. – British Commonwealth Air Training Plan
Co. – Company
D.F.C. – Distinguished Flying Cross
E.F.T.S. – Elementary Flight Training School
F/E – Flight Engineer
F.I.S. – Flying Instructor School
F/O – Flying Officer
F/L – Flight Lieutenant
F/Sgt. – Flight Sergeant
H.C.U. – Heavy Conversion Unit
I.T.S. – Initial Training School
M.P.H. – Miles per Hour
MU/AG – Mid-Upper Air Gunner
NAV – Navigator
N.C.O. – Non-Commissioned Officer
O.T.U. – Operational Training Unit
P/O – Pilot Officer
P.O. – Post Office
P.O.W. – Prisoner of War
P.S.I. – Pounds per Square Inch
RAF – Royal Air Force
R/AG – Rear Air Gunner
RCAF – Royal Canadian Air Force
R.P.M. – Revolutions per Minute
S.F.T.S. – Service Flying Training School
S.M. – Sergeant Major
Sgt. – Sergeant
WOP/AG – Wireless Operator/Air Gunner

Notes

Chapter Three – Over There

1. Canadian Directorate of History and Heritage, Report No. 131: Canadian Participation in the Operations in North-West Europe, 6 June – 31 July 44, paragraph 28.
2. Ibid and paragraph 29
3. Canadian Directorate of History and Heritage, Report No. 131: Canadian Participation In The Operations In North-West Europe, 6 June – 31 July 44, Appendix "C"
4. Commonwealth Air Training Museum Inc., *They Shall Not Grow Old*, p. 686

Chapter Four – Heavy Conversion Unit Training

1. Canadian Directorate of History and Heritage, Report No. 169: Canadian Participation in the Operations in North-West Europe, 1944. Part III: Canadian Operations, 1 – 23 August, paragraph 124
2. Canadian Directorate of History and Heritage, Report No. 169: Canadian Participation in the Operations in North-West Europe, 1944. Part III: Canadian Operations, 1 – 23 August, paragraph 12
3. Middlebrook, Martin and Chris Everitt, *The Bomber Command War Diaries*, (New York 1985) p. 557
4. Canadian Directorate of History and Heritage, Report No. 169: Canadian Participation in the Operations in North-West Europe, 1944. Part III: Canadian Operations, 1 – 23 August, paragraph 203
5. Canadian Directorate of History and Heritage, Report No. 169: Canadian Participation in the Operations in North-West Europe, 1944. Part III: Canadian Operations, 1 – 23 August, paragraph 202

Chapter Five – Combat Ready

1. Library and Archives Canada, Operations Record Book (ORB) No. 434 Squadron, Jan. 1943 - Aug. 1944, microfilm reel. C-12309
2. Library and Archives Canada, ORB No. 434 Squadron, Aug. 1944, microfilm reel C-12309

3. Library and Archives Canada, ORB No. 434 Squadron, Jan. 1943 – Apr. 1945 microfilm reel C-12309 and C-12310
4. Ibid.
5. Library and Archives Canada, ORB No. 434 Squadron, June – Sept., 1944, microfilm reel C-12309
6. Interview with Frank Welsh, May 2008
7. Library and Archives Canada, ORB No. 434 Squadron, Sept. 15, 1944, microfilm reel C-12309
8. Ibid.
9. Flying Log Book, Sgt. Ronald Pyves, Sept. 17, 1944
10. Pilot and Engineer's Notes, Air Publication 1719 C & G, Air Ministry March 1944
11. Interview with Frank Welsh, May 2008
12. Pilot and Engineer's Notes, Air Publication 1719C & G, Air Ministry March 1944
13. Letter from Ron Pyves to Kay Eason
14. Pilot and Engineer's Notes, Air Publication 1719C & G, Air Ministry March 1944
15. Library and Archives Canada, ORB No. 434 Squadron, Sept. 20, 1944, microfilm reel C-12309
16. Flying Log Book, Sgt. Ronald Pyves, Sept. 20, 1944
17. Flying Log Book, F/O Frank Welsh, Sept. 20, 1944
18. Library and Archives Canada, ORB No. 434 Squadron, Sept. 20, 1944, microfilm reel C-12309 and www.6grouprcaf.com/Sept-44operations.html
19. Library and Archives Canada, ORB No. 434 Squadron, Sept. 20, 1944, microfilm reel C-12309
20. Flying Log Book, Sgt. Ronald Pyves, Sept. 20, 1944
21. Ibid.
22. Flying Log Book, Sgt. Ronald Pyves, Sept. 23, 1944
23. Canadian Directorate of History and Heritage, Report No. 184: Canadian Participation In The Operations in North-West Europe 1944. Part V: Clearing the Channel Ports, 3 Sept 44 – 6 Feb. 45, paragraph 111
24. Written by Frank Welsh. Used with permission 2009
25. Flying Log Book, Sgt. Ronald Pyves, Sept. 25, 1944

26. Flying Log Book, F/O Frank Welsh, Sept. 25, 1944
27. Ibid.
28. Library and Archives Canada, ORB No. 434 Squadron, Sept. 25, 1944, microfilm reel C-12309
29. Ibid. and www.6grouprcaf.com/Sept44operations.html
30. Middlebrook, Martin and Chris Everitt, *The Bomber Command War Diaries*, (New York 1985) p. 589
31. Flying Log Book, Sgt. Ronald Pyves, Sept. 26, 1944
32. Library and Archives Canada, ORB No. 434 Squadron, Sept. 26, 1944, microfilm reel C-12309
33. Ibid.
34. Library and Archives Canada, ORB No. 434 Squadron, Sept. 26, 1944, microfilm reel C-12309 and www.6grouprcaf.com/Sept-44operations.html
35. www.6grouprcaf.com/Sept44operations.html
36. Canadian Directorate of History and Heritage, Report No. 184: Canadian Participation In The Operations in North-West Europe 1944. Part V: Clearing the Channel Ports, 3 Sept 44 – 6 Feb. 45, paragraph 115
37. Flying Log Book, Sgt. Ronald Pyves, Sept. 26, 1944
38. www.rcaf434squadron.com/crew-downloads/
39. Library and Archives Canada, ORB No. 434 Squadron, June 16, 1944, microfilm reel C-12309
40. Library and Archives Canada, ORB No. 434 Squadron Sept. 27, 1944, microfilm reels C-12309
41. Library and Archives Canada, ORB No. 434 Squadron, Sept. 27, 1944 – April 30, 1945, microfilm reels C-12309 and C-12310
42. www.6grouprcaf.com/Sept44operations.html
43. Middlebrook, Martin and Chris Everitt, *The Bomber Command War Diaries*, (New York 1985) p. 590
44. Flying Log Book, F/O Frank Welsh, Sept. 27, 1944
45. Ibid.
46. Ibid.
47. Library and Archives Canada, ORB No. 434 Squadron, Sept. 28, 1944, microfilm reel C-12309
48. www.6grouprcaf.com/Sept44operations.html

49. Canadian Directorate of History and Heritage, Report No. 184: Canadian Participation In The Operations in North-West Europe 1944. Part V: Clearing the Channel Ports, 3 Sept 44 – 6 Feb. 45, paragraph 117

50. Canadian Directorate of History and Heritage, Report No. 184: Canadian Participation In The Operations in North-West Europe 1944. Part V: Clearing the Channel Ports, 3 Sept 44 – 6 Feb. 45, paragraph 118

51. Canadian Directorate of History and Heritage, Report No. 184: Canadian Participation In The Operations in North-West Europe 1944. Part V: Clearing the Channel Ports, 3 Sept 44 – 6 Feb. 45, paragraph 123

52. Flying Log Book, F/O Frank Welsh, Sept. 28, 1944.

53. Interview with Frank Welsh, May 2008

54. Library and Archives Canada, ORB No. 434 Squadron, Sept. 28, 1944, microfilm reel C-12309

55. Flying Log Book, Sgt. Ronald Pyves, Sept. 28, 1944

56. Library and Archives Canada, ORB No. 434 Squadron, Sept. 28, 1944, microfilm reel C-12309

57. Library and Archives Canada, ORB No. 434 Squadron, Jan. 1943 – April 1945

Chapter Six – Cat and Mouse

1. Library and Archives Canada, ORB No. 434 Squadron, Sept. 30, 1944, microfilm reel C-12309

2. Flying Log Book, Sgt. Ronald Pyves, Oct. 1,1944

3. Library and Archives Canada, ORB 431 Squadron, Oct. 4, 1944, microfilm reeel C-12305

4. Flying Log Book, Sgt. Ronald Pyves, Oct. 4, 1944

5. Library and Archives Canada, ORB No. 434 Squadron, Oct. 4, 1944, microfilm reel C-12309

6. www.6grouprcaf.com/Oct1944operations.html

7. Library and Archives Canada, ORB No. 434 Squadron, Oct. 4, 1944, microfilm reel C-12309

8. Interview with Frank Welsh, December 2006

9. www.6grouprcaf/Oct1944operations.html

10. Library and Archives Canada, ORB 434 Squadron, Oct. 4, 1944, microfilm reeel C-12309
11. Library and Archives Canada, ORB 431 Squadron, Oct. 4, 1944, microfilm reeel C-12305
12. www.6grouprcaf.com/Oct44operations.html
13. Ibid.
14. Library and Archives Canada, ORB No. 431 Squadron, Oct. 6, 1944, microfilm reel C-12305
15. Library and Archives Canada, ORB No. 434 Squadron, Oct. 1944, microfilm reel C-12309
16. Library and Archives Canada, ORB No. 434 Squadron, Oct. 12, 1944, microfilm reel C-12309
17. Flying Log Book, F/O Frank Welsh, Oct. 14, 1944
18. Library and Archives Canada, ORB No. 434 Squadron, Oct. 14, 1944, microfilm reel C-12309
19. Library and Archives Canada, ORB No. 434 Squadron, Oct. 14, 1944, microfilm reel C-12309 and www.6grouprcaf.com/Oct-44operations.html
20. Library and Archives Canada, Bomber Command Report on Night Operations, 14/15 October 1944
21. Library and Archives Canada, ORB No. 434 Squadron, Oct. 14, 1944, microfilm reel C-12309
22. Library and Archives Canada, Bomber Command Report on Night Operations, 14/15 October 1944
23. Flying Log Book, Sgt. Ronald Pyves, Oct. 14, 1944
24. www.6grouprcaf.com/Oct44operations.html
25. Library and Archives Canada, ORB No. 434 Squadron, Oct. 14, 1944, microfilm reel C-12309
26. Ibid.
27. Ibid and www.6grouprcaf.com/Oct44operations.html
28. Library and Archives Canada, Bomber Command Report on Night Operations, 14/15 October 1944
29. www.6grouprcaf.com/Oct44operations.html
30. Library and Archives Canada, ORB No. 434 Squadron, Oct. 14, 1944, microfilm reel C-12309
31. Flying Log Book, Sgt. Ronald Pyves, Oct. 14, 1944

32. Ibid.
33. Library and Archives Canada, Bomber Command Report on Night Operations, 14/15 October 1944
34. Ibid.
35. Canadian Directorate of History and Heritage, Report No. 188: Part IV: The Clearing of the Scheldt Estuary. 1 Oct. – 8 Nov. 1944, paragraph 304
36. Middlebrook, Martin and Chris Everitt, *The Bomber Command War Diaries*, (New York 1985) p. 603 – 606 and p. 608 – 610
37. Canadian Directorate of History and Heritage, Report No. 188: Part IV: The Clearing of the Scheldt Estuary. 1 Oct. – 8 Nov. 1944, paragraph 308

Chapter Seven – A Lucky Fellow

1. Flying Log Book, Sgt. Ronald Pyves, Oct. 17, 1944
2. Library and Archives Canada, ORB No. 434 Squadron, Oct. 23, 1944, microfilm reel C-12309
3. Library and Archives Canada, Bomber Command Report on Night Operations 23/24 October 1944
4. Library and Archives Canada, ORB No. 434 and 431 Squadrons, Oct. 23, 1944, microfilm reels C-12309 and C-12305
5. Library and Archives Canada, ORB No. 434 Squadron, Oct.23,1944, microfilm reel C-12309
6. Library and Archives Canada, Bomber Command Report on Night Operations 23/24 October 1944
7. Library and Archives Canada, ORB No. 434 Squadron, Oct. 23, 1944, microfilm reel C-12309
8. www.6grouprcaf.com/Oct44operations.html
9. Library and Archives Canada, ORB No. 434 Squadron, June 1944 – April 1945, microfilm reel C-12309 and C-12310
10. Library and Archives Canada, ORB No. 434 and 431 Squadrons, Oct. 25, 1944, microfilm reel C-12309
11. Middlebrook, Martin and Chris Everitt, *The Bomber Command War Diaries*, (New York 1985) p. 607
12. Flying Log Book, F/O Frank Welsh, Oct. 25, 1944
13. Library and Archives Canada, ORB No. 434 Squadron, Oct. 25,

1944, microfilm reel C-12309

14. Flying Log Book, Sgt. Ronald Pyves, Oct. 25, 1944

15. www.6grouprcaf.com/Oct44operations.html

16. Library and Archives Canada, ORB No. 434 Squadron, Oct. 26, 1944, microfilm reel C-12309

17. Library and Archives Canada, ORB No. 434 Squadron, Oct. 27, 1944, microfilm reel C-12309

18. *An Hour Never Passes*, written by Jimmy Kennedy. Used by Permission of Shapiro, Bernstein & Co., Inc. 2011. All Rights Reserved. International Copyright Secured.

19. Library and Archives Canada, ORB No. 434 Squadron, Oct. 28, 1944, microfilm reel C-12309

20. Middlebrook, Martin and Chris Everitt, *The Bomber Command War Diaries* (New York 1985) p. 608 and www.6grouprcaf.com/Oct44operations.html

21. Library and Archives Canada, ORB No. 434 Squadron, Oct. 28, 1944, microfilm reel C-12309

22. Ibid.

23. www.6grouprcaf.com/Oct44operations.html

24. Ibid.

25. Library and Archives Canada, ORB No. 434 Squadron, Oct. 30, 1944, microfilm reel C-12309

26. Library and Archives Canada, Bomber Command Report on Night Operations 30/31 October 1944

27. Library and Archives Canada, ORB No. 434 Squadron, Oct. 30, 1944, microfilm reel C-12309

28. Library and Archives Canada: Bomber Command Report on Night Operations 30/31 October 1944

29. Library and Archives Canada, ORB No. 434 Squadron, Oct. 30, 1944, microfilm reel. C-12309

30. Ibid.

31. Ibid.

32. Library and Archives Canada, ORB No. 434 Squadron, Oct. 31, 1944, microfilm reel C-12309

33. www.6grouprcaf.com/Oct44operations.html

Chapter Eight – Lucky Number Thirteen

1. Flying Log Book, F/O Frank Welsh, Nov. 1, 1944
2. Library and Archives Canada, ORB No. 434 Squadron, Nov. 1, 1944, microfilm reel C-12309 and www.6grouprcaf.com/Nov44operations.html
3. Middlebrook, Martin and Chris Everitt, *The Bomber Command War Diaries* (New York 1985) p.612
4. Library and Archives Canada, ORB No. 434 Squadron, Nov. 1, 1944, microfilm reel C-12309
5. Ibid.
6. www.6grouprcaf.com/Nov44operations.html
7. Library and Archives Canada, ORB No. 434 Squadron, Questionnaire For Returned Aircrew Loss of Bomber Aircraft, POW Questionnaire dated May 13, 1945, microfilm reel C-12310
8. Ibid.
9. Ibid.
10. www.6grouprcaf.com/Nov44operations.html
11. Flying Log Book, Sgt. Ronald Pyves Nov. 1,1944
12. Note from Frank Welsh dated May 6, 2008_
13. www.6grouprcaf.com/Nov44operations/.html
14. Ibid.
15. Flying Log Book, Sgt. Ronald Pyves, Nov. 2, 1944
16. Library and Archives Canada, ORB No. 434 Squadron, Nov. 2, 1944, microfilm reel C-12309 and www.6grouprcaf.com/Nov44operations.html
17. www.6grouprcaf.com/Nov44operations.html
18. Library and Archives Canada, Bomber Command Report on Night Operations 4/5 November 1944
19. Ibid.
20. Interview with Hal Ward, June 2008
21. www.6grouprcaf.com/Nov44operations.html
22. Library and Archives Canada, ORB No. 434 Squadron, Nov. 4, 1944, microfilm reel C-12309
23. Library and Archives Canada, Bomber Command Report on Night Operations 4/5 November 1944 and www.6grouprcaf.com/Nov44operations.html

24. Library and Archives Canada, ORB No. 434 Squadron, Nov. 4, 1944, microfilm reel C-12309

25. Flying Log Book, Sgt. Ronald Pyves, Nov. 6, 1944

26. Middlebrook, Martin and Chris Everitt, *The Bomber Command War Diaries* (New York 1985) p.614 and Library and Archives Canada, ORB No. 434 Squadron, Nov. 6, 1944, microfilm reel C-12309

27. Library and Archives Canada, ORB No. 434 Squadron, Nov. 6, 1944, microfilm reel C-12309

28. Ibid.

29. Ibid.

30. Ibid.

31. www.6grouprcaf.com/Nov44operations.html

32. Library and Archives Canada, ORB No. 434 Squadron, Nov., 1944, microfilm reel C-12309

33. Ibid.

34. Library and Archives Canada, ORB No. 434 Squadron, Nov. 16, 1944, microfilm reel C-12309

Chapter Nine – Fighter Attack

1. Flying Log Book, F/O Frank Welsh, Nov. 27, 1944

2. Library and Archives Canada, ORB No. 434 Squadron, Nov. 27, 1944, microfilm reel C-12309

3. Library and Archives Canada, ORB No. 431 Squadron, Nov. 27, 1944, microfilm reel C-12305

4. Library and Archives Canada, ORB No. 434 and 431 Squadrons, Nov. 27, 1944, microfilm reel C-12309 and C-12305

5. Middlebrook, Martin and Chris Everitt, *The Bomber Command War Diaries* (New York 1985) p.623

6. Library and Archives Canada, ORB No. 434 Squadron, Nov. 27, 1944, microfilm reel C-12309

7. Ibid

8. Library and Archives Canada, Combat Report 434 Squadron Nov. 27, 1944

9. Ibid.

10. Ibid.

11. Library and Archives Canada, ORB No. 434 Squadron, Nov. 27,

1944, microfilm reel C-12309
12. Library and Archives Canada, ORB No. 431 Squadron, Nov. 27, 1944, microfilm reel C-12305
13. Flying Log Book, F/ Sgt. Ronald Pyves, Nov. 28, 1944
14. Library and Archives Canada: Bomber Command Report on Night Operations, 30[th]Nov/1[st]December, 1944
15. Library and Archives Canada, ORB No. 434 and 431 Squadrons, Nov. 30, 1944, microfilm reels C-12309 and C-12305
16. Library and Archives Canada, ORB No. 434 Squadron, Nov. 30, 1944, microfilm reel C-12309
17. Ibid.
18. Library and Archives Canada, ORB No. 431 Squadron, Nov. 30, 1944, microfilm reel C-12305
19. Interview with Frank Welsh, May 2008
20. Ibid.
21. Ibid.
22. Library and Archives Canada, ORB No. 434 Squadron, Nov. 30, 1944, microfilm reel C-12309
23. www.6grouprcaf.com/Nov44operations.html
24. Library and Archives Canada, ORB No. 431 Squadron, Nov. 30, 1944, microfilm reel C-12305
25. www.6grouprcaf.com/Nov44operations.html
26. Ibid and www.6grouprcaf.com/Oct44operations.html
27. Library and Archives Canada, ORB No. 434 Squadron, Nov. 1944, microfilm reel C-12309
28. Library and Archives Canada, ORB No. 434 Squadron, Nov. 30, 1944, microfilm reel C-12309
29. Flying Log Book, F/ Sgt. Ronald Pyves, Nov. 30, 1944
30. Library and Archives Canada, ORB No. 434 Squadron, Nov. 30, 1944, microfilm reel C-12310

Chapter Ten – Birthday over Germany

1. Flying Log Book, F/ Sgt. Ronald Pyves, Dec. 2, 1944
2. Library and Archives Canada, ORB No. 434 Squadron, Dec. 2, 1944, microfilm reel C-12310
3. Library and Archives Canada, ORB No. 434 Squadron and No.

431 Squadron, Dec. 2, 1944, microfilm reels C-12310 and C-12305 and www.6grouprcaf.com/Dec1944operations.html

4. Library and Archives Canada, Bomber Command Report on Night Operations, 2/3rd December 1944

5. Library and Archives Canada, ORB No. 434 Squadron, Dec. 2, 1944, microfilm reel C-12310

6. Library and Archives Canada, ORB No. 431 Squadron, Dec. 2, 1944, microfilm reel C-12305

7. www.6grouprcaf.com/Dec44operations.html

8. Library and Archives Canada, Combat Report 434 Squadron December 2, 1944

9. Ibid.

10. Ibid.

11. Ibid.

12. Ibid.

13. Ibid.

14. Library and Archives Canada, ORB No. 434 Squadron, Dec. 2, 1944, microfilm reel C-12310

15. Library and Archives Canada, Bomber Command Report on Night Operations, 2/3rd December 1944

16. Library and Archives Canada, ORB No. 434 Squadron, Dec. 2, 1944, microfilm reel C-12310

17. www.6grouprcaf.com/Dec44operations.html

18. Interview with Bill Thomson, August 2001

19. Library and Archives Canada, ORB No. 431 Squadron, Dec. 4, 1944, microfilm reel C-12305

20. Flying Log Book, F/Sgt. Ronald Pyves, Dec. 5, 1944

21. Library and Archives Canada, ORB No. 431 Squadron, Dec. 5, 1944, microfilm reel C-12305

22. www.6grouprcaf.com/Dec44operations.html

23. Library and Archives Canada, ORB No. 434 Squadron, Dec. 5, 1944, microfilm reel C-12310

24. Library and Archives Canada, Bomber Command Report on Night Operations, 5/6th December 1944

25. www.6grouprcaf.com/Dec44operations.html

26. Ibid.

27. Library and Archives Canada, Bomber Command Report on Night Operations, 5/6ᵗʰ December 1944
28. Library and Archives Canada, ORB No. 434 Squadron, Dec. 5, 1944, microfilm reel C-12310
29. Library and Archives Canada, ORB No. 431 Squadron, Dec. 5, 1944, microfilm reel C-12305
30. www.6grouprcaf.com/Dec44operations.html
31. Ibid.
32. Ibid.
33. Ibid.
34. Library and Archives Canada, ORB No. 434 Squadron, Dec. 5, 1944, microfilm reel C-12310
35. Flying Log Book, F/ Sgt. Ronald Pyves, Dec. 6, 1944
36. Middlebrook, Martin and Chris Everitt, *The Bomber Command War Diaries* (New York 1985) p.628 and www.6grouprcaf.com/Dec44operations.html
37. Library and Archives Canada, ORB No. 434 Squadron, Dec. 6, 1944, microfilm reel C-12310
38. Library and Archives Canada, ORB No. 431 Squadron, Dec. 6, 1944, microfilm reel C-12305
39. www.6grouprcaf.com/Dec44operations.html
40. Flying Log Book, F/O Frank Welsh, Dec. 2, 1944
41. www.6grouprcaf.com/Dec44operations.html
42. Interview with Hal Ward, June 2008
43. Ibid.
44. Ibid.
45. Library and Archives Canada, ORB No. 431 Squadron, Dec. 6, 1944, microfilm reel C-12305
46. www.6grouprcaf.com/Dec44operations.html
47. Todd, A.A.B., *Pilgrimages of Grace* (Darlington 1993), p. 157

Chapter Eleven – Goodbye Halifax

1. Greenhous, Brereton, Stephen J. Harris, William C. Johnston and William G. Rawling, The *Crucible of War 1939-1945: The Official History of the Royal Canadian Air Force* (Canada 1994), p.755
2. Flying Log Book, F/ Sgt. Ronald Pyves, Dec. 9, 1944

3. Todd, A.A.B., *Pilgrimages of Grace* (Darlington 1993), p. 157
4. Flying Log Book, F/Sgt. Ronald Pyves, Dec. 12, 1944
5. Flying Log Book, F/Sgt. Ronald Pyves, Dec. 17, 1944
6. Library and Archives Canada, ORB No. 434 Squadron, Dec. 18, 1944, microfilm reel C-12310
7. Library and Archives Canada, ORB No. 431 Squadron, Dec. 18, 1944, microfilm reel C-12305
8. Library and Archives Canada, ORB No. 434 Squadron, Dec. 19, 1944, microfilm reel C-12310
9. Interview with Tom Edgerton, June 21, 2011
10. www.6grouprcaf.com/Dec44operations.html
11. Library and Archives Canada, ORB No. 434 Squadron, Dec. 29, 1944, microfilm reel C-12310
12. Library and Archives Canada, ORB No. 434 Squadron, Dec.17, 1944, microfilm reel C-12310 and www.6grouprcaf.com/dec-44operations.html
13. www.6grouprcaf.com/Oct44operations.html thru www.6grouprcaf.com/Dec44operations.html
14. Library and Archives Canada, ORB No. 434 Squadron, Dec. 30, 1944, microfilm reel C-12310
15. Library and Archives Canada, Bomber Command Report on Night Operations, 30/31st December 1944
16. www.6grouprcaf.com/Dec44operations.html
17. Library and Archives Canada, ORB No. 434 Squadron Dec. 30, 1944, microfilm reel C-12310
18. Ibid.
19. Library and Archives Canada, Bomber Command Report on Night Operations, 30/31st December 1944
20. Library and Archives Canada: ORB No. 431 Squadron, Dec. 30, 1944, microfilm reel C-12305
21. www.6grouprcaf.com/Nov44operations.html and www.6grouprcaf.com/Dec44operations.html
22. Flying Log Book, F/Sgt. Ronald Pyves, Dec. 31, 1944

Chapter Twelve – A New Year

1. Library and Archives Canada, ORB No. 434 Squadron, Jan. 1,

1945, microfilm reel C-12310 and www.6grouprcaf.com/Jan-45operations.html

2. www.6grouprcaf.com/Jan45operations.html

3. Library and Archives Canada, ORB No. 434 Squadron, Sept. – Oct. 1943, microfilm reel C-12309

4. Library and Archives Canada, ORB No. 431 Squadron, Jan. 5, 1945, microfilm reel C-12305

5. Ibid.

6. www.6grouprcaf.com/Jan45operations.html

7. Library and Archives Canada, ORB No. 434 Squadron, Jan. 5, 1945, microfilm reel C-12310

8. Ibid.

9. Library and Archives Canada, Bomber Command Report on Night Operations, 5/6th January 1945

10. Library and Archives Canada, ORB No. 434 Squadron, Jan. 5, 1945, microfilm reel C-12310

11. Ibid.

12. Ibid.

13. Ibid.

14. www.6grouprcaf.com/Jan45operations.html

15. Library and Archives Canada, Bomber Command Report on Night Operations, 5/6th January 1945

16. Ibid

17. www.6grouprcaf.com/Jan45operations.html

18. Library and Archives Canada, ORB No. 431 Squadron, Jan. 5, 1945, microfilm reel C-12305

19. www.6grouprcaf.com/Jan45operations.html

20. Ibid.

21. Ibid.

22. Middlebrook, Martin and Chris Everitt, *The Bomber Command War Diaries* (New York 1985) p.649 and www.6grouprcaf.com/Jan45operations.html

23. www.6grouprcaf.com/Jan45operations.html

24. Library and Archives Canada, ORB No. 434 Squadron, Jan 9-12, 1945, microfilm reel C-12310

25. Library and Archives Canada, ORB No. 434 Squadron, Jan 12,

1945, microfilm reel C-12310

26. Ibid.

27. Library and Archives Canada, ORB No. 434 Squadron, Jan 14, 1945, microfilm reel C-12310

28. Ibid.

29. Ibid.

30. Flying Log Book, F/Sgt. Ronald Pyves, Jan. 14, 1945

31. Library and Archives Canada, ORB No. 434 Squadron, Jan. 14, 1945, microfilm reel C-12310

32. www.6grouprcaf.com/Jan45operations.html

33. Library and Archives Canada, Bomber Command Report on Night Operations, 14/15th January 1945

34. Library and Archives Canada, ORB No. 431 Squadron, Jan. 14, 1945, microfilm reel C-12305

35. Ibid. and Library and Archives Canada, ORB No. 434 Squadron, Jan. 14, 1945, microfilm reel C-12310

36. Library and Archives Canada, ORB No. 434 Squadron, Jan. 14, 1945, microfilm reel C-12310

37. Ibid.

38. Ibid and www.6grouprcaf.com/Jan45operations.html

39. Library and Archives Canada, ORB No. 431 Squadron, Jan. 14, 1945, microfilm reel C-12305

40. Library and Archives Canada, ORB No. 434 Squadron, Jan. 14, 1945, microfilm reel C-12310

41. Ibid

42. Flying Log Book, F/Sgt. Ronald Pyves, Jan. 14, 1945

43. www.6grouprcaf.com/Jan45operations.html

44. Library and Archives Canada, ORB No. 431 Squadron, Jan. 14, 1945, microfilm reel C-12305

45. www.6grouprcaf.com/Jan45operations.html

46. Library and Archives Canada, ORB No. 434 Squadron, Jan. 16, 1945, microfilm reel C-12310

47. Ibid.

48. Ibid.

49. Ibid.

50. Library and Archives Canada, Bomber Command Report on

Night Operations, 16/17 January 1945

51. www.6grouprcaf.com/Jan45operations.html

52. Ibid.

53. Ibid.

54. Library and Archives Canada, Bomber Command Report on Night Operations, 28/29th January 1945

55. Library and Archives Canada, ORB No. 434 Squadron, Jan. 28, 1944, microfilm reel C-12310

56. Ibid.

57. Library and Archives Canada, ORB No. 431 Squadron, Jan. 28, 1945, microfilm reel C-12305

58. Interview with Hal Ward, June 2008

59. www.6grouprcaf.com/Jan45operations.html

60. Flying Log Book, F/Sgt. Ronald Pyves, Jan. 31, 1945

61. www.6grouprcaf.com/Jan45operations.html

62. Ibid.

63. Ibid.

64. Library and Archives Canada, ORB No. 434 Squadron, Jan. 30, 1945, microfilm reel C-12310

65. Ibid.

66. Personal recollections of Ronald Pyves

67. www.6grouprcaf.com/Jan45operations.html

68. Library and Archives Canada, ORB No. 434 Squadron, Jan. 31, 1945, microfilm reel C-12310

69. Ibid.

Chapter Thirteen – Night Madness

1. Canadian Directorate of History and Heritage, Report No. 185: Operation Veritable: The Winter Offensive Between the Maas and the Rhine, 8-25 Feb. 45, paragraphs 199 and 206

2. Library and Archives Canada, ORB No. 434 Squadron, Feb. 1, 1945, microfilm reel C-12310

3. Library and Archives Canada, ORB No. 434 Squadron, Feb. 2, 1945, microfilm reel C-12310

4. www.6grouprcaf.com/Feb45operations.html

5. Ibid.

6. Library and Archives Canada, ORB No. 434 Squadron, Feb. 3, 1945, microfilm reel C-12310
7. Flying Log Book, P/O Ronald Pyves, Feb. 4, 1945
8. Library and Archives Canada, ORB No. 434 Squadron, Feb. 4, 1945, microfilm reel C-12310
9. Ibid.
10. Library and Archives Canada, Bomber Command Report on Night Operations, 4/5th February 1945
11. Flying Log Book, F/O Frank Welsh, Feb. 4, 1945
12. Library and Archives Canada, ORB No. 431 Squadron, Feb. 4, 1945, microfilm reel C-12305
13. Ibid.
14. Library and Archives Canada, ORB No. 434 Squadron, Feb. 4, 1945, microfilm reel C-12310
15. Library and Archives Canada, ORB No. 431 Squadron, Feb. 4, 1945, microfilm reel C-12305
16. www.6grouprcaf.com/Feb45operations.html
17. Library and Archives Canada, ORB No.434 Squadron, Feb. 7, 1945, microfilm reel C-12310
18. Taylor, Frederick (2004), *Dresden*. p. 194, 200
19. Library and Archives Canada, Bomber Command Report on Night Operations, 13/14th February 1945
20. Taylor, Frederick (2004), *Dresden*, p. 256-7
21. 'Timewitnesses,' moderated by Tom Halloway, *The Fire-bombing of Dresden*, an eyewitness account of Lothar Metzger, recorded May 1999 in Berlin. Used with permission by Tom Holloway and Lothar Metzger 2010.
22. Library and Archives Canada, Bomber Command Report on Night Operations, 13/14th February 1945
23. Ibid.
24. Flying Log Book, P/O Ronald Pyves, Feb. 13, 1945
25. Ibid and www.6grouprcaf.com/Feb45operations.html
26. Library and Archives Canada, Bomber Command Report on Night Operations, 13/14th February 1945
27. Library and Archives Canada, ORB No. 434 Squadron, Feb. 13, 1945, microfilm reel C-12310

28. Ibid.
29. Ibid.
30. Ibid.
31. Margaret Freyer, survivor, cited in *1945: The Devil's Tinderbox (2000)*, pps. 172-174 by Alexander McKee. Used with permission by Souvenir Press 2010.
32. B.B.C., Peter Nicholson, W.W.2. People's War, W/O Nick Nicholson – 35 Squadron Pathfinder
33. www.6grouprcaf.com/Feb45operations.html
34. Flying Log Book, P/O Ronald Pyves, Feb. 13, 1945
35. www.6grouprcaf.com/Feb45operations.html
36. Taylor, Frederick (2004), *Dresden*, p. 317
37. Taylor, Frederick (2004), *Dresden*, p. 329
38. Source of English translation, Johannes Steinhoff, Peter Pechel and Dennis Showalter, *Voices From the Third Reich*, Regenery Gateway (1989). Used by Permission of Dennis Showalter and Goetz Bergander 2010.
39. USAF Historical Division, Research Studies Institute, Air University. Historical Analysis of the 14-15 February 1945 Bombings of Dresden, paragraph 25
40. USAF Historical Division, Research Studies Institute, Air University. Historical Analysis of the 14-15 February 1945 Bombings of Dresden, paragraph 9
41. Library and Archives Canada, ORB No. 434 Squadron, Feb. 14, 1945, microfilm reel C-12310
42. Library and Archives Canada, ORB No. 434 Squadron, Feb. 14, 1945, microfilm reel C-12310
43. Ibid.
44. Ibid.
45. Ibid.
46. Ibid. and www.6grouprcaf.com/Feb45operations.html
47. www.6grouprcaf.com/Feb45operations.html
48. Library and Archives Canada, ORB No. 434 Squadron, Feb. 15, 1945, microfilm reel C-12310
49. Library and Archives Canada, ORB No. 434 Squadron, Feb. 15-18, 1945, microfilm reel C-12310

50. Library and Archives Canada, ORB No. 434 Squadron, Feb. 19, 1945, microfilm reel C-12310

51. Ibid and Library and Archives Canada, ORB No. 431 Squadron, Feb. 19, 1945 microfilm reel C-12305

52. Ibid.

53. Flying Log Book, F/O Frank Welsh, Feb. 20, 1945

54. Library and Archives Canada, ORB No. 431 Squadron, February 20, 1945, microfilm reel C-12305

55. www.6grouprcaf.com/Feb45operations.html

56. Library and Archives Canada, Bomber Command Report on Night Operations, 20/21st February 1945

57. Ibid and www.6grouprcaf.com/Feb45operations.html

58. Library and Archives Canada, Bomber Command Report on Night Operations, 20/21st February 1945

59. Library and Archives Canada, ORB No. 434 Squadron, Feb. 20, 1945, microfilm reel C-12310

60. Ibid.

61. Flying Log Book, P/O Ronald Pyves, Feb. 20, 1945

62. Library and Archives Canada, ORB No. 431 Squadron, February 20, 1945, microfilm reel C-12305

63. www.6grouprcaf.com/Feb45operations.html

64. Library and Archives Canada, Bomber Command Report on Night Operations, 20/21st February 1945

65. www.6grouprcaf.com/Feb45operations.html

66. Ibid.

67. Library and Archives Canada, Bomber Command Report on Night Operations, 20/21st February 1945

68. Ibid.

69. Flying Log Book, P/O Ronald Pyves, Feb. 21, 1945

70. Library and Archives Canada, Bomber Command Report on Night Operations, 21/22nd February 1945

71. Ibid.

72. Library and Archives Canada, ORB No. 434 Squadron, Feb. 21, 1945, microfilm reel C-12310

73. Flying Log Book, P/O Ronald Pyves, Feb. 21, 1945

74. www.6grouprcaf.com/Feb45operations.html

75. Library and Archives Canada, ORB No. 434 Squadron, Feb. 21, 1945, microfilm reel C-12310
76. www.6grouprcaf.com/Feb45operations.html
77. Flying Log Book, F/O Frank Welsh, Feb. 23, 1945
78. www.6grouprcaf.com/Feb45operations/.html
79. Library and Archives Canada, ORB No. 434 Squadron, Feb. 27, 1945, microfilm reel C-12310
80. Ibid.
81. Library and Archives Canada, ORB No. 434 Squadron, Feb. 28, 1945, microfilm reel C-12310

Chapter Fourteen – Screened

1. Flying Log Book, F/O Frank Welsh, Mar. 1, 1945
2. Library and Archives Canada, ORB No. 434 Squadron, Mar. 1, 1945, microfilm reel C-12310
3. Library and Archives Canada, ORB No. 431 Squadron, Mar. 1, 1945, microfilm reel C-12305
4. Ibid.
5. www.6grouprcaf.com/Mar45operations.html
6. Library and Archives Canada, ORB No. 434 and 431 Squadrons, Mar. 1, 1945, microfilm reels C-12310 and C-12305
7. Middlebrook, Martin and Chris Everitt, *The Bomber Command War Diaries*, (New York 1985) p. 672
8. Flying Log Book, F/O Frank Welsh, Mar. 1, 1945
9. Library and Archives Canada, ORB No. 434 Squadron, Mar. 1, 1945, microfilm reel C-12310
10. Library and Archives Canada, ORB No. 431 Squadron, Mar. 1, 1945, microfilm reel C-12305
11. www.6grouprcaf.com/Mar45operations.html
12. Library and Archives Canada, ORB No. 434 Squadron, Mar. 2, 1945, microfilm reel C-12310
13. Library and Archives Canada, ORB No. 431 Squadron, Mar. 2, 1945, microfilm reel C-12305
14. Flying Log Book, P/O Ronald Pyves, Oct. 28-30, 1944 and Dec. 30, 1944
15. Flying Log Book, P/O Ronald Pyves,, Mar. 2, 1945

16. Library and Archives Canada, ORB No. 434 Squadron, Mar. 2, 1945, microfilm reel C-12310

17. Middlebrook, Martin and Chris Everitt, *The Bomber Command War Diaries*, (New York 1985) p. 673

18. www.6grouprcaf.com/Mar45operations.html

19. Library and Archives Canada, ORB No. 434 Squadron, Mar. 2, 1945, microfilm reel C-12310

20. www.6grouprcaf.com/Mar45operations.html

21. Library and Archives Canada, ORB No. 431 Squadron, Mar. 2, 1945, microfilm reel C-12305

22. Library and Archives Canada, ORB No. 434 Squadron, Mar. 2, 1945, microfilm reel C-12310

23. Library and Archives Canada, ORB No. 434 Squadron, Mar. 4, 1945, microfilm reel C-12310

24. Ibid.

25. Ibid.

26. Library and Archives Canada, ORB No. 434 Squadron, Mar. 5, 1945, microfilm reel C-12310

27. Flying Log Book, P/O Hal Ward, Mar. 5, 1945

28. www.6grouprcaf.com/Mar45operations.html

29. Ibid.

30. Library and Archives Canada, ORB No. 434 Squadron, Mar. 5, 1944, microfilm reel C-12310

31. Interview with Hal Ward, June 2008

32. www.6grouprcaf.com/Mar45operations.html

33. Interview with Hal Ward, June 2008

34. Library and Archives Canada, Combat Report March 5, 1945

35. Ibid.

36. Ibid.

37. Ibid.

38. Ibid.

39. Interview with Hal Ward, June 2008

40. Ibid.

41. Ibid.

42. Library and Archives Canada, ORB No. 434 Squadron, Mar. 5, 1945, microfilm reel C-12310

43. Interview with Hal Ward, June 2008

44. www.6grouprcaf.com/Mar45operations.html

45. Ibid.

46. Ibid.

47. www.6grouprcaf.com/Mar45operations.html and Middlebrook, Martin and Chris Everitt, *The Bomber Command War Diaries*, (New York 1985) p. 675

48. www.6grouprcaf.com/Mar45operations.html and Middlebrook, Martin and Chris Everitt, *The Bomber Command War Diaries*, (New York 1985) p. 676

49. Ibid.

50. Library and Archives Canada, ORB No. 434 Squadron, Nov. 22, 1943 – Feb. 15, 1944, microfilm reel C-12309

51. Library and Archives Canada, ORB No. 434 Squadron, Mar. 7, 1945, microfilm reel C-12310

52. Ibid.

53. www.6grouprcaf.com/Mar45operations.html

54. Library and Archives Canada, ORB No. 434 Squadron, Mar. 7, 1945, microfilm reel C-12310

55. www.6grouprcaf.com/Mar45operations.html

56. Flying Log Book, P/O Ronald Pyves, Mar. 8, 1945

57. Library and Archives Canada, ORB No. 434 Squadron, Mar. 9, 1945, microfilm reel C-12310

58. Ibid.

59. www.6grouprcaf.com/Mar45operations.html

60. Ibid. and Library and Archives Canada, ORB No. 434 Squadron, Mar. 11, 1945, microfilm reel C-12310 and Middlebrook, Martin and Chris Everitt, *The Bomber Command War Diaries*, (New York 1985) p. 678

61. www.6grouprcaf.com/Mar45operations.html

62. Middlebrook, Martin and Chris Everitt, *The Bomber Command War Diaries*, (New York 1985) p. 679 and www.6grouprcaf.com/Mar45operations.html

63. Flying Log Book, F/O Frank Welsh, Mar. 12, 1945

64. Library and Archives Canada, ORB No. 434 Squadron, Mar. 12, 1945, microfilm reel C-12310

65. www.6grouprcaf.com/Mar45operations.html
66. Flying Log Book, P/O Ronald Pyves, Mar. 12, 1945
67. Middlebrook, Martin and Chris Everitt, *The Bomber Command War Diaries*, (New York 1985) p. 679 and www.6grouprcaf.com/Mar45operations.html
68. www.6grouprcaf.com/Mar45operations.html
69. Ibid.
70. Library and Archives Canada, ORB No. 434 and 431 Squadrons, Mar. 14, 1945, microfilm reel C-12310 and C-12305
71. Library and Archives Canada, ORB No. 431 Squadron, Mar. 14, 1945, microfilm reel C-12305
72. Flying Log Book, P/O Ronald Pyves, Mar. 17, 1945
73. Ibid. and Library and Archives Canada, ORB No. 431 Squadron, Mar. 17, 1945, microfilm reel C-12305
74. Ibid.
75. Middlebrook, Martin and Chris Everitt, *The Bomber Command War Diaries*, (New York 1985) p. 684
76. Flying Log Book, P/O Ronald Pyves, Mar. 20, 1945
77. Library and Archives Canada, ORB No. 434 Squadron, Mar. 22, 1945, microfilm reel C-12310
78. Ibid.
79. Ibid.
80. Ibid.
81. www.6grouprcaf.com/Mar45operations.html
82. Ibid.
83. Ibid and Library and Archives Canada, ORB No. 434 Squadron, Mar. 24, 1945, microfilm reel C-12310
84. Library and Archives Canada, ORB No. 434 Squadron, Mar. 24, 1945, microfilm reel C-12310 and Middlebrook, Martin and Chris Everitt, *The Bomber Command War Diaries*, (New York 1985) p. 687
85. Flying Log Book, P/O Ronald Pyves, Mar. 24, 1945
86. Flying Log Book, F/O Frank Welsh, Mar. 24, 1945
87. Interview with Frank Welsh, May 2008
88. Library and Archives Canada, ORB No. 434 Squadron, Mar. 24, 1945, microfilm reel C-12310

89. Flying Log Book, P/O Ronald Pyves, Mar. 24, 1945
90. Library and Archives Canada, ORB No.434 Squadron, Mar. 24 – Apr. 25, 1945, microfilm reel C-12310
91. Interview with Hal Ward, June 2008
92. Flying Log Book, P/O Ronald Pyves, Mar. 31, 1945
93. www.6grouprcaf.com/Sept44operations.html thru www.6grouprcaf.com/Mar45operations.html
94. Ibid.
95. Ibid.
96. Library and Archives Canada, ORB No. 434 Squadron, Mar. 31, 1945, microfilm reel C-12310
97. Library and Archives Canada, ORB No. 434 Squadron, April 30, 1945, microfilm reel C-12310
98. Ibid.

Chapter Fifteen – Reunion

1. archives.cbs.ca/war_conflict/second_world_war/clips/11573/
2. Ibid.
3. Ibid.
4. Churchill, Winston. Speech broadcast from the House of Commons, London on May 8, 1945
5. Hastings,Max, *Bomber Command:Churchill's Epic Campaign*, (New York, 1989), pps.372-374
6. The United States Strategic Bombing Survey Summary Report (European War) 1945, p.4
7. Ibid
8. Library and Archives Canada, RCAF Personnel Files for Ronald Pyves, May 1945, Can J93149
9. Library and Archives Canada, RCAF Personnel Files for Ronald Pyves August 1945, Can J93149

Chapter Sixteen – Post Traumatic Stress Disorder

1. *Toronto Star*, September 24, 2000, Sarah Jane Growe, Post Traumatic Stress Disorder
2. Canadian Mental Health Association, B.C. Division, Primer Fact Sheets (2008*), Learn About Post-Traumatic Stress Disorder,* p.2

3. Statistics Canada. *The Canadian Forces 2002 Canadian Community Health Survey Supplement*
4. *Montreal Mirror* (2005), Vol. 21 No. 16, Patrick Lejtenzi, *War Zone Burnout*
5. Statistics Canada. *The Canadian Forces 2002 Canadian Community Health Survey Supplement*
6. www.legionmagazine.com/en/index.php/2009/12/minds-at-war-operational-stress-injuries
7. Ibid.
8. Canadian Mental Health Association, B.C. Division, Primer Fact Sheets (2008*), Learn About Post-Traumatic Stress Disorder,* p.3
9. DND/CF Ombudsman Special Report, *Systematic Treatment of CF Members with PTSD*, Complainant: Christian McEachen, p.25
10. DND/CF Ombudsman Special Report, *Systematic Treatment of CF Members with PTSD*, Complainant: Christian McEachen, p. 8
11. www.npr.org/templates/story/story.php?Id=128467680, Rachel Martin, *VA Eases Claims Process For PTSD Treatment*
12. www.thecanadianencyclopedia.com/articles/romeo-dallaire
13. Ibid.
14. Ibid.
15. Ibid.
16. www.cbc.ca/news/background/dallaire, updated March 9, 2005.
17. www.liberalsenateforum.ca/news/10793_Senate-Subcommittee-on-Veterans-Affairs-announces-Senator-Romeo-Dallaire-as-the-new-chairman

Chapter Seventeen – A New Beginning

1. Story written by Kathleen Pyves based on personal recollections, 1948

Chapter Nineteen – Passing the Torch

1. Dr. Jacques Voyer Expert Psychiatric Opinion for Ronald Pyves p.2 (Translation by Colleen Pyves of original document in French, used with permission 2010)
2. Veterans Affairs Canada, Volume II of the Disability Pension Pro-

gram Evaluation, Section 2.3 – Differing Approval Rates at First Application and Appeal Levels

3. Veteran Affairs Canada, Decision 6679551, letter to Kathleen Pyves dated 16 February 2000

4. Ibid.

5. Veteran Affairs Canada, Volume II of the Disability Pension Program Evaluation, Section 2.1.1 – Definitions and Findings

6. Letter to Kathleen Pyves from Dr. Jacques Voyer, M.D., F.R.C.P.

7. Royal Canadian Legion, Quebec Provincial Command, letter to Kathleen Pyves dated April 26, 2001

8. Veteran Review and Appeal Board Canada, HO file No. 5305800, Entitlement Review, May 23, 2001

9. Dr. Jacques Voyer Expert Psychiatric Opinion for Ronald Pyves p.6 (Translation by Colleen Pyves of original document in French, used with permission 2010)

10. Veterans Review and Appeal Board letter to Kathleen Pyves dated 23 May 2001

11. Royal Canadian Legion, Quebec Provincial Command, letter to Kathleen Pyves dated November 06, 2001

12. Veteran Review and Appeal Board Canada, HO file No. 5305800, Reconsideration of Assessment Appeal, April 4, 2002

13. Veteran Review and Appeal Board Canada, HO file No. 5305800, Reconsideration of Assessment Appeal, January 28, 2004

Bibliography

Addison, Paul and Jeremy A. Crang. *Firestorm: The Bombing of Dresden, 1945*. London: Pimlico, 2006.

Ambrose, Stephen E. *The Wild Blue: The Men and Boys Who Flew The B-24's Over Germany 1944-45*. New York: Touchstone, 2001.

Bashow, David L. *No Prouder Place: Canadians and the Bomber Command Experience 1939-1945*. St. Catherine's: Vanwell Publishing Ltd., 2005.

Bessal, Richard. *Germany 1945: From War to Peace*. New York: HarperCollins Publishers, 2009.

Bowman, Martin W. and Theo Boiten. *Raiders of the Reich: Air Battle Western Europe: 1942-45*. Osceola: Motorbooks International Publishers, 1996.

Bowyer, Chaz. *Guns in the Sky: The Air Gunners of World War Two*. London: J.M. Dent & Sons Ltd., 1979.

Bruhl, Marshall De. *Firestorm: Allied Airpower and the Destruction of Dresden*. New York: Random House, 2006.

Caidin, Martin. *Black Thursday: The Epic Story of the Schweinfurt Raid*. New York: Bantam Books Inc., 1987.

Coleman, Penny. *Flashback: Posttraumatic Stress Disorder, Suicide, and the Lessons of War*. Boston: Beacon Press, 2006

Comer, John. *Combat Crew: The True Story of One Man's Part in World War II's Allied Bomber Offensive*. London: Warner Books, 2001.

Cooper, Alan W. *Bombers over Berlin*. Shrewsbury: AirLife Publishing Ltd., 2003.

Dallaire, Lt. General Romeo A. with Major Brent Bearsley. *Shake*

Hands With the Devil: The Failure of Humanity in Rwanda. Toronto: Random House of Canada Ltd., 2003.

Darling, Ian. *Amazing Airmen: Canadian Flyers in the Second World War.* Toronto: Dundurn Press, 2009.

Dunmore, Spencer and William Carter. *Reap The Whirlwind: The Untold Story of 6 Group, Canada's Bomber Force of World War II.* Toronto: McClelland & Stewart Inc., 1993.

Friedrich, Jorg. *The Fire: The Bombing of Germany 1940-1945.* New York: Columbia University Press, 2006.

Garbett M. and B. Goulding. *Lancaster.* China: The Promotional Reprint Company Ltd., 1979.

Gray, Philip. *Ghosts of Targets Past: The Lives and Losses of a Lancaster Crew in 1944-1945.* London: Grub Street, 2009.

Grayling, A.C. *Among The Dead Cities: The History and Legacy of the WWII Bombing of Civilians in Germany and Japan.* New York: Walker & Company, 2006.

Greenhous, Bereton, Stephen J. Harris, William C. Johnston and William G.P. Rawling. *The Crucible of War 1939-1945: The Official History of the Royal Canadian Air Force, Volume III.* Toronto: University of Toronto Press, 1994.

Hansen, Handall. *Fire and Fury: The Allied Bombing of Germany 1942-1945.* New York: New American Library, 2008.

Harris, Sir Arthur. *Bomber Offensive: The Memoirs of one of the Greatest – and Most Controversial – Commanders of World War II.* London: Greenhill Books, Lionel Leventhal Ltd., 1998.

McCafferty, Dan. *Battlefields in the Air: Canadians in the Allied Bomber Command.* Toronto: James Lorimer & Company Ltd., Publishers, 1995.

McKee, Alexander. *1945: The Devil's Tinderbox.* London: Souvenir Press Ltd., 2000.

Middlebrook, Martin. *The Battle of Hamburg: The Firestorm Raid.* London: Cassell Military Paperbacks, 2000.

Middlebrook, Martin and Chris Everitt. *The Bomber Command War Diaries: An Operational Reference Book, 1939-1945.* New York: Viking, 1985.

Milberry, Larry and Hugh Halliday. *The Royal Canadian Air Force at War 1939-1945.* Toronto: Canav Books, 1990.

Milberry. *Canada's Air Force: At War and Peace, Volume Two.* Toronto: Canav Books, 2000.

Miller, Donald L. *Masters of the Air: America's Bomber Boys Who Fought the Air War Against Nazi Germany.* New York: Simon & Schuster, Inc., 2006.

Motiuk, Laurence. *Thunderbirds at War: Diary of a Bomber Squadron.* Nepean: Larmot Associates, 1998.

Nijboer, Donald and Dan Patterson. *Gunner: An Illustrated History of World War II Aircraft Turrets and Gun Positions.* Erin: The Boston Mill Press, 2006.

Otter, Patrick. *Yorkshire Airfields in the Second World War.* Newbury: Countryside Books, 1998.

Peden, Murray. *A Thousand Shall Fall.* Toronto: Stoddart, 1979.

Roberts, Leslie. *There Shall Be Wings: A History of the Canadian Air Force.* Toronto: Clarke, Irwin & Company Ltd., 1959.

Rolfe, Mel. *Looking Into Hell: Experiences of the Bomber Command War.* London: Rigel Publications, 2004.

Shores, Christopher. *History of the Royal Canadian Air Force.* Toronto: Royce Publications, 1984.

Smith, Ron. *Rear Gunner Pathfinders.* Wilmslow: Crecy Publishing Ltd, 1997.

Stachiw, Anthony L. and Andrew Tattersall. *Handley Paige Halifax*. St. Catherines, Vanwell Publishing Ltd., 2005.

Steinhoof, Johannes, Peter Pechel and Dennis Showalter. *Voices from the Third Reich: An Oral History*. Washington: Regnery Gateway, 1989.

Sweetman, John. *Bomber Crew: Taking on the Reich*. London: Abacus, 2005.

Taylor, Frederick. *Dresden: Thursday, February 13, 1945*. New York: Harper Collins Publishers Inc., 2004.

Taylor, James and Martin Davidson. *Bomber Crew: Survivors of Bomber Command Tell Their Own Story*. London: Hodder and Stroughton Ltd., 2005.

Todd, A.A.B. *Pilgrimages of Grace: A History of Croft Aerodrome*. Darlington: Alan Todd Associates, 1993.

Tripp, Miles. *The Eighth Passenger: A Flight of Recollection and Discovery*. London: MacMillan London Ltd. 1969.

Williston, Floyd. *Through Footless Halls of Air: The Stories of a Few of the Many Who Failed to Return*. Burnstown: General Store Publishing House, 1996.

Wilson, Kevin. *Men of Air: The Doomed Youth of Bomber Command*. London: Phoenix, 2008.

Index

A

Air Gunnery Training School, No. 4, 13-14
aircrew, members, 25-26, 39, 45
    Casavant, Joe (Flight Engineer), 266-67
    Coleman, Al (Navigator), 268-70
    Henry, Bob (Pilot), 57-58, 76, 274-76
    Henry, Jack (Pilot), 271-73
    last mission, 212-15
    Thomson, Bill (Mid-upper Gunner), 277-78
    Toronto reunion, 246
    Ward, Hal (Wireless Operator), 201-3, 279-81
    Welsh, Frank (Bomb Aimer), 69-70, 194-95, 282-83
    See also combat missions
American Eighth Tactical Air Force, 56, 58
Antwerp, Port of, 92-93
atomic bombs dropped, 230

B

Benedetto, Andrew, 235
Bergander, Goetz, 185-86
Bergen-Belsen concentration camp, 157
Bergen, sixth mission, 82-84
Beurling, George Frederick "Buzz", 24-25
Bluenose Squadron (434), 56-57, 105, 134, 152
    See also aircrew, members
Bochum, fourteenth mission, 112, 114-15
Bomber Group 6, 28, 55, 56, 153
    Chemnitz attack, 201-3
Bombing and Gunnery School, No. 4, 8-11
Bombing and Gunnery School, No. 9, 13
bombing missions *See* combat missions
bombs, 64
    incendiary, 107-8
    unmanned flying, 36-37
Bonn, twenty-sixth mission, 176-77
Bournemouth, England, 18-21

British Commonwealth Air Training Plan (B.C.A.T.P.), 8
Browning machine gun, 13

C

Calais, France, 61, 75-76
   first mission, 60-65
   second mission, 68-71
   third mission, 72-73
Canadian Navy, 17
Cap Gris Nez, France, 61, 76-77
   fifth mission, 76-77
Casavant, Joe, 266-67
Churchill, Winston, radio speech, 225
Coleman, Al, 268-70
Cologne, Germany, 101, 103
   eleventh mission, 101, 103
   twelfth mission, 104-5
   twenty-first mission, 152-53
   thirty-first mission, 200
combat missions, 57
   first (Calais), 60-65
   second (Calais), 68-71
   third (Calais), 72-73
   fourth (Sterkrade), 74-75
   fifth (Cap Gris Nez), 76-77
   sixth (Bergen), 82-84
   seventh (Duisburg), 86-87, 89
   eighth (Duisburg), 89-91
   ninth (Krupp Steel Works), 95, 96-98
   tenth (Homberg), 98-100
   eleventh (Cologne), 101, 103
   twelfth (Cologne), 104-5
   thirteenth (Oberhausen), 107-10
   fourteenth (Bochum), 112, 114-15
   fifteenth (Gelsenkirchen), 116-17
   sixteenth (Neuss), 127, 129-30
   seventeenth (Duisburg), 130-31, 133
   eighteenth (Hagen), 135, 137-38, 140
   nineteenth (Soest), 140-42
   twentieth (Osnabruck), 143-45
   twenty-first (Cologne), 152-53

twenty-second (Hannover), 155-57, 159
twenty-third (Merseberg), 161, 163
twenty-fourth (Zeitz), 165-66
twenty-fifth (Kornwestheim), 169, 171
twenty-sixth (Bonn), 176-77
twenty-seventh (Dresden), 180-85
twenty-eighth (Dortmund), 189-92
twenty-ninth (Duisburg), 192, 194
thirtieth (Mannheim), 198-99
thirty-first (Cologne), 200
thirty-second (Dessau), 203, 205-6
thirty-third (Dortmund), 207-8
thirty-fourth, (Heide), 209, 211
thirty-fifth (Bottrop), 212-13
compensation for veterans, 250-51
conscription, 174-75
Croft-on-Tees, Yorkshire, 53
    air base, 57
    attack on air base, 201
    Lancaster WL-F explosion, 211-12

D
D-Day invasion (Normandy), 18, 29-30, 32-33, 47-48
Dakota twin engine aircraft, 114
Dallaire, Romeo, 236
doodlebugs, 36-37
Dortmund, twenty-eighth mission, 189-92
Dresden, Germany, 180-86, 248
    twenty-seventh mission, 180-85
Duisburg, Germany, 86
    seventh mission, 86-87, 89
    eighth mission, 89-91
    seventeenth mission, 130-31, 133
    twenty-ninth mission, 192, 194

E
Eason, Kathleen Emily (Kay), 14-16
    death, 259-60
    marriage and family, 231, 238, 239-42
    widowhood and retirement, 251, 254-55
    work history after marriage, 239, 240, 242

Edgerton, Tom, 149-50

F
Freyer, Margaret, 183-84

G
GEE radio navigation system, 138
Gelsenkirchen, fifteenth mission, 116-17
German 88-mm artillery gun, 70-71
German surrender, 224-25
Grenadier Guards, 5-6

H
Hagen, eighteenth mission, 135, 137-38, 140
Halifax bombers, 49-50, 63, 146
Hannover, twenty-second mission, 155-57, 159
Hart, Fred, 103
Heavy Conversion Unit Training (Topcliffe), 40, 48-49
    training missions, 52
Henry, Bob, 57-58, 76, 274-76
Henry, Jack, 271-73
Homberg, tenth mission, 98-100
housing shortage, 237
hypnotism, 240-41

I
I.G. Farben chemical factory, 154
Ile de France, 227

K
Kornwestheim, twenty-fifth mission, 169, 171
Krupp Steel Works (Essen), 95
    ninth mission, 95, 96-98

L
Lancaster bombers, 99, 146-47
legislation for veterans, 250
letters, 18, 22-24, 27, 34
London, England, 21-22, 36, 149
loss (survival) rates, 73-74, 159, 173, 226

M

Mackenzie King, William Lyon, radio speech, 224-25
Mannheim, thirtieth mission, 198-99
Merseberg, twenty-third mission, 161, 163
Messerschmitt Me-109 bombers, 65
Metzger, Lothar, 181
morale, 235
Mosquito bombers, 64

N

Neuss, sixteenth mission, 127, 129-30
Nissen huts, 81
Normandy, invasion of Europe, 18, 29-30, 32-33, 47-48
Norway, 81-82
nose art, 51

O

Oberhausen, thirteenth mission, 107-10
Operation Hurricane, 86-87, 89-91
Operational Training Unit (O.T.U.) No. 22, 25
    training missions, 28, 31, 34-36, 37-38, 40
Osnabruck, twentieth mission, 143-45

P

pensions for veterans, 251-52
    appeal process, 256-57
    pension claim denial, 255-56
    pension claim process, 252-54
    Request for Reconsideration, 258
    second appeal, 257-58
Post Traumatic Stress Disorder (PTSD), 232-33, 249
    among soldiers, 233-34, 252
    awareness of, 236
    and Ron Pyves, 253-54
    treatment, 234-35
Pyves, Colleen, 253
Pyves, Kay See Eason, Kathleen Emily (Kay)
Pyves, Ronald Leslie, 1-3
    career in drafting, 238-39, 240-41
    depression, 243-45
    desire to commit suicide, 246-47

drinking problem, 245-46
enlistment Grenadier Guards, 4-6
enlistment RCAF, 6-7
enlistment Tiger Force, 215, 228-29, 230
family, 238, 239-42
feelings of guilt, 248
final illness and death, 248-49
homecoming, 227-28
last mission, 212-15
marriage, 231
overdose, 246
pressure of combat, 207-8
twentieth birthday, 140
war medical record, 230

Q
Queen Mary, 3

R
radar technology, 79-80
RAF Bomber Command, 55-56, 248
RCAF ring, 18
Robertson, Robbie, 252, 253, 256, 257
Roney, Katharine, 257, 258
Royal Canadian Air Force (RCAF), 6
    Air Force Reserve, 239
    enlistment, 6-7
    mission policy change, 177-78
    pilot training school, 11-13
Ruhr Valley, 95, 97

S
shell shock, 232
Soest, nineteenth mission, 140-42
St. Elmo's fire, 39
Sterkrade, fourth mission, 74-75

T
Thomson, Bill, 277-78
training missions, 28, 31, 34-36, 37-38, 40, 52

U
U-boats, 135

V
Victory Bonds, 84-85
Voyer, Dr. Jacques, 253-54, 256-57, 258

W
Ward, Hal, 201-3, 279-81
Wellington bombers, 28
Welsh, Frank, 69-70, 194-95, 282-83
World War Two, 3-4, 5, 8
  Allied Expeditionary Force, 55
  Ardennes attack, 175
  atomic bombs dropped on Japan, 230
  Calais, 60-65, 68-71, 72-73, 75-76
  Canadian casualties, 18, 33, 36, 47-48
  casualties, 226
  German surrender, 224-25
  Germany on defensive, 112, 174, 196-97
  invasion of Europe (Normandy), 18, 29-30, 32-33, 47-48
  Market Garden campaign, 58-59

Z
Zeitz, twenty-fourth mission, 165-66
zoot-suiters, 30-31